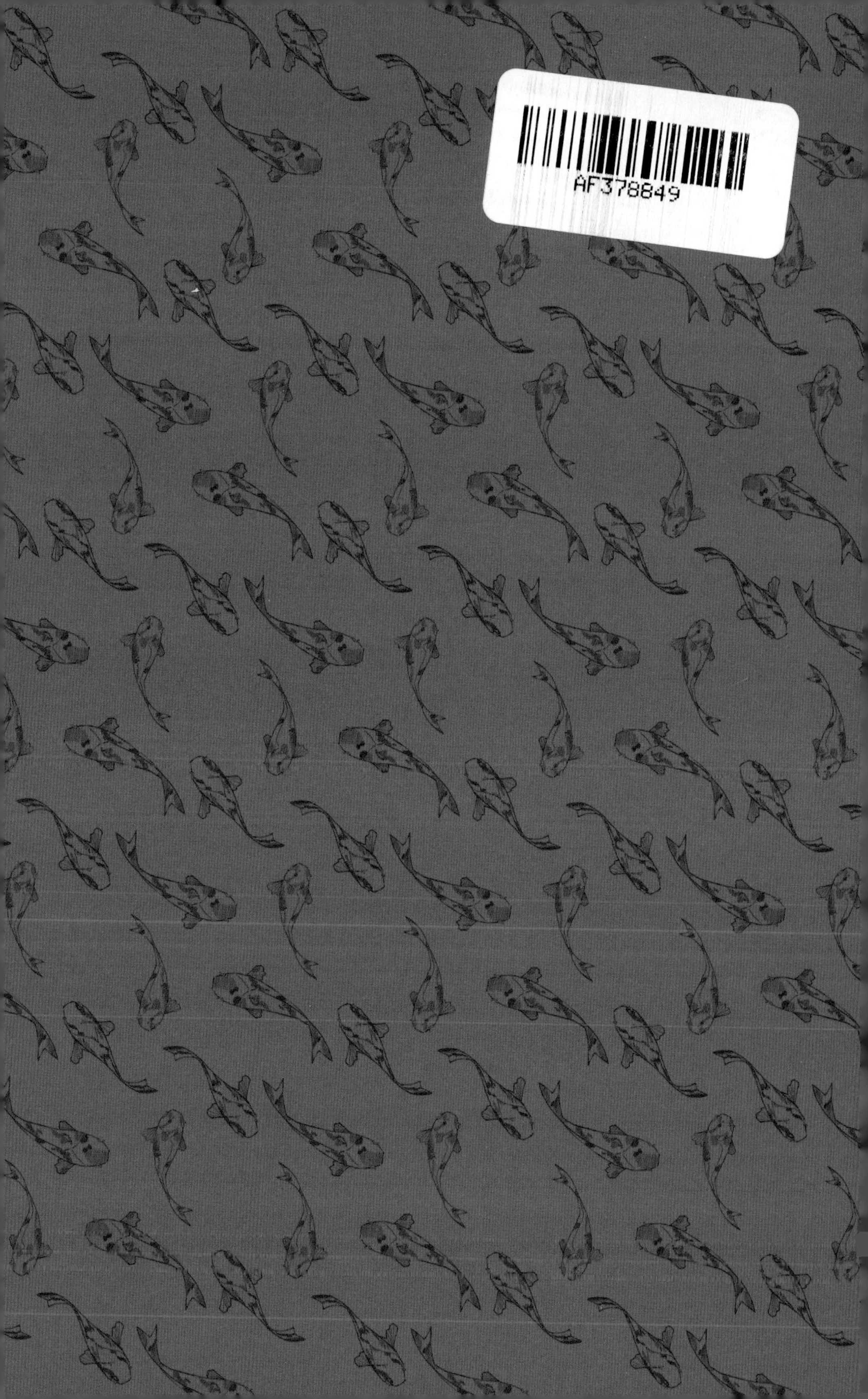
AF378849

A Japanese Art Journey

Meher McArthur

TUTTLE Publishing
Tokyo | Rutland, Vermont | Singapore

Published by Tuttle Publishing, an imprint of Periplus Editions (HK) Ltd.

www.tuttlepublishing.com

Copyright © 2025 Meher McArthur

ISBN: 978-4-8053-1990-1

First edition
28 27 26 25
10 9 8 7 6 5 4 3 2 1   2507CM

Printed in China

Distributed By

North America, Latin America & Europe
Tuttle Publishing
364 Innovation Drive
North Clarendon, VT 05759-9436 U.S.A.
Tel: (802) 773-8930
Fax: (802) 773-6993
info@tuttlepublishing.com
www.tuttlepublishing.com

Japan
Tuttle Publishing
Yaekari Building, 3rd Floor
5-4-12 Osaki, Shinagawa-ku
Tokyo 141 0032
Tel: (81) 3 5437-0171
Fax: (81) 3 5437-0755
sales@tuttle.co.jp
www.tuttle.co.jp

Asia Pacific
Berkeley Books Pte. Ltd.
3 Kallang Sector, #04-01
Singapore 349278
Tel: (65) 6280-1330
Fax: (65) 6280-6290
inquiries@periplus.com.sg
www.tuttlepublishing.com

GPSR representative
Matt Parsons
matt.parsons@upi2mbooks.hr
UPI-2M PLUS d.o.o., Medulićeva 20
10000 Zagreb, Croatia

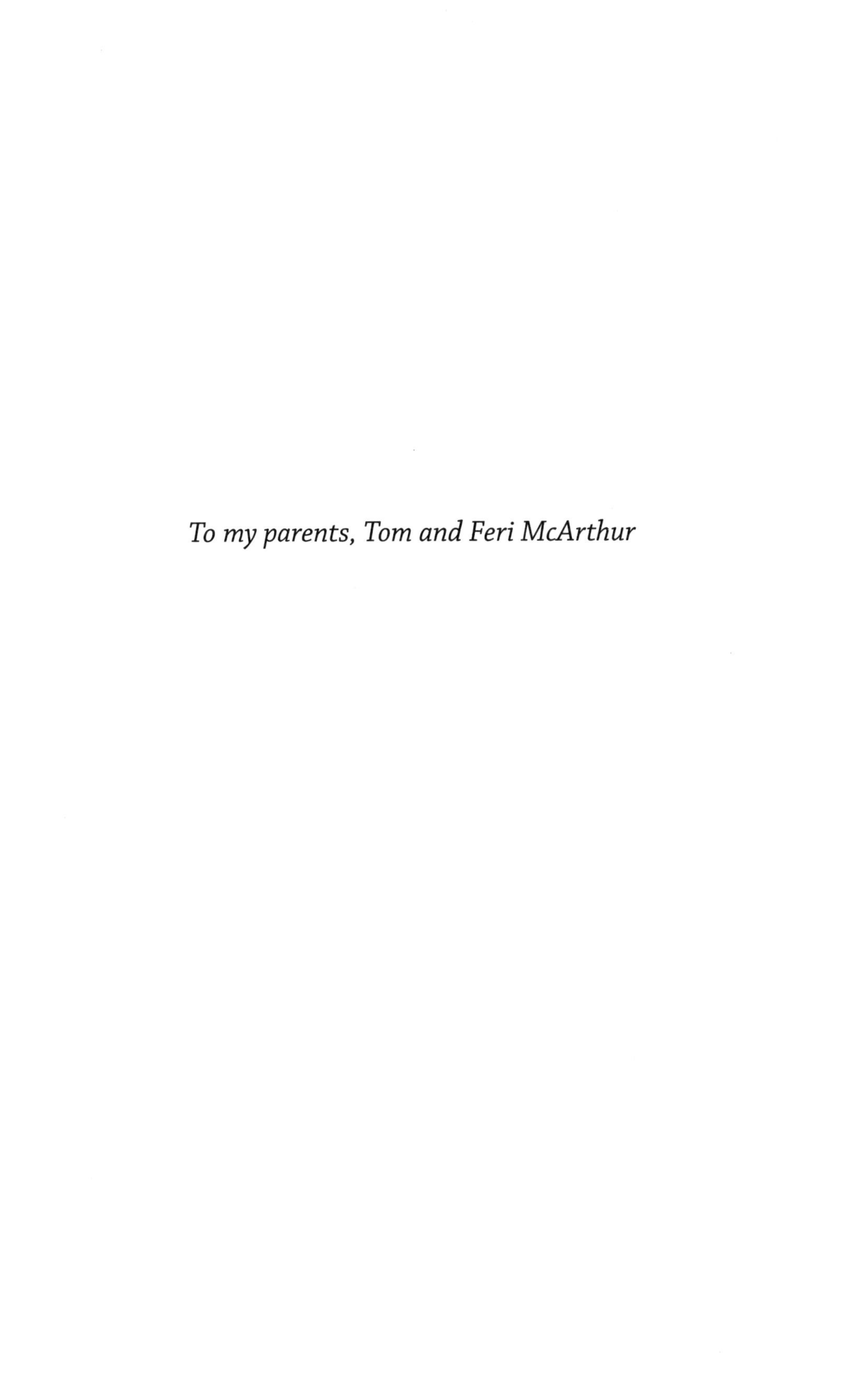

To my parents, Tom and Feri McArthur

Contents

Braiding Our Many Homes Together

Much like the author of this warm and affectingly open-hearted memoir, I grew up the only dark-skinned child in all my English classrooms, preyed upon by "Paki-bashers" even though my Indian parents couldn't have been further from Pakistani. But I, like Meher McArthur, came to see that I was blessed to have many worlds within me and many sets of eyes through which to observe our ever more mingled planet. Like her, I came to love in particular the delicacy, grace and courtesy of Japan, in which—as we read here—a scholar will present a thousand-year-old print to a stranger so that it can take on a new life far away.

Yet, even after thirty-seven years of basing myself in Western Japan, I never knew till reading *A Japanese Art Journey* that there are at least fifty words in Japanese for rain! On page after page, McArthur opens doors to my adopted home with a sense of poetry and beauty that captures much of what I love most deeply about Japan. I had been reading the works of Santoka since 1988 without ever encountering the poem that illuminates this work, or reading of his life in quite the light we see here.

It's hard not to be quickened—and touched—as McArthur cross-cuts her excitement in discovering kindness and beauty in Japan with the challenges of being far from home as loved ones fall ill. All of which makes a special blessing of those loyal and generous presences—Takeshi, Toshie, the memory of Sadako Sasaki—that keep coming back in these pages. Even as she leads us through many of the essential concepts that guide Japan, this writer brings them into the here and now by showing us a young boy last seen in Kyushu suddenly appearing in a Pasadena garden, dancing, and reminding us how that latest hot anime is lit up by the same attention to detail we associate with Hiroshige.

So many foreign writers on Japan chafe and even rage against the way that it can be very different from the world we know "back home." McArthur is the happy soul who exults in the difference, and can point out how the modesty, patience and kindness we meet in Japan may not be so foreign after all. In both East and West here, we meet collectors who offer their treasures to museums and scholars who share their wisdom without a second thought.

The result is an honest and humane celebration of generosity that takes us far beyond easy divisions of East and West. The author's family comes to seem as wise and thoughtful as the community she befriends in Japan, and a certain Buddhist realism about the reality of suffering helps to guide even a Scottish-Iranian woman who spent her infancy in India. Her parents were far-sighted indeed, all those years ago, to see Meher McArthur as a hopeful being from the future, a global citizen; in her life and in her writing she reminds us how Japan can be a part of all of us, wherever we happen to reside.

—Pico Iyer
Nara, Japan
December, 2024

Introduction

Oh, East is East, and West is West, and never the twain shall meet,
Till Earth and Sky stand presently at God's great Judgment Seat;
But there is neither East nor West, Border, nor Breed, nor Birth,
When two strong men stand face to face, though they come from the
*   ends of the earth!*

These lines are the first verse of the poem *The Ballad of East and West*, written in 1889 by Rudyard Kipling, a British writer born in India. Though the first two lines suggest that people from different cultures will never truly know each other, the remainder of the poem—about a British soldier and Indian chieftain who appear close to coming to blows, but in the end discover mutual respect—argues the very opposite. The ballad suggests that, rather than race and ethnicity, character and integrity should be the criteria by which we judge and accept each other. Because I was born in India, and my parents were Scottish and Persian, my father shared this poem with me to illustrate their global perspective on humanity.

All of my life, I have looked different from most of the people around me, and for the majority of my life, I have spoken with a different accent—one suggesting another land. As a result, the question I have been asked more than any other is, "Where are you from?" Although I have now lived in Southern California for almost thirty years, and it is no longer considered acceptable to ask non-white people where they come from, I still hear the question on a regular basis. By becoming a Japanese art historian and curator of Japanese art, I complicated things further and set myself up for another persistent question, "How did you become interested in Japanese art?"

As in many love stories, I didn't see this love affair coming, but once I fell, I fell hard, and the love has endured for decades. Japan's ceramics traditions—some of which evolved from those of the mainland, but many of which are unique native creations—probably drew me in first. But I have also become passionate about many of the country's paper-based art forms, from woodblock prints to origami and recently, sculptures made from traditional handmade *washi* paper. I am also regularly captivated by aspects of Japanese contemporary art, from the vibrant sculptures, paintings and installations of Yayoi Kusama to the animated films of Hayao Miyazaki and Makoto Shinkai.

Memoirs are typically written by famous people, or by those who have lived through harrowing times—or both. This is not one of those. Instead, it is one that acknowledges the deeply transformative effect that art can have on a single life, and in this case the powerful influence that Japanese artistic creativity has had on a person born of many other cultures. By journeying through the many worlds of Japanese art and sharing them with others, I have learned that there truly is "neither East nor West, Border, nor Breed, nor Birth."

—Meher McArthur
Pasadena, CA
June, 2025

Discovering and Learning

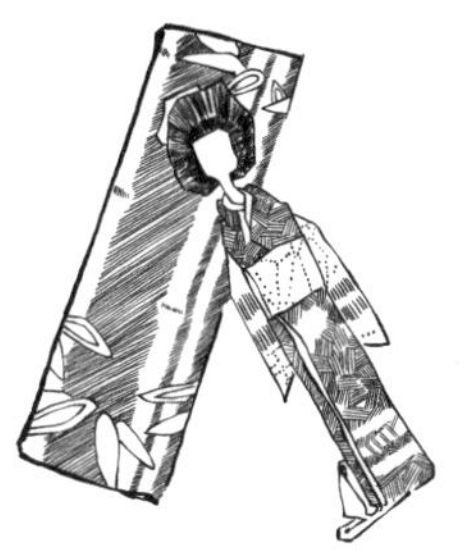

CHAPTER 1

The Paper Doll

"A little something." "Nothing special." "Just a trifle, a boring thing." These are all possible translations for *tsumaranai mono desuga*, a phrase traditionally used in Japan when someone is presenting a gift. Often, the gift isn't a dull, trifling thing at all. It may in fact be rather special, extremely expensive and even quite spectacular. By uttering the phrase, the giver expresses humility, honors the receiver and also indicates that the relationship between the giver and receiver is more important than the value of the gift itself.

In my experience, the smallest of gifts can have a profound effect, perhaps enriching the receiver's life in ways that only become obvious much later. First as a child, then as a student of Japanese language, culture and art, and later as a Japanese art historian, I have received many gifts from Japanese friends, colleagues and even people I've just met for the first time. Some gifts are beautiful items, and others are delightful experiences. Though usually given modestly, none have been trifling, and all have fueled my love for Japanese art and culture, and my understanding and appreciation of the country's rich artistic traditions.

———◆———

Some of the names in this story have been changed to protect identities.

"What has a brown person ever invented?"

The phrase was spat out at me one day at school by Gillian, a lanky girl with sandy brown hair, freckled white skin and piercing blue eyes. She stood with her hands on her hips and a smug expression on her face, staring at me expectantly, eyebrows raised. Gillian was in my circle of friends, but she could sometimes be a bit mean, one minute telling me how lucky I was not to get sunburned like she did, but the next, teasing me for being so dark.

My mouth opened to respond, as I always did when I was being taunted for the color of my skin, but this time no words came out. I was dismayed to realize that I didn't have a good comeback for her barb. Nothing in our history or science books had mentioned inventions by brown people. From what I could recall from history class, white Scottish people had invented almost everything important, like the steam engine, the telephone and the television.

Deflated, I trudged back toward the classroom, kicking at the gravel on the playground surface as I approached the steps. I was sure brown and other non-white people must have invented some important things, but even though I was already eleven years old, I had no idea what they were. The ancient Egyptians, Greeks and Romans were brown or brownish, but other than pyramids and aqueducts, which weren't part of modern daily life, I couldn't name anything else important that they had invented. I swore to myself that I would learn of something soon so that I would be ready for the next attack.

Name-calling and remarks about my skin color were an ongoing occurrence while I was growing up in Scotland. My family lived in Longniddry, a coastal village a few miles east of Edinburgh that was best known for its golf course. It had a railway station, a post office, a grocery shop and a sweet shop right next to the dental clinic, as well as a pub, church and community center. Its population was around two thousand five hundred people, and for the seven years that we called this village our home, my younger sister, Roshan, and brother, Alan, and I were the only mixed-race, non-white children there.

Dad was Scottish and very white, so he didn't stand out at all, but Mum was Persian and the only fully non-white person in the village. This was the 1970s, and at that time, there were very few people of color in Scotland, not even very many immigrants from India, Pakistan or other former British colonies. With her thick, lustrous black hair, deep brown eyes, olive skin, and a slender long nose, Mum attracted quite a bit of attention, and we often heard our neighbors, friends and shopkeepers refer to her as "beautiful" and "exotic." I had darker skin than all of my classmates, and I had the added distinction of having been born in India—a far-away country full of brown people—so I felt dark and very different, but rarely in a positive way. My classmates called me many things, but never "beautiful" or "exotic."

The insults began when I was about six years old, when a boy, probably one of the Ferguson boys who lived down the long road to school, ran after me shouting, "Coca-Cola Face!" I yelled back at him, "Shut up, Lemonade Face!" I was proud of my clever retort, though it still didn't stop his insults. On another occasion, I was so furious at the same boy and his name-calling that I tried to throw my bicycle at him. I wasn't strong enough to hurl it anywhere near him, and, instead of triumphantly crushing my abuser under its wheels, I found myself standing over my poor dented bike, feeling more frustrated than ever and struggling to hold back my tears. When I mentioned these encounters to my parents, Mum reminded me that, "sticks and stones can break your bones, but words will never hurt you." Dad told me that I should ignore them and not let them get to me. "If you react to their insults, they will keep on using them," he explained, "but if you don't react, they will eventually stop."

But all the names did hurt. They hurt a lot. They may have been just silly words, but they stung deeply and shook my sense of who I was. I couldn't ignore them. So, I yelled back. And Dad was right. The insults didn't stop.

My despair at these insults shaped one of my earliest school essays. In Primary 1 (think Kindergarten), we were given an assignment to write about our appearance. I described my brown eyes, brown hair and brown skin, and summed up my essay with the sentence, "I like myself, but I wish I was white." My teacher marked the essay with a big checkmark and made no comments. When my parents read it, however, they sat me down for a chat. With worried eyes but kind smiles, they explained that there was nothing wrong with my skin color. "You three kids are children of the future, global citizens," they reassured me. "When you get older, you'll meet other mixed-race kids. We've met so many mixed couples over the years—like Barry and Rie, the American and Japanese couple whom we shared a houseboat with in Kashmir. Remember them? Soon, there will be a lot of 'global children' like you. We promise." I wasn't completely convinced, but their words were encouraging. I opened my essay book and erased the last sentence of my essay, perhaps in an attempt to erase my doubts about myself and finally accept my skin color. But my younger self had pressed her emotions so deeply into the paper that even today, I can still see the ghost of those heartfelt words on the page and remember the shame that compelled me to write them. This early essay has served as a sort of touchstone in my journey toward self-acceptance.

As the years passed, the insults became more racially specific, like "Paki," an abbreviation of Pakistani. Since the 1950s and 60s, growing communities of Pakistanis lived in Britain's larger towns and cities. Presumably some of the kids in my school had seen them and decided that I looked quite like them. More bafflingly, though, when I was about ten years old and our class was studying American history and slavery, some of my classmates pointed at me and giggled, "Ha-ha! Negro Slave!" Another called me the "N-word!" For those comments, all I could do was shake my head in disbelief. Though I was young, I knew that they were wrong in so many ways.

In my final year of primary school, one of my snickering classmates, Donald, crassly joked to his neighbor Grant that I was brown because my father had used a chocolate wrapper instead of a condom. Perhaps in an attempt to find out the meaning of "condom," I mentioned his joke to my parents that evening. They did not laugh. Nor did they suggest I just ignore the joke. Instead, my father immediately called Mr. King, the principal. The next day, Donald was summoned out of class by Mr. King and belted three times on his left palm. Instead of being pleased that my parents made sure Donald was punished for his racist joke, I was mortified that I had caused him such terrible trouble! He wasn't a bad person and was just trying to be funny, but at that age, I didn't fully understand how dangerous and destructive such jokes can be. Despite everything my parents told me at home, fitting in at school was everything, and my brown skin seemed to be stopping me from being like the other kids. It felt like a handicap, or even a curse. At that moment, rather than being grateful for my parents' support, I blamed and resented them for making me so different.

Thankfully, however, these moments of resentment toward my parents were relatively rare. Much of the time—usually when I was not at school—I not only didn't mind my color, but I actually enjoyed not being completely Scottish or white. Sometimes, being different from others felt special. At home, Mum made delicious dinners—much tastier, I thought, and more elaborate than the Scottish meals most of our friends ate at home. She made Persian chicken, vegetable, and rice dishes that she had learned to make by watching her own family meals being prepared while she was growing up. As we sat and did our homework after school, we would be tantalized by delicious smells wafting out of the kitchen and throughout the house. As soon as Mum placed those dinners on the table, the three of us fought over the crispiest and largest piece of *tadig*—the slices of potato she fried at the bottom of the pot of rice, which were served on top of a big mound of rice at the table. We would grab at the thick potato chips, sprinkle salt on them and munch them down greedily. Mum frequently used bay leaves, turmeric, cumin and other spices to recreate the curries that she and Dad had eaten while they lived in India, and she often cooked dishes with unusual vegetables like *aubergines* (eggplants) and *courgettes* (zucchini) that few people in Scotland knew about in the 1970s. They are still my favorites today. Whenever Persian relatives came to visit or sent us packages in the post, we would dive into the included bags full of pistachios and dried cherries. We always looked forward to these exotic treats. That we were the only kids in our school who were sent snacks like these from faraway lands made them even more delicious!

Although Mum shared the food of her homeland with us, she chose not to teach us her mother tongue, Farsi, and we had no interest in learning the language. Mum was totally committed to her new home in Scotland, as well as its culture and language, an attitude that per-haps reflected the relatively cosmopolitan worldview with which she had been raised. Her family in Tehran had dealt in traditional Persian carpets, but her parents had been untraditional in other ways. Both were members of the Bahá'í faith, a religion that had broken away from Islam in the mid-nineteenth century and promoted a strong universal-ist worldview. One of her brothers had moved to England and married an English woman, and her other brother and sister later sent their teenagers abroad to study. Keen to see the world, Mum, the youngest of four, also left her country at eighteen years old. She flew to England to stay with her brother and learn English, and soon found that she had no desire to go back to Iran to live.

What little Farsi we did pick up was taught to us by Dad. He over-flowed with a passion and aptitude for languages that made him very different from his working-class family in Glasgow. Unlike his parents and brother, his mind hungered for new information and experiences, and his feet itched for travel. He read passionately and was the first in his family to go to university. At Glasgow University, he studied Classics (Latin and Greek) and joined the International Club, further fueling his curiosity about the world. After a few years in the British army, he left to seek a more global community, joined a group of Bahá'ís near Birmingham, England, and then met and fell in love with Mum. They married and then moved to Bombay (Mumbai), India.

For four years, Mum and Dad lived in Bombay, where Dad taught English in a private high school. Mum became pregnant with me during that time and carried me around inside her on the many adventures she and Dad had in India, including an interview my father did with His Holiness, the Dalai Lama, during which I received His blessing *in utero*! When I was just one year old, however, my parents chose to leave India and build a life as a family in Scotland. Though I have no memories of India, as a young child, Dad regaled us with countless colorful stories about their life there, which involved such fascinating characters as pet squirrels, cockroaches in ketchup bottles, holy men, and powerful gods and goddesses. The floors of our modest home were covered with colorful Persian carpets from Mum's family, and its walls and bookshelves were decorated with characters brought back from India—a brass sculpture of Shiva, Lord of the Dance, a wooden carving of Ganesha, the elephant-headed Lord of Obstacles, as well as a serene sculpture of the Buddha, gazing calmly out from beneath half-closed eyelids. Once settled in Scotland, our family welcomed my sister, Roshan, and then my brother, Alan. Dad completed a PhD in English Language and Linguistics at Edinburgh University and began instructing foreign EFL teachers how to teach English as a foreign language, as well as running courses in yoga and Indian philosophy.

As a teacher, Dad brought together his work life and his family life, partnering with Mum to open up many worlds to the three of us. Many of my favorite childhood memories were the programs Mum and Dad organized for his local and international students—in part because they were spent with other people who looked different or were curious about different cultures. There were the occasional events that we kids called the "Curry Seminars"—actually seminars that Dad taught on yoga and Indian philosophy, for which Mum cooked a huge quantity of curry, dahl, rice and papadum. Roshan, Alan and I loved the food at these events, but were not so interested in the contents of these classes, which were mostly meant for adults. At one of these gatherings, the three of us sat outside one of the classrooms giggling at the sound of people inside chanting "Om" together. It seemed very weird.

We much preferred the Burns Night celebrations and other Scots Evenings that Mum and Dad arranged for his foreign students to introduce them to the food, drink, poetry, and songs of Scotland. A tall, gray-haired and rugged friend of theirs, Ron, recited Scotland's national poet Robert Burns' most famous poems including *Address to a Haggis* and *Holy Willie's Prayer* with great energy and humor. Though many of Dad's foreign students had no idea what the Scots words in the poems meant, his lively expressions and dynamic gestures had them roaring with laughter. One of our neighbors, Sheila, a full-figured woman with jet-black hair, joined the Scots Evenings to share haunting Scottish ballads and love songs in her powerful soprano. Mum baked scones, shortbread and other delicious Scottish treats (because she had mastered Scottish food too!) and Dad, wearing his McArthur tartan trousers and tie, vigorously sang Scottish folk songs, sometimes accompanied by the "Persian Highlanders"—his three brown-skinned children wearing kilts and singing in Gaelic. The evenings were quite the family productions. By sharing these joyful, multi-cultural events with us and involving us as performers too, Mum and Dad truly did make us feel like we were citizens of the world. The guests all cheered us on enthusiastically. The other kids at school knew nothing about this part of our lives, where we were not strange so much as special.

In the summers, Mum and Dad invited his EFL class students to our home in Longniddry for parties in the back garden to celebrate the end of the academic year. These gatherings were a chance to say goodbye to them all before they scattered again all over the world, armed with their newly acquired English-teaching skills. Our back garden was rather small. Mum used about a third of the area to grow broad beans, rhubarb, raspberries and other fruits and vegetables, so that only left a small patio and a square of grass about thirty feet by thirty feet for entertaining guests. Nonetheless, the gatherings were lively, packed with young, interesting people with all colors of hair and skin. The air was filled with cheerful chatter in a mix of accents and languages as guests munched on Mum's sandwiches, scones and cakes, sipped tea, and shared memories and plans with each other. They came from countries as diverse as Spain, Peru, Italy, Iraq, and various parts of Asia, and some brought with them gifts from their home countries for Mum and Dad and for us children as well. It was at one of these gatherings in our little back garden in Longniddry that I experienced my first encounter with a work of Japanese art.

That summer, two of his students were young Japanese women. They are the only students of his whose names I still remember—Kaoru and Hideko. Dressed casually in jeans and t-shirts, both young women wore their hair short, which struck me as unusual for Japanese women. The Japanese women I had seen on TV and had met before always had long, straight hair. When they arrived, they greeted our whole family with enthusiastic smiles and bows and with English that still had a thick Japanese accent. Once in the back garden, Kaoru held up a cloth bag, and Hideko reached inside it. She pulled out three pretty, little, well-wrapped packages and smiled as she handed one each to Roshan, Alan and me. She spoke very slowly and carefully in what seemed to be well-rehearsed English. "These are just some small, trifling things from Japan."

I can't remember what they gave Alan, but Roshan and I each received a narrow little package. We eagerly unwrapped them and each found inside a paper box about four inches (ten centimeters) long and decorated with colorful patterns. We lifted the lids to reveal a little paper doll lying inside. I gasped at how small and exquisite the figure was—a beautiful miniature person crafted solely from paper. Mine had a completely white face and a full black bouffant hairdo tied at the back, and she was wearing a black, brown and white kimono tied with a pink, purple and white belt that hung down her back, forming a long triangle. The figure was folded a bit like origami, which I already knew about from an origami instruction book my parents had recently bought me. I had already spent hours studying the instructions for folding flat squares of paper into animals, birds and boxes, and had mastered a few of the forms. Inside the box was a little sheet of paper with indecipherable (to me) Japanese writing about the doll, words that remained unread for years. Enchanted by these little handmade paper dolls, my sister and I thanked Kaoru and Hideko. This time Kaoru spoke, "These are from Tokyo. Maybe someday, you will visit."

Sometime shortly after the party, the two young women presumably returned to Japan to become English teachers. We never saw or heard from them again, but I squirreled away my Japanese paper doll with my other childhood treasures. I still have her today—almost 50 years later—in her little paper box. Over those decades, unbeknownst to Kaoru and Hideko, I went on to learn the Japanese language and then to study Japanese art. As an art historian, I encountered many different kinds of Japanese dolls, or *ningyo*, some with porcelain faces and bodies wrapped in miniature silk kimonos, others as painted cylindrical wooden dolls known as *kokeshi*, and several types of paper dolls. I recently opened up the little slip of paper that accompanied my paper doll and strained my eyes (and brain) to read the tiny Japanese characters. Although my eyes are not as sharp today as they were in my youth, with the help of my reading glasses, my now-educated brain can finally read the formerly mystifying characters. The paper explains that this little folded paper doll is called a *Chiyogami Ningyo* (literally, a "Thousand-Year Paper Doll"), a craft product made in the Yanaka neighborhood of Tokyo.

Chiyogami is a type of Japanese hand-made paper that has been printed with intricate designs, often based on textile patterns, made since the Edo period (1603–1868). These decorative papers had many uses, including being folded into kimonos for small paper dolls, hence the name *Chiyogami Ningyo*. They are also known as *Anesama Ningyo* (or "Older Sister Dolls"). Apparently, the dolls were originally made by mothers and given to their daughters, who then passed them down to (or made new ones for) their own daughters. Their faces were left blank so that girls could fill in their features themselves. These dolls are still made in Tokyo today by specialist artists, and according to the little slip of paper, mine was made by a fourth-generation artist of the Isetatsu family of Chiyogami makers in Tokyo. A little research revealed to me that since the late Edo period, the Isetatsu family has made decorative papers used for wrapping gifts and everyday goods, using engraved wood blocks to print the designs onto the handmade paper. At their store, they still sell sheets of decorative papers, as well as jewelry boxes coated with the papers—and probably little dolls like mine.

When Kaoru and Hideko handed their gift to my sister and me, they had called the dolls "small, trifling things from Japan," their English translation of *tsumaranai mono desu*. My doll was indeed small and perhaps didn't cost a large sum of money at the Isetatsu shop in Tokyo, where I imagine the young women went to buy gifts to take with them when they traveled to Scotland. However, the gift was not at all trivial to me. In fact, the object was the first work of Japanese art that I ever held in my hands, my first Japanese treasure.

I can't say for sure that the paper doll inspired me to become a Japanese art historian some twenty years later, but I know that it contributed to an interest in other languages and cultures that ultimately led me to study the Japanese language and then Japanese art history. It also introduced me to the ingenuity of Japanese artists, demonstrating quite clearly that people other than white people could create spectacular things. I will always be grateful to these two young Japanese women—these Japanese "Older Sisters"—for wanting to share their culture and art with young children in a country so far away from their own. For children, such gifts can be portals into other worlds.

Today, when I look at this little doll and remember the circumstances that brought her to me, I am also deeply thankful for a much larger gift that I received as a child—the gift of exposure to a wide range of people, customs and beliefs, and the knowledge that I was a child of multiple cultures. What seemed such a curse at times was actually a blessing. As a child, I routinely felt that my darker skin and international family story meant that I didn't belong in Longniddry, but, as I would find out in due course, it wasn't that I didn't belong there. I did belong there, *and* I belonged in a lot of other places too. I may not have realized its value when I was a child, but while I was struggling to find my place at school and among my Scottish peers, my parents were sharing their curiosity and passion for other cultures to help me embrace my own global identity. Their gifts to me of a global perspective, an open mind and curiosity for other cultures equipped me to find my place in the world as an adult.

And that is no trifling thing either.

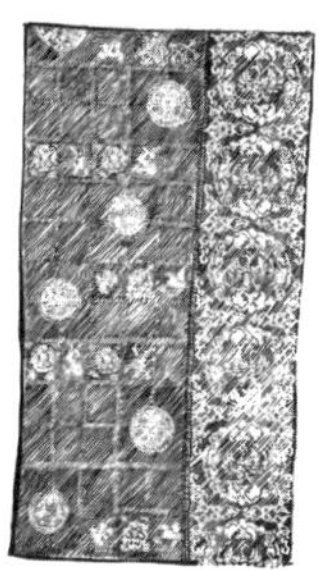

CHAPTER 2

The Obi Sample

The Japanese word *musubu* means to bind, connect, unite or tie together. The verb is often used not only in conversations about cords, hair, ropes and sashes, but also in discussions of contracts, treaties, friendships and marriage. A girl can tie a ribbon in her hair—*kami o ribon de musubu*—and two countries can forge an alliance—*dōmei o musubu*. In Japanese, the verb is written 結ぶ—a combination of the *kanji*, or Chinese character, read *musu* and meaning "to tie," followed by the Japanese *hiragana* syllable *bu*.

Because it illustrates the concept of tying, the character has the Chinese root character for thread, 糸 (read *ito* in Japanese) on the left side, but more surprisingly, on the right side is the character read *kichi* in Japanese, meaning "good luck" or "good fortune." This suggests that for centuries in East Asia, the delightful idea has existed that the most important connections in our lives—friendships, treaties and marriages—are created with lucky threads.

At the age of twenty-one, I found myself cycling around the ancient city of Kyoto on a bike in the sticky heat of the rainy season, wondering why I was the only person dripping with sweat. It was late in the afternoon and the cicadas were buzzing rhythmically in the trees as the sun began its retreat behind the mountains. Looking at the map, my ride home hadn't seemed that far—only ten blocks or so—but the blocks in this well-planned, once-imperial city were very long. Experiencing the city from a bicycle made it clear exactly how large the metropolis was and how hard it must have been to traverse a thousand years ago, when it was the Imperial capital. After much determined pedaling, I arrived at my destination and hopped off the bike. I was shocked to see that my turquoise cotton sundress was drenched with sweat in places and was now two different shades of blue! I wheeled my bike around to the side of the house and searched in my purse for the little key that locked the wheel. I slid open the front door. "*Tada ima!*" I announced as I entered the house. "I'm home."

My "home" was a modern Japanese house that belonged to the Endo family, located in the northwest part of Kyoto. Mr. Endo owned a kimono company and a couple of traditional Japanese restaurants in Kyoto. He always wore a business suit, even on the hottest, most humid days of the Kyoto summer. He was middle-aged and slightly plump with wavy black hair, black-rimmed glasses and a toothy grin, which he seemed to wear most of the time. Mrs. Endo was a petite woman who, like her husband, always seemed to be smiling or laughing. She flitted busily from room to room, making sure that her all her family members and I were comfortable and had plenty of green tea to sip and goodies to eat. She looked after Mr. Endo's elderly mother, an even tinier woman with silver hair, who wore indigo cotton kimonos and played a three-stringed instrument called a *shamisen*. Their son was a college student who was always out with his friends, so I rarely saw him. But I did spend some time with their daughter, Keiko, a shy girl who was a little younger than me, who had long, straight black hair. She aspired to be a kindergarten teacher. Almost no one in the Endo family spoke any English, so I had to rely on the conversational Japanese I had absorbed over the last two years studying the language at Cambridge. I had studied hard, learning quite a lot, but speaking it every day with a family I barely knew was much harder than I had expected. I felt pushed to my limits, and the summer heat made it all the more exhausting.

It hadn't been my original plan to study Japanese at college. I'd planned to study French because I was already familiar with it. Several years earlier, when we were living in Scotland, my father had been offered a job in Quebec, so we had uprooted our lives to move across the Atlantic into a completely different culture. After four years at an English-language school in a predominantly French-speaking province, we had all picked up quite a lot of French. Then, when Dad was offered the chance to edit a journal about the English language for Cambridge University Press, the whole family moved back across the Atlantic, this time to England. I kept studying French and was interested in using the language for business. So, before taking my final high school exams, I applied to various universities to study French and business. However, my exam results came back better than I expected, which made me reconsider my possibilities. I wondered if studying a more challenging language like Arabic, Chinese or Japanese might give me a competitive edge in the business world. Because the Japanese economy was still booming in the late 1980s, and jobs for Japanese speakers were plentiful, I chose Japanese.

Only four universities in the country offered degrees in Japanese Studies at that time. One was Cambridge University, just three miles from our home. I had been working as a waitress at Emmanuel College, one of Cambridge University's less famous (so, less tourist-infested) colleges, and I liked the students and the general atmosphere of the place. The college was founded in 1584 and has an elegant, domed chapel built by Christopher Wren, beautiful gardens with the oldest outdoor swimming pool in the country, and many illustrious alumni, including John Harvard. It was also one of the more liberal colleges of the university—the first, in fact, to eliminate the elitist Oxbridge exams as a requirement for entry. Once I entered the college, I came to know the Master, Professor Derek Brewer, an English professor who had a deep affinity for Japan and who was thrilled that his college finally had a student of Japanese. Toward the end of my first year, he invited me to work over the summer helping a group of Japanese students who were attending a summer school at Emmanuel. They were from a college in Osaka. A family of one of the students taking this course—the Endos—generously offered to host me for a homestay the following summer. They lived in Kyoto. I couldn't believe my luck!

Within seconds of my entering the house, Mrs. Endo appeared almost running from the direction of the kitchen to greet me at the front door. "*O-kaeri nasai!*" she called out cheerfully. "Welcome home." As usual, her smile was so wide that her eyes seem to disappear into it. She clearly could still see me and my sweaty dress, though, as she remarked, "Ah. Kyoto so hot!" She quickly switched to Japanese and explained that Mr. Endo wasn't home yet. I would have time to change before dinner. It was a busy time of the year, she went on. We were getting close to *O-bon*, the time when the spirits of ancestors are believed to come home, and at *O-bon* and during New Year's celebrations, Japanese people exchange lots of gifts. Because Mr. Endo had many clients in Kyoto, he was taking a variety of gifts to some of his clients to thank them for their business that year. She slid open a door to one of the traditional rooms. The tatami-mat floor was almost covered with stacks of boxes—all carefully wrapped. I had never seen so many gifts in one place —even at Christmas. In Kyoto, she explained, gift-giving was a very important part of the culture.

"Kyoto old city," she added, reverting to her broken English. "Old style."

Kyoto was the home of the Imperial Court for over one thousand years. Though not always politically powerful, the court had considerable wealth and cultural influence. It was the patron of many Buddhist temples and Shinto shrines, some nearly a thousand years old and homes to many of the country's national treasures. While block-like buildings, electrical wires, and neon signs dominate much of the city's center today, interspersed among the modern buildings are several large temples, a single-story castle, and the old imperial palace. And on the outskirts, countless historic temples nestle in the hills in the north (Kitayama) and east (Higashiyama) of the city. In these areas, surrounded by ancient buildings, bamboo groves and narrow streets with tea shops and traditional restaurants, it is easy to imagine you have gone back in time. I was surprised that these structures had survived World War II. During the war, American bomber crews had apparently been instructed by their commanders not to drop bombs on Kyoto. So, thankfully, much of the city's imperial past was preserved.

It was exciting to be surrounded by so much traditional Japanese culture. Kyoto was a beautiful, exotic setting for achieving my main goal for the summer, which was to immerse myself in Japanese life and learn as much Japanese as I could before I joined the rest of my class in

Tokyo for a term studying the language at a Japanese university. Even after a few days, I could feel my Japanese improving. Pulling all the words and phrases I had absorbed from my textbooks out of my brain had been a struggle at first, but as my mouth became used to forming them, they started coming to life, becoming real and meaningful. The Endos were very kind to welcome me into their home and allow me to practice my shaky Japanese on them. However, Mr. Endo seemed to want me to learn more than just the language while I was in Kyoto. As soon as I moved into their home, despite his busy work schedule, he insisted on taking me all over the city. He proudly showed me the Sanjusangendo, Kinkakuji, Ryoanji and Daikakuji Temples, as well as the Heian Shrine, the temples on Mt. Hiei and the scenery of Arashi-yama. Then, he took me to the Kyoto National Museum, the Kyoto Handicraft Center and the Kawai Kanjiro Museum, located in the home of one of the city's most famous ceramic artists. It was the middle of July, so he wanted to make sure I experienced Kyoto's famous Gion Festival, in which colorful floats, or *hoko*, are pulled around the city in the sweltering heat to appease the god of pestilence. It was soon clear to me what an extraordinary city Kyoto was, what a rich history it had, and how proud Mr. Endo was of being part of it. Though I was grateful that he wanted to share it with me, I was initially anxious that these outings didn't leave me much time to study my *kanji* (Chinese characters), grammar and vocabulary. I needed to put in several hours a day to be able to improve, and all this sight-seeing was taking up a lot of my study time.

One day that first week, Mr. Endo drove me in his elegant car through the narrow streets of Nishijin, on the west side of the city, where his kimono company was located. Throughout Japan's history, the Imperial Court also supported many of Japan's finest art forms, including calligraphy, painting, metalwork, lacquerware and a rich array of woven, dyed and embroidered silk textiles. So, for centuries, Kyoto has been the epicenter of many Japanese artistic developments. Even today, Kyoto remains the heart of the Japanese textile industry. Textiles are mostly produced in the district of Nishijin, where woven silk fabrics, known as "Nishijin-ori" (Nishijin weaving), have been made since the Heian period (794–1185). That day, we stopped at various textile-related studios and shops, where Mr. Endo introduced me to businesses that were often hundreds of years old, some originally created to serve the Imperial Court. I met textile artists who painted silk cloth for use in kimonos for special occasions and weavers who used complex looms to create the elaborate brocades for wedding kimono and *obi*, the sashes that are worn around the kimono waist. We stopped by his own company office, and he instructed his staff to take my measurements and asked me to choose from a selection of brightly colored bolts of cotton. He was going to have a summer kimono, or *yukata*, made for me. My own custom-made kimono—I couldn't believe his generosity!

The next day, he took me the Kiyomizu District, a bustling hub of ceramics studios and shops, where he introduced me to ceramic artists and arranged for me to have a ceramics class with one of his potter friends. This wasn't exactly what I'd had in mind for my summer. My goal was to get a better understanding of the Japanese language, not ceramics! I was uneasy at first, sitting in a studio with people I hardly knew and couldn't communicate well with, but soon my hands were covered in clay as I was gleefully trying to throw a teacup on a spinning wheel. Then I learned how to shave off the excess clay when it was nearly dried using a metal tool, so that it actually looked like a proper cup. I may not have been able to study many *kanji* that day, but by listening to the potter explaining what to do and asking questions, I found myself exercising my vocabulary and practicing my grammar—all while making something I could use! It dawned on me that by showing me some of the highlights of Kyoto—essentially giving me my first immersive introduction to Japanese art and culture and its makers, Mr. Endo was causing me to learn so much more Japanese than I would have sitting in my room just studying *kanji* and grammar!

In the third week of my stay, Mr. Endo arranged for me to take lessons in *kumihimo*, or silk braiding, a centuries-old art form that was integral to the accessories for kimonos and other valuable items. *Kumihimo* means "gathered threads," and the art form dates back to the seventh century, when monks in Buddhist temples braided cords for use as a type of temple decor that facilitated meditation. Later, braided silk cords were used in samurai armor to bind together the lacquered metal plates, as well as to wrap sword handles and assemble armor for horses. Much later, they became part of women's kimono ensemble as the *obijime,* elaborate cords that are worn over the *obi,* or sash, to keep it in position.

Over four days, I sat in a rather drab-looking modern workroom with several very friendly women who patiently taught me how to braid the most gorgeous, lustrous silk threads into *obijime.* For my cord, I chose a deep burgundy color and was offered a gilt chain as one of the threads to add a touch of glamor. With their help, I tied together the silk threads and brought them up through the central hole in the round braiding frame, or *marudai.* I then separated the threads into sixteen separate strands, each with a wooden bobbin attached to the end. Very carefully and deliberately, I passed the threads across and over and around each other, again and again in a specific order to build my braid. Almost magically, a silken snake gradually emerged from the underside of the frame, born from my concentration and growing with the rhythm of my hands and the click-clack of clattering bobbins. With the encouragement of my instructors and my deep concentration, my braided cord looked so good that no one could believe I'd made it— least of all me!

Toward the end of my stay in Kyoto, Mr. Endo took me to one of his shops, opened a drawer full of colorful fabrics and told me to choose one as a gift. He explained that they were sample fabrics for *obi,* or kimono sashes. Because traditional Japanese kimono have no buttons or fasteners, *obi* are an important element of the kimono ensemble. They are wrapped around the waist of a kimono and tied in a bow at the back. While serving to keep the kimono tightly closed, they also further embellish the kimono—often with auspicious patterns and glittering gold threads. The samples were each about twelve inches (thirty centimeters) wide—the standard width for most formal women's *obi*—and were cut to about twenty-four inches (sixty centimeters) in length, and each would have been shown to someone interested in ordering a sumptuous *obi* to wear to a wedding, graduation or other special occasion. They featured designs of birds, flowers and natural motifs, geometric patterns, or a combination of both. This cloth was called *nishiki,* Mr. Endo explained, but the name was meaningless to me. Later, I learned that *nishiki* is the Japanese term for silk brocade, a type of decorative fabric with an intricate woven design that had a sheen like that of embroidery. At the time, I was just wowed by its beauty.

I sat on the tatami mat sifting through dozens of silk *obi* samples, overwhelmed by Mr. Endo's seemingly endless generosity and the dazzling array of designs before me. I ran my fingers over the surface of each of the samples, marveling at the smoothness of the beautiful, shiny patterns. I was amazed to see that designs were made up not only of silk but also gold threads. Mr. Endo explained that this type of *nishiki* cloth is called *kinran,* and it is one of the most luxurious fabrics made in Kyoto's Nishijin District. I recognized the word *kin*, meaning "gold." The gold threads, he told me, were in fact silk threads wrapped in paper coated with gold leaf. When I turned the cloths over in my hands, I noticed wide patches of what looked like hundreds of gold threads just floating over the surface, forming an almost abstract design. These areas, according to Mr. Endo, were the areas where gold wasn't used to create the design on the front, so the threads just hung loosely, floating on the back side of the cloth. Normally, in a finished *obi*, the back of the cloth would be hidden inside the lining of the *obi*. Having so much gold in the fabric made an *obi* quite heavy and, of course, very expensive. A standard woman's obi can be about twelve feet long and can often cost more than the kimono itself—sometimes thousands of dollars. I couldn't believe Mr. Endo was offering me something so valuable.

With so many exquisite cloths before me, I found it impossible to choose just one. I had narrowed them down to three: one with flowers in a brownish palette and gold detailing dancing over the surface; another had a black background and diagonal silver stripes and an assortment of flowers and butterflies; the third, the most luxurious of them all, featured a golden grid of squares dotted and bordered with roundels containing birds and flowers on a background that resembled mysterious clouds. I now know that the grid pattern, the roundels and the phoenix motifs on this piece of fabric were inspired by Chinese textiles in the Shōsōin Imperial Repository in Nara. This famous collection of many thousands of treasures belonged to the Emperor Shōmu (724–749) and includes gifts he received from foreign dignitaries when he consecrated the Great Buddha at the Tōdaiji Temple in Nara. An *obi* featuring such a design would hint at Japan's rich imperial history and cultural connections with the larger world.

"Okay—three!" snapped Mr. Endo suddenly, no doubt getting a little impatient with me and hungry for lunch. He picked up the three samples, rolled them up, and wrapped them in a khaki-colored cloth and handed them to me. I tried to close my gaping mouth and stammered out what I hoped was the politest expression for "thank you" in Japanese. *Domo arigato gozaimasu.* We left his kimono shop and made our way to one of his restaurants for a delicious tofu lunch.

At the end of August, my stay with the Endo family came to an end, and I heavy-heartedly left Kyoto for Tokyo to begin a Japanese language course at a university there. My three months there were not as magical as my time in Kyoto. In Tokyo, I was able to spend a lot of my time in the classroom and at home studying vocabulary and grammar, and I felt my Japanese improving considerably, but I missed the rich cultural outings that I'd been treated to by Mr. Endo. In late November, when the university course ended, it was time to leave Japan. I returned to Cambridge with a suitcase bulging full of ceramics, tea, charms from temples and shrines, and cute souvenirs from gift shops. I was also carrying an impressive collection of kimonos, a custom-made cotton summer *yukata*, my own *kumihimo* braids and the three *obi* samples—some of the lucky threads that had begun to bind my heart—*kokoro o musubu*—to Japan. At home in my bedroom, I laid out some of the objects I'd acquired in Kyoto—the ceramic cup I'd made in Kiyomizu, the *kumihimo* belt and the beautiful obi samples from Nishijin and gazed at them fondly, allowing them to transport me back to my summer in Kyoto.

When college started again in January, I struggled to get myself back into the swing of student life. I was bursting with experiences I wanted to talk about, but I kept them inside because I didn't want to bore my boyfriend or my friends with "another Japan story." Instead, I bottled them up inside and tried to be interested in the world around me. But everything seemed gray and dull by comparison, and I felt an awkwardness in my relationship with my boyfriend and my interactions with friends. I even had trouble enjoying my Japanese classes. I was unmotivated to learn the language, and I even started wondering why I was studying the language and what I wanted to go into business for. I felt like I had lost myself and was starting to unravel. A friend suggested that I might be depressed. I was surprised at his "diagnosis" because I had just experienced one of the most exciting, stimulating experiences of my life. Deep down, however, I realized he was onto something. Perhaps, after an amazing time in Japan, I was experiencing some sort of "re-entry shock" or reverse culture shock. It did make sense, but even when I understood what was wrong with me, I had no idea how to snap myself out of my funk and pull all the strands of "me" back together.

This struggle in my head went on for several months, until one Saturday evening toward the end of the academic year, when in the middle of a party in my college house, the phone rang. It was my father. It was very unusual for him to be calling me.

"Your mother is in the hospital having emergency surgery." His voice sounded thin and shaky. "I'm coming to pick you up, so we can both be there when she wakes up."

The words hit me like a slap. About twenty minutes later, I got into the car with Dad, and we drove to the ER and waited anxiously to hear how Mum was. She made it through the surgery, but we found out then that she had leukemia (cancer of the blood), and her odds of beating it were not good. Immediately, all the self-pity and depression I had been feeling were replaced with fear for my mother, and all the threads I had felt unraveling began to weave themselves tightly back together again, as if to give me the strength to face the horrors of our new reality.

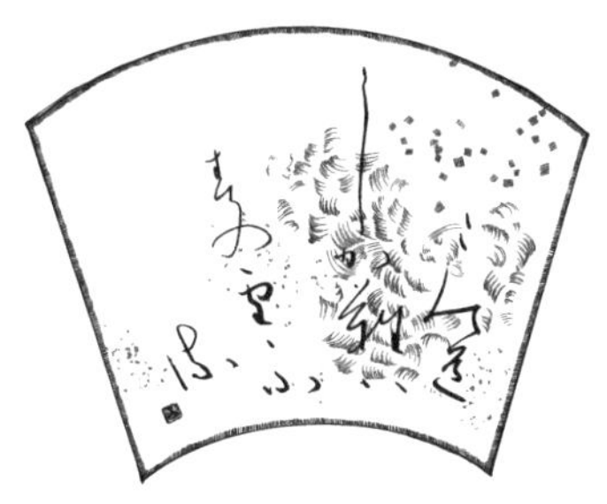

CHAPTER 3

The Calligraphy

For the Japanese, the idea of a "path" or a "way" is very important and profound. It is represented by the kanji 道, which can be read either *dō* or *michi*. Read *michi*, the word is typically used literally to mean a road or a pathway that is walked, cycled or driven along, such as the *Tetsugaku no michi*, or "Philosophy Path," that runs along a narrow channel in the Eastern Hills of Kyoto and is known for its exquisite cherry blossoms. As a suffix, *-dō* can mean a road or highway, as in the famous Tōkaidō, the "Eastern Sea Route," which historically connected the military capital Edo (now Tokyo) with the ancient Imperial capital of Kyoto.

Read *dō*, the character can also have a more philosophical meaning, as in the Chinese philosophical tradition Daoism (Dōkyō in Japanese), which stresses living in harmony with a larger, more cosmic "Way" (Dao in Chinese, Dō in Japanese). Understanding the importance of finding one's spiritual path, the Japanese have long used the suffix *dō* to refer to a discipline or practice that is followed as a way to train both physically and spiritually, as in *Bushidō* ("The Way of the Warrior"), *Judō* ("The Gentle Way") or *Chadō* ("The Way of Tea"), because these disciplines are considered paths one takes to reach a level of mastery or perfection—and also to cultivate one's spiritual self.

33

I stood in the women's clothing section of the John Lewis department store, sorting through the scarves that hung neatly on a metal rack. None of them looked right. The store's lights were too bright, and the air felt stifling. I normally avoided department stores as I disliked the dry air, artificial lighting and sterile environment, and I considered the clothes there rather frumpy. But Mum liked this shop and she had asked me to go there and buy her a scarf. Her hair had started falling out from the leukemia treatment. She would soon be bald, so she needed a scarf to cover her head. As I stared at the rack, I felt the tears welling up. I had no idea what would look good—the black and gray striped one, the one with the brown paisley designs, something floral? Which one, for goodness' sake? I couldn't imagine what Mum would look like bald. How could I possibly know what scarf would frame her face best with no hair? It was so unfair that after all the pain she was going through, she was going to lose her hair as well—such a beautiful woman. I broke down sobbing—right in the middle of the store! I'd thought I was becoming an adult, but here I was crying in public over not being able to choose a scarf. I was not ready to lose my mother.

The summer after my third year in college was a blur of hospital visits, time with the family at home, talking a lot and processing reality. It was all very hard to fathom. Mum was only 45 years old and had led a very healthy lifestyle, so how could she be so ill? She had acute myeloid leukemia, and the doctors warned us that her chances of surviving it were about fifty percent. Mum was always so kind and thoughtful to others. She did not deserve this. It was so cruel and unfair. The whole family felt derailed by the diagnosis and her gloomy prognosis, but we did our best to support her through her hospitalization, her harsh chemotherapy treatments and their unpleasant side effects—including losing her hair.

I did finally chose a scarf—the one with the brown paisley pattern. Mum wore it, and it looked pretty good framing her beautiful, tired face. In the months following her first round of treatment, she gradually started to heal. Miraculously, it seemed, she was doing much better by autumn, and her hair started to grow back—soft gray fuzz on her perfectly smooth, round head. I returned to college for my final year. The shock of Mum's illness had jolted me out of my "re-entry shock" depression, and now, the relief that Mum was on the mend freed me to get back to my learning. I was fired up again and determined to make the most of my final year of college. Mum would want me to do that. I took courses in classical Japanese literature and Tokugawa-period philosophy, and I dove into my final dissertation on folk literature. By the time I completed my degree, Mum was able to attend my graduation—with a full head of thick, gray hair. She may have been proud of her daughter for graduating from university, but I was even prouder of my mother for fighting her illness and being there to see me accept my diploma.

Before graduation, I had applied for a job in Japan that seemed perfect. I'd been excited when I learned I'd got the job, but I was worried about leaving Mum and the family. Had she truly been cured, or would she relapse? She urged me to go. This was my chance to spread my wings and find my way in the world, she insisted, just as she and Dad had done when they were my age. She had looked me straight in the eyes and explained that sometimes that meant leaving your family behind and traveling halfway around the world. She reminded me that she had left Iran when even younger than me to follow her dreams. So, armed with my college degree and a mix of youthful determination, anxiety and guilt—but also reassured that Mum had Dad, Roshan and Alan with her—I headed off to Japan again, this time to live and work.

My position was a Coordinator of International Relations, or CIR, on the Japan Exchange and Teaching (JET) Program. The program was established by the Japanese government in 1987 to "internationalize" Japan by placing English-speaking college graduates (later other languages too) in schools, government offices and international centers around Japan. CIRs were required to know the Japanese language. In my application, I had asked to live in Kyoto. Apparently, so did everyone else. Instead, I was posted to Hita, a city in western Oita Prefecture in Kyushu, Japan's southernmost main island—far from Japan's main cities, Tokyo, Kyoto and Osaka, and far from the Endos and other people who had been so kind to me when I was a student.

My disappointment was short-lived. A rural city of about 85,000 people, Hita is surrounded by mountains and has two major rivers running through it. Some of its streets are lined with rows of old wooden buildings that reminded me of parts of Kyoto I had explored as a student. In fact, it is one of several towns in Japan known as

"Sho-Kyoto" or "Little Kyoto." When I arrived in late July, the town was abuzz with its Gion Festival, and men from different neighborhoods dressed in white shorts and cotton jackets were pulling large, colorful floats around the city—something similar to the big Gion Festival Mr. Endo had taken me to in Kyoto. It was spectacular. In my first days there, I was guided through the narrow old streets of the old section of town, called Mameda, to the three-hundred-year-old Shimaya restaurant with its delicious *dango jiru*, or "flat noodle soup," to the Kuncho sake factory, where I sampled the local brew, and to the Kusano Honke, the old home of one of the city's wealthy old families, now a museum with a famous doll collection. Within a day or two, I was completely charmed.

I rented a small apartment on the second floor of a modern apartment building just outside the center of Hita. My main room was six tatami mats in size (a little over one hundred square feet) and had a French window that looked out over a rice field. I could often hear frogs chirping down below, and the sound would help me fall asleep at nights. In the mornings, I fixed myself coffee and toast in my tiny kitchen, got dressed and then hopped on my bike for a short ride to work. Mostly, the rides were delightful, as the roads were flat, and the city was surrounded by picturesque mountains covered in cedar trees. Even when it was raining, the scenery took on a hazy beauty, and the scent of cedar permeated the damp air. On one rainy morning, I noticed a small frog sitting on my right shoulder. It had hitched a ride on my raincoat. I stopped by a rice field and placed the bright green creature on some rice, hoping that he would be able to find a new home there.

My place of work was the General Affairs Office of the City Hall, a tired-looking, three-story post-war building. Some twenty people worked in the open-plan office, and most of them smoked, so the air was always thick with cigarette smoke. The office chief, Mr. Suetsugu, was positioned at a large desk by the window so he could watch over his team. I occasionally looked over and saw him gazing dreamily out of the window toward the mountains. I wondered where his mind was. My supervisor, Mr. Suetake, was a thoughtful, good-humored man in his forties, blessed with the patience and dry sense of humor necessary to manage a young, foreign employee alongside his other responsibilities. He mostly spoke to me in Japanese, but, because his English was quite good, we occasionally spoke in English. When he made a mistake, his face would crack into a huge smile as he chuckled at himself. He introduced me to all the different offices of the City Hall, from the Mayor and City Assembly to the Departments of Education, Forestry and Tourism, and explained that I would be teaching an English class once a week to City Hall employees and another class to citizens in the city's brand-new community center. I would also be visiting schools and various local groups to talk to them about my country, my impressions of Japan, and what it means to be international.

The job was really all about connecting with the local people, many of whom had never spoken to foreigner before, and talking to them about the similarities and differences between our worlds. I visited schools and local businesses—from the fire department to farms—and community groups like the Rotary Club, where I was asked to share my impressions of Japan, both good and bad. I became a regular visitor to a couple of preschools, where I taught English nursery rhymes and English animal sounds to the smallest and cutest residents of Hita. The little ones loved saying "woof, woof" like a British dog, instead of "wan, wan" like a Japanese one! A group of housewives in the neighboring pottery village of Onta invited me to teach them British cooking. My cooking repertoire was extremely limited and not very British, so I taught them to make curry and shortbread (borrowed from Mum's repertoire) and a pasta dish. They were gracious, warm and forgiving of my limited skills and happily cooked along with me, sharing food of their own with me too.

Whenever foreign visitors came to Hita, I was part of the welcome committee that showed them around the city. These included a group of Korean students, members of the British Council, and a Spanish ceramic artist who came to study with the Onta potters. The potter, Carmen, and I became great friends and compared notes on our experiences with the locals, as well as our language struggles. The local newspaper reporters followed me around. They were there when I was visiting an elementary school, dancing in a festival dressed in my *yukata*, and wading knee-deep in a muddy field learning how to plant rice. Soon, my picture appeared regularly in local newspapers, and interviews with me about my experiences and impressions of Hita were broadcast on the local TV channel. I had become a local celebrity! It was surreal to have such a prominent position in the community. With it came more responsibility to do my job there well. Some evenings, I staggered exhausted up the stairs to my apartment after a day of non-stop socializing in Japanese. But the next morning, I was excited again for my next adventures.

My evenings quickly became full too, with invitations to people's homes for dinner and with three very stimulating art classes. The first was *ikebana*, or flower arranging, with my supervisor's mother-in-law, Mrs. Shimizu, who was the head of the Ikenobō school of *ikebana* in Hita. I hadn't planned to learn flower arranging, but when this elegant, silver-haired woman with a warm heart and a mischievous smile invited me to join her class, I couldn't say no. Shimizu-sensei lived with Mr. Suetake and his family and had turned one of their tatami-mat rooms into a classroom. Every Wednesday evening, I had dinner with the Suetakes and then joined a group of ladies who had been taking the class with her for years. I marveled at the exquisitely balanced arrangements she and her senior students could assemble using a seemingly random assortment flowers, branches and grasses. These arrangements would then be placed in their own homes, artfully bringing the outside world into their inside spaces.

Shimizu-sensei taught me that *ikebana* was also known as *Kadō*, the "Way of Flowers," a name that indicated that it was an artistic discipline with a spiritual aspect. Leaning over her vase and inserting a tall branch into the center, she explained that each arrangement was about harmony between aspects of nature. The tallest branch was *Shin* (symbolizing Heaven), followed by *Soe* (the medium branch or flower representing humanity) and *Tai* (the shortest, representing Earth). As she picked up a flower, she said its name in Japanese and had me repeat it, and soon I knew more flower names in Japanese than in English. Shimizu-sensei was always thoughtful, warm and patient with me—except for on one occasion, when she surprised me with something close to anger. I showed her an *ikebana* book someone had given me from the Sōgetsu school (a newer school with a more contemporary approach to floral arrangement than the more traditional Ikenobō School), and she frowned and snapped, "*Sōgetsu wa dame desu!*" meaning "Sōgetsu is no good!" From that outburst, I learned of the rivalry that can exist between traditional Japanese cultural schools. Each school believes their school is the true path within the tradition.

My second teacher was Mr. Anai, a ceramic artist who wasn't part of a lineage of potters, as is common in Japan, but had chosen ceramics as a profession. He lived outside Hita in an old farmhouse and had built a kiln next to it to fire his wares, which he then sold at a stall in the Mameda District. After a school visit one afternoon, I had been invited for tea in Mameda by one of the class parents, and we met Mr. Anai selling his ceramics on a table in front of the tea shop. Some of his wares were earth-toned with dark speckles, and others had a gorgeous, rich purple glaze. I had thrown some pots in college as well as in Kyoto, and was interested in studying ceramics in Japan, so I asked him if he taught classes. He didn't usually, but he offered to teach me once a week, on Thursdays, starting right away. I couldn't wait to learn from him how to throw pots on the wheel. However, Anai-sensei had other plans. "First *tebineri*." Hand-building. This way, he explained, would help me truly understand the clay. Every week, I worked for two hours forming clay sausages and coiling them into bowls, cups and vases. When he wasn't teaching me or working on his own pieces, Anai-sensei would stand smoking his cigarette, staring into the night sky and contemplating something profound and beautiful, I was sure. And my gentle, wise teacher was right. Though I was initially frustrated that I wasn't getting to throw pots, over the weeks and months, hand building became surprisingly natural and easy and very calming. I recently tried it again after a couple of decades, and the familiar movements came right back to me.

My third class, on Monday evenings, was calligraphy, or *Shodō*, the "Way of Writing," with Mrs. Miyake, an accomplished calligrapher who had shown her work in calligraphy exhibitions around Kyushu and beyond. In East Asia, calligraphy is on par with painting as one of the most respected art forms. In both the religious and secular realms, being able to write beautifully with a brush is an admired skill and has long been considered a sign of sophistication. Mrs. Miyake specialized in *kana* calligraphy—a very slender, cursive script composed mostly of Japanese syllabic characters known as *kana*, which evolved from Chinese characters, or *kanji*. This fluid writing style was originally used by the ladies of Japan's Imperial Court during the Heian period. Their writing was largely confined to letters and poetry, though some composed diaries as well. One court lady—Murasaki Shikibu—authored the world's first novel, *The Tale of Genji*, entirely in *kana*. I took to Mrs. Miyake right away. She was not what I had expected a calligrapher to be like—someone serious, maybe stiff and composed like those Heian court ladies. Miyake-sensei loved to joke, laughed boisterously—often at herself—and was warm and encouraging. She insisted that I call her Takako, even in class. I accepted her invitation enthusiastically.

Every Monday evening, I cycled over to Takako's classroom in the old part of town, climbed up a dark, steep wooden staircase to a low-ceilinged tatami-mat room on the second floor and sat with about eight middle and high school students who practiced writing large Chinese characters or slender-lined poems on sheets of white paper with soot-black ink. The sweet scent of the ink infused the room like incense, rising upward from the labor and concentration of the students, who began each calligraphy session with five minutes of ink grinding. We all sat in front of our low desks, rubbing a black stick of solid ink against the smooth surface of an inkstone, back and forth and in and out of the small well of water in the stone. The pool of water in the well darkened and thickened with each motion. We had all come here from a full day of school or work, so grinding the ink helped to settle our minds before beginning the practice of calligraphy—the writing of beautiful letters.

For the first few sessions, Takako had me practice getting used to writing with a brush. As a child, I'd been good at drawing, but had struggled with painting, finding it hard to draw with a soft point. I still found controlling the brush challenging, so Takako made me write line after line of connected Vs zig-zagging across the page, or lines of connected loops—this went on for several weeks. She made me practice writing wet strokes, with the brush heavy with ink, and then dry strokes, using hardly any ink to create lines that were often broken and rough in appearance. Then, she had me copy specific characters and simple *kana* phrases. I thought of the Heian court ladies sitting on the floors of their palaces dressed in layers of silk kimonos, writing with slender brushes on poetry cards. These women were basically trapped in their elegant court lives, unable to go outside and see the world. Yet, the poems they wrote were often very worldly and poignant. They wrote *waka*, or "Japanese poems," and these were typically short poems called *tanka* that were made up of thirty-one syllables—an ancestor of the seventeen-syllable *haiku* poetry form. One of the most famous waka poets, Ono no Komachi (active from around 833–854), wrote:

花の色はうつりにけりないたづらに
わが身世にふるながめせしまに

Hana no iro, utsuri ni kerina itazura ni waga
mi yo ni furu nagame seshi ma ni

> The color of this flower
> Has already faded away,
> While in idle thoughts
> My life goes by,
> As I watch the long rains fall.

Over the first few weeks, my progress felt slow, and my brushwork looked ugly and clumsy to me. But eventually I felt a shift in the way I handled my brush, and my writing began to flow. It was satisfying to be feeling some progress and exciting to be learning an art form that was not only elegant but made me feel connected to Japanese court ladies from over 1,000 years ago!

In the late autumn, several months after I arrived in Hita, I received another heart-stopping phone call from home. Dad broke the news to me that Mum had relapsed. She was back in hospital and about to start another round of chemotherapy. The news was like a punch in the gut. It took the wind out of the sails that I had felt filling up with so much air over the past few months. I asked Dad if I should come home. He reassured me that because she had done well with the chemo the first time, the doctors were confident they could get her back into remission. He told me to stay for now. I flew home at Christmas. Mum's spirits seemed strong, even though her body was clearly worn out by the illness and all the chemicals she'd been absorbing. "Go back to Japan!" she ordered me. "You have to live your life. Don't worry about me." I followed her first order. I went back to Japan, but I couldn't follow the second one. I worried about her constantly and called home often. I threw myself into my work and into my classes to distract myself and to "live my life," as she had instructed me to do. In calligraphy class in particular, I focused hard on every brush stroke as a way to calm my fears. For those moments, I could lose myself in the soft rhythm of brush touching paper, the scent of the ink, and the words of long-ago poets.

Then, two months later, I got a call from Dad. It wasn't the regular time for our weekly call, so I was immediately worried. His voice sounded even more weary than usual.

"I don't know how to tell you this..." he faltered. And Dad's speech rarely faltered.

"Oh God. Mum! What's happened?" My blood ran cold.

"No. Your mother's okay. It's Alan. He's in hospital now. He has leukemia too."

"What?" I didn't think I'd heard him correctly. "How is that possible?"

He went on to explain that my brother hadn't been feeling well and his skin had started turning yellowish. The doctors thought he might have hepatitis, but when they ran some tests, they discovered that, not only did he have hepatitis, he also had a form of leukemia called acute lymphoblastic leukemia, one that usually affected children, even though he was nineteen years old. They said it was completely unrelated to Mum's leukemia, and he had a good chance of recovering. But this was unimaginable. Mum was still receiving treatment for her leukemia. Apparently, even the nurses in Mum's ward cried when they found out.

"Oh my God!" was all I could muster.

I couldn't get my head around this impossible news. I would have to go back home. I couldn't keep working here in Hita while my family was suffering at home—two out of the five of us sick! Even though I loved my life in Hita, and I had the responsibility of a job here, Alan was ill now too, so I couldn't keep doing what I was doing. It wasn't right for me to be enjoying myself and growing so much while he was suffering. I started crying into the phone, my heart breaking for my brother who was now gravely ill, my mother who was still recovering and who now had a son who was going through what she was. I shed tears too for my Dad and sister who were dealing with the pain and anxiety of this awful situation every day. It was too much.

"I'll come back home," I finally sputtered.

"No," came Dad's response, firm and certain. "You stay there and keep doing what you're doing. There's really nothing you can do here to help. At least if you're having adventures in Japan, you can call us and share them with us—it'll be something positive that can cheer us all up. One of us needs to be doing that. It will help us all."

I couldn't believe Dad's generosity. Surely he could use my help at home right now. Surely that's where I should be.

My sister, Roshan, was there, he explained, and she was being wonderful, very supportive. She was helping him with everyday tasks and emotional care, and he wanted me to help from Japan in a different way—one that would serve as a reminder to the whole family that life could still be full and enjoyable.

I could barely think straight. When I hung up the phone, I cried some more. Dad had now given me my instructions, and his advice had always been very wise. I knew I needed to follow it and live my life for my whole family here in Hita. I threw myself into my CIR job, adding a few other activities of my own to my work schedule, including an International Club, with regular programs featuring guests, music and food from different cultures. I held a Scots Evening, modeled on my parents' gatherings in Edinburgh, with similar songs, poetry recitals, dancing, and food. I also wrote a column in the City Hall's newsletter on my observations of Japanese life—from my admiration for the Japanese respect toward the elderly to the wastefulness of disposable chopsticks. I called home regularly, and in the summer returned to Cambridge. Mum was in remission again. Alan had recovered from his first round of chemo, but he was looking thin. He had lost his hair too, but he was starting to regain his strength. It was painful to see him struck down right as he was entering his adult life. When I told them how guilty I felt living a life of adventure while he was suffering so much, my parents reassured me that both Mum and Alan were now healing, and I should renew my contract and spend another year in Japan. It was much harder, though, for Alan that I would be going back to Japan while he was ill. I hoped that my parents were right.

So, I returned for a second year in Hita, determined to make my time in Japan count. I decided to do something big and meaningful for as many people as possible and proposed a trip to the UK to students in my English classes. Some of them had become dear friends by that time and had been supporting me emotionally over the last year. In April of 1992, at the age of twenty-five, I organized and led fifteen of them around England and Scotland for two weeks. Choosing places to visit and activities that would interest fifteen people of different ages and making sure no one got lost, injured or robbed was exhausting, but also exhilarating. The emotional climax was bringing them to Cambridge and introducing them to my family. They had all joined in my worry about my mother and brother, while also supporting me and making sure I felt cared for in Hita. Several of them, including Mrs. Suetake and a dear older friend, Mrs. Yokota, had welcomed me into their families, regularly cooking dinner for me and checking in on me, like my local Japanese *okāsan* (mothers).

Though the Japanese traditionally don't hug, when they met my parents, they hugged them hard. Mum and Dad could tell how close I had become to my students and how much I had done for them and they seemed proud of the work I'd been doing in Japan. My students' English hadn't improved much from my classes, but those two weeks in the UK were life-changing for several of them—especially those who had never left Japan before. Afterward, a few of them felt confident enough to travel other countries alone or in groups, and a small group traveled to my wedding in California some years later. I liked to think some serious "internationalizing" happened on that trip.

Once back in Hita, my CIR work and my class schedules got busier than ever, particularly because I had decided to return home after completing my second year there. My ikebana arrangements seemed to be becoming more elegant, as if my hands now knew where to place the flowers to create the most balance between branch and bloom. My hand-built ceramic bowls, cups and vases were becoming smoother and sturdier, and I was becoming more expressive with the forms I built.

However, it was in calligraphy where I seemed to have made the most improvement. Takako told me she wanted me to try a *rinsho*, the exercise of directly copying the calligraphy of a master. She assigned me a poem by the legendary eighth-century poet Ki no Tsurayuki, a male courtier who famously adopted *kana* and even wrote one work in the traditionally female script, writing in the voice of a woman. By "copy," she meant that I had to not only mimic the form of his characters, but also use more ink where his ink was heavy and less ink for the characters that were faint. It seemed unlikely to me that I would be able to create anything as exquisite as his handwriting.

I worked hard on the poem for several weeks, practicing with a very slender brush, lifting the brush where I imagined he had lifted his and pressing down harder where his strokes were thicker. The action of pressing down and lifting the brush to vary the strokes was not only a neat artistic trick, but I noticed that it was very calming. As I wrote out the poem over and over again, I began to understand how truly meditative calligraphy could be and how it could capture my focus and soothe my heart. I wondered if those Heian court ladies had also found the practice soothing when they were feeling isolated or broken hearted, buried under layers of silk gowns and trapped in their gilded cages.

At last Takako seemed to think I was ready and gave me some small squares of elegant, sand colored paper. I wrote out the poem on several sheets, from which she chose one that she declared "beri beri goodo!" in her limited, heavily accented English. She had me impress my seal in the corner and then sent it to the scroll makers to be mounted, something I knew made it special and ready to be displayed formally.

As the end of my stay in Hita approached, Takako wrote out another poem in her beautiful writing and told me she wanted me to copy her version onto decorative paper—a soft yellow parchment with areas that looked to be sprinkled with blue pigment—that had been cut into the shape of a fan. This exercise was not as formal as the *rinsho* of the Tsurayuki poem I had worked on, but it seemed very special to be copying her writing now.

> *Kono michi shika nai*
> *Haru no yuki furu*
> There is only this path,
> Spring snow falls.

The verse was written by Santoka Taneda (1882–1940), a free-verse haiku poet, whose verses didn't conform to the traditional rules of haiku—i.e. three lines of 5-7-5 syllables each. Santoka lived a challenging life; when he was a child, his mother killed herself, and, as an adult, he struggled with alcoholism and a failed marriage. In his forties, he became a Zen Buddhist monk and spent many months at a time walking, begging for food and writing poems, eventually becoming one of Japan's most beloved modern poets. His poem was all the more poignant to me when I learned about his hard life.

For me, this simple poem conjures up an image of someone pushing doggedly forward through the snowy cold, following a path that will only become clearer and easier with the advent of spring and warmer days. The verse wasn't as long or complex as the Tsurayuki poem, which I couldn't read or understand. But with this short poem, I could say each word to myself as I wrote it. "*Kono michi shika nai...*There is only this path." "*Haru no yuki furu...*Spring snow falls" The rhythm of these words helped guide my hand to brush each line onto the paper, fluidly and fluently. I pressed harder with the brush where Takako had pressed hard, and I lifted the brush where I could see she had lifted hers. My final version seemed adequately balanced, and I remember gazing down at it with pride. Takako was delighted and framed the work for me. As a special send-off before I left Hita, she collaborated with Shimizu-sensei and Anai-sensei to mount an exhibition of my ikebana, ceramics and calligraphy at my farewell party. No one was more stunned than I was to see how much I had learned and how much my work had improved in two years.

My time in Hita left me profoundly transformed. I had arrived there as a college-fresh twenty-four-year-old with an international background, expecting to teach the residents of Hita how to be more global. However, during my time there, I was the one who did the most growing and changing. My language skills had improved immensely, and I had even learned some of the local dialect. Living and working in rural Japan for two years had given me a knowledge of the country and its culture that cannot be acquired from a textbook, from my relation-ships with my co-workers to all the groups of people I met through my job. Studying flower arrangement, ceramics and calligraphy had taken me even deeper into Japanese culture, allowing me to feel how art is created and how it can impact lives. My classes had taught me that art has the power not only to beautify a space, but also to connect us with other times and places and to strengthen the heart and soothe the soul.

Most importantly, I had learned the power of true kindness and generosity. At a time when I was missing my own family and wavering about where I was supposed to be in the world, my friends, students, colleagues and teachers in this rural Japanese city had embraced me fully and shared their town, their culture and their lives with me. And my own family, despite their suffering, had generously given me the space and freedom to accept the gifts being offered to me in Hita. Both of my families—in Cambridge and in Hita—helped me live and work and grow, so that my time in Japan would not be wasted and I could be armed with skills I could somehow share with others. Despite my sadness at leaving Hita and my ongoing concerns about my mother and my brother, I had a stronger sense of myself, and I was beginning to be able to see the direction I wanted to take in my life—as if the snow was beginning to melt away and my path was coming into view.

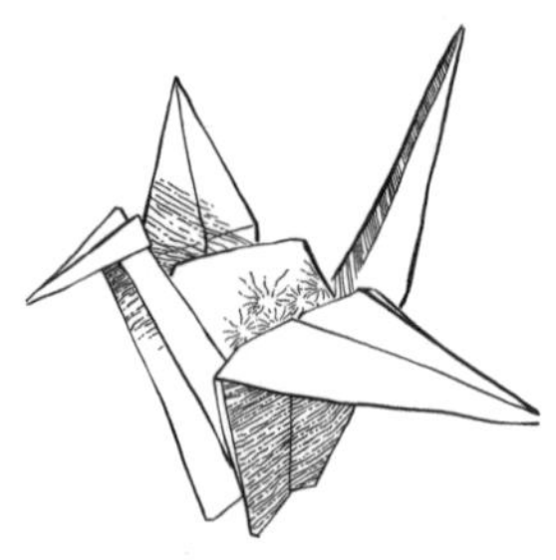

CHAPTER 4

The Origami Cranes

The Japanese have a word, *ikigai*, that refers to the thing that gives your life meaning, purpose or value. Written with the characters *iki* (生き) meaning "alive" or "life," and *gai* (甲斐), which can mean "benefit," "fruit," "use" or "worth," it is similar to the French expression *"raison d'être"* or "reason for being." The concept of *ikigai* has long existed in Japanese culture, but it was first popularized in 1966 by Japanese psychiatrist and academic Mieko Kamiya in her book *On the Meaning of Life* (生きがい について, *Ikigai ni tsuite*). For Kamiya, the word *ikigai* refers to both the thing that gives a person a sense of purpose and the sense of purpose itself. She believed that spending one's life fulfilling a duty that completely differs from one's *ikigai* can lead to neurosis, depression and even suicide.

More recently, the word has gained attention again after several foreign researchers suggested that having *ikigai*—such as work, hobbies and community activities—is what has enabled members of certain Japanese communities, particularly in Okinawa, to live exceptionally long, healthy lives. In response to the worldwide attention the Japanese concept has garnered, the Japanese government has created a page on their website: *Ikigai: The Japanese Secret to a Joyful Life* (2022) https:// www.japan.go.jp/kizuna/2022/03/ikigai_japanese_secret_to_a_joyful_ life.html

I sat on the toilet seat staring between my knees at the floor and wondering what the heck had happened to my life. I looked up at the back of the stall door for some sort of message from the universe, perhaps a scribbled cry from someone in a similar state of existential distress. The surface was blank, completely clean of markings, or any sort of detail that I could read into as some sort of sign. I let out a sigh. Everything seemed so dull and flat. For several months now, I had been coming in here to escape my new reality. I worked at a desk in a windowless, basement office, feeling incompetent and undermotivated. With each passing week, I was feeling my sense of direction slipping away from me more and more. I'd been ducking out of the office so often now that my colleagues probably thought I had some sort of bladder or intestinal problem, but my suffering was more emotional than physical. I had returned to England six months ago. I had known it was time for me to leave Japan and be back home close to my family again, and I had been determined to put my experiences in Japan to work here in London, to "shine my light" and make a difference in a bigger city. But it wasn't working out the way I had hoped. Instead, I seemed to have gone from an enriching job in an exciting, colorful setting—where I was treated like a star!—to a feeling of utter professional inadequacy and insignificance. How had this happened? Had I just had a lucky couple of years in Japan, outside of reality? Was I now back in "the real world?" Was this what adulthood was actually like?

I kept telling myself I should be feeling more positive and thankful. My mother and my brother both seemed to be healing again. Just a few weeks after my return from Japan, Mum had relapsed again, and this time was extremely weak and frail. It felt like we might lose her at any moment. The timing was awful. We were a few weeks away from the launch of the biggest book of Dad's career, *The Oxford Companion to the English Language.* As an English language scholar, he had compiled a comprehensive study of the English language, involving experts from around the world. He was working with a major publisher, and the book was to be his crowning academic achievement to date. Mum had played a critical role in preparing the book too, working by his side as the managing editor before and during her struggles with leukemia. The book represented many years of work and life and loving partnership. The idea that Mum might not be able to celebrate the launch with Dad was heart-breaking. With Mum looking so weak and uncomfortable, a feeling of dread had hung over us all, instead of excitement. But Mum surprised us again with her strong, stubborn will, somehow finding the power to drag her exhausted body back into remission again, for the third time. When the day of the book launch at Heffers Bookshop in Cambridge arrived, Mum was there, shaky, her head again wrapped in a scarf. But she was smiling, clearly proud to be able to celebrate the fruits of years of hard and meaningful work with her life partner. Alan was also in remission from his leukemia. He had been regaining some of his physical strength and was much more energetic. Like Mum, he too had lost his wonderful head of thick, almost black hair, and now it was coming back, lighter in color and finer in texture. Things were looking promising for him again, and he was talking about going back to college and finishing his degree.

I should have been feeling grateful that I had managed to get a job in London at all, with Japan's current economic situation. Two years before, when I had moved to Japan, there had been plenty of jobs for Japanese speakers in companies, law firms and the art and culture sphere. However, around the exact time that I left Hita to return to the UK, Japan's economic bubble had burst. It had been a huge shock to me and many others, though financial experts had presumably seen it coming. The value of the yen plummeted, greatly reducing the value of my hard-earned Japanese savings. But, worse still, all those companies—Japanese and European—that had been hiring Japanese speakers just a few months ago had lost their incentive to invest in Japan. It was the end of Japan's economic boom, and, just like the currency, my Japanese degree was now considerably less valuable in the world of business or international relations than it had been. Nevertheless, I had managed to land the one job I did apply for. It was with a Japanese newspaper, the *Nihon Keizai Shinbun* (*Nikkei*), as a financial news translator for their "Nikkei News Bulletin." I applied for the position, took some difficult translation tests, and then a few days later they offered me the job. At first, I was amazed to have secured the position and excited to start working as a Japanese financial news translator in London. The position seemed very grown-up and even a little glamorous. However, the reality of the job soon became apparent.

The office was located in the basement of the *Financial Times* building on the South Bank of the River Thames, and I traveled there underground on the Tube, so I saw very little sunlight on my working days. My Japanese boss, an elegant man with gray hair and glasses that he wore low on his nose, had limited English-speaking ability, but his translation skills were excellent. As an editor, he was brutal and covered each of my Japanese-to-English translations with blood-red corrections. My two colleagues, who had been working at the *Nikkei* for a few years, were so much better at translating than I was, and their work was less blood-spattered. Even though I had just spent two years living and working in Japan, and my Japanese was pretty good, it wasn't up to the expected level of translation work, and financial news translation is a very specific skill. Determined to improve, I worked hard to build up the vocabulary, grammar and business terminology fluency I needed to pick up my pace, and my work started to come back with less red on it. But, to be honest, I wasn't really very excited that "Company A's pretax profits had fallen eight percent in the first quarter due to slow public sector widget sales." In fact, I found it really hard to care about any of the stories I was writing about, or the world of business as a whole—a world I'd thought I'd wanted to work in just a few years before! I could sense that this was not the right place for me. While I was living in Japan I had learned the word *ikigai*—or "sense of purpose"—and this did not seem to be mine.

What was my *ikigai* then? I spun the roll of toilet paper round and round on its spindle, as if the spinning might somehow help spark some insight. I let the thin paper spill out in layers onto the bathroom floor. Although I had worked hard in Japan, my job hadn't been a "real job" in some ways, but more of an internship created by the Japanese government for foreigners who spoke some Japanese. It hadn't really provided me with skills that could lead to a professional position back home, especially now that Japan's economy had collapsed! In Japan, I was special because, as a foreigner with a different perspective, I had something to say that the people of a small rural city in Kyushu wanted to hear. Here, I had nothing to say that people would pay to hear. I wasn't special at all. I didn't have any sort of real use or purpose. I sighed again heavily. Other than just the language, surely I must have learned something else in Japan that I could use here!

I stared at the heap of toilet paper on the floor beside me and thought back to what I'd enjoyed learning most while living in Japan.

By experiencing the festivals, temple visits, martial arts, flower arranging, kimonos and poetry, I had learned how the Japanese people expressed their deepest beliefs, and I found this very interesting. Maybe other people would too. It dawned on me that I could keep studying Japanese culture and religion until I was good enough to teach others about it. And I could do this by studying the art—because, art, I had learned from my various teachers, was a vehicle of spiritual and cultural expression. Yes, that was it! That's what I needed to learn so that I could have a purpose in this country! I quickly re-rolled all the unspooled toilet paper, stood up triumphantly, and headed back to the office. That was my final phony bathroom break.

I hunted for courses in Japanese art history at colleges in London. There were not many, but I found a postgraduate diploma course in Asian art run jointly by Sotheby's, the auction house, and London University's School of Oriental and African Studies (SOAS). The course offered modules in the arts of India, China, Japan, Korea and the Islamic world. The instructors were art history professors, museum curators, auction house experts and gallery owners, and there would be opportunities to handle actual artworks at places like the British Museum and the Victoria and Albert Museum ("the V&A"). It looked very enticing. The more I read through the course brochures, the more convinced I became that this was indeed what I wanted to do next. But it was expensive. It wasn't a regular college course, but an intensive course with many classes a day for a small number of students. I thought hard, talked to my parents, and looked at my bank account. I would have to spend all my savings on this one-year course and a year of accommodation in London, with no guarantee of a job at the end. It was risky, but I was excited about the future again. I would make this work.

I packed up my desk at the basement office at *Nikkei* and thanked my boss for the opportunity to work there. He understood that financial news translating was not my calling and wished me well. I spent some time back in Cambridge visiting the family. Alan was doing much better and was completing his final year at college, and my sister Roshan was finishing her master's degree. Although we knew we couldn't take Mum's health for granted, she seemed to be doing better and we were all feeling hopeful. I found an inexpensive room with a family in Camden Town, a very trendy part of London not too far from where the course would be held. I could take the bus straight into class, so no more journeys underground on the Tube. Life was already feeling better.

I showed up at the first class and met students from all over the world, many of them clearly from quite wealthy backgrounds—a couple of Italian women with impeccable outfits, makeup and hair, an elegant businesslike woman from Singapore who was already working as a museum curator there, and a glamorous Californian woman who seemed to have walked right out of a classic Hollywood movie. I was a little intimidated by my classmates at first, but it soon became clear that they were all as excited to be taking this course as I was. They either wanted to become academics, work in museums, galleries and auction houses, or learn more about their own art collections. Our origins were diverse, but we all shared a common passion for Asian art that united us during this very intense, high-speed introduction to the subject. Over the twelve months of the course, we all worked diligently to learn everything we could from our specialist teachers.

The first term, devoted to the arts of India, was filled with Buddhist art, Hindu art, temples, sculptures and cave paintings. There were dynastic names and artistic styles that were mostly new to me, but a few were familiar from stories Mum and Dad had shared over the years. We had three or four lectures a day from some of the top experts in the field. One elderly scholar of Indian art, with wisps of white hair and crooked spectacles, could talk for hours without notes about the Hindu temples of Southern India, as well as the rulers who commissioned them and the ornate details of the sculptures carved into their exteriors. He had clearly spent many years in India studying its architectural heritage, and his passion was contagious. He seemed to love what he was talking about and he relished sharing it with others. I took notes furiously and increasingly found myself trying to draw the temples and deities in my notebook so that I wouldn't forget the images I was scribbling about. I was desperate to imprint everything into my brain. The information itself was all fascinating, and I was beginning to imagine myself like this professor, standing in a room full of keen young people teaching them about a culture I loved.

Even more captivating were the visits to the storerooms of the British Museum, the V&A, and Sotheby's to examine and sometimes even handle some of the ancient objects. In secret rooms behind locked doors where visitors usually weren't allowed, we were presented with several ancient statues arranged on a table. After donning gloves, we were passed one object at a time to examine. One day, in a Sotheby's sale room, as I held an ancient, curvaceous gray stone figure of an Indian goddess in my gloved hands, it wasn't just the weight of the stone that I felt, but the weight of the figure's antiquity and importance, artistically and spiritually. She had belonged in a temple and been worshiped by thousands of people for many centuries. I had heard about Hindu gods and goddesses from my parents when I was younger, so I knew how powerful they were and their significance in Indian culture, even today. To be able to hold her and feel a connection across the centuries and the distance seemed almost miraculous. This had my heart racing. I couldn't wait to share these experiences with Mum and Dad. They had experienced India and would understand why I was so excited. Over the phone and on the weekends when I returned to Cambridge, I told Mum and Dad about my classes and museum visits and showed them pictures of the temples and deities I'd been studying. In return, they shared memories of temples and statues they'd seen in India. I felt as if many different aspects of my life were coming together. I could feel myself getting close to finding out what I should be doing with my life. It was all starting to make sense.

But it was during one of these visits home in the autumn of 1993 that my parents shared the shocking news that Mum's cancer was back. And this time she had decided she didn't want to go through the chemotherapy again. She had been fighting for over four years now. Sickness, chemo, remission, relapse. More chemo, then remission, then relapse again. She had now relapsed—for the third time. It was painfully clear that the chemo wouldn't completely cure her but just buy her a few months of health each year. Mum never complained to us about what she had been going through, but we all could see that the treatments had taken a physical and emotional toll on her. She had been suffering for years now and had done her best to stay alive for us all, but she was paying a high price in pain and discomfort. She had decided she had had enough, and we couldn't ask her to keep suffering like this, year after year. We felt defeated. We had hoped she would beat the disease, that the remission would stick this time, that the disease wouldn't come back, that maybe researchers would find the silver bullet in time to destroy the cancer cells without ravaging the rest of her body too. But this was not our story. We were going to lose her.

I felt useless. Dad had been right years ago when he'd told me to stay in Japan because there was nothing I could do to help Mum get better. I had no medical knowledge, and I wasn't much of a caregiver. Mum had always taken care of me, and I had next to no skills that I could use to look after her. All I could do was sit with her and keep her company, talk when she felt like listening and listen when she felt like talking. She didn't like to talk about herself and what she was going through; she preferred to listen to what we all had to say, to know how our days were going. One of the days I was with her, anxious for something to do with my hands while I was sitting at her bedside, I picked up a square of paper and folded an origami crane. I'd learned the folklore in Japan that if you fold one thousand cranes, your wish will come true. Maybe folding cranes for her could help somehow. It seemed better than doing nothing at all. I handed it to Mum, and she smiled.

"Thank you. It's lovely," she said softly. "You learned to make these from the origami book we gave you when you were a child."

"Yes," I replied. "I can't believe that was nearly twenty years ago! It's incredible that I can still remember how to make them!"

The Japanese have been folding paper for more than a millennium. Origami (折紙) meaning "folding paper" or "folded paper" was likely first practiced in Shinto shrines, where folded white paper strips were attached to wooden wands used in purification rituals. Later, elaborately folded envelopes were used in the Imperial Court to hold gifts, and folded butterflies were used to decorate sake bottles used in weddings. Eventually, as paper became more widely available, people started folding it into various creatures like birds and frogs, and objects like boats and samurai helmets. Most popular of all the origami forms is the crane, or *tsuru*, and every child in Japan learns to make *orizuru* ("folded cranes") out of paper at some point in school. Around four hundred to five hundred years ago, the belief arose that folding one thousand cranes out of squares of paper would guarantee the granting of a wish, particularly for a happy marriage, since cranes mate for life. Because of the East Asian myth that cranes live for a thousand years, these birds are also associated with long life, so garlands of 1,000 cranes are often made as a wedding gift—for a long and happy marriage.

In recent decades, the practice of folding paper cranes has spread well beyond Japan, and its meaning has broadened too, mainly because of Sadako Sasaki, a Japanese girl who was a victim of the atomic bombing of Hiroshima and became sick with leukemia as a result of radiation poisoning. When her friend told her that folding cranes can make a wish come true, Sadako folded more than one thousand origami cranes while in hospital in the hope of recovering from leukemia. She made them out of any available material—sometimes even candy wrappers. Some of her cranes were so tiny that she had to use a needle to fold them. Sadly, the disease ultimately claimed her life, but her efforts inspired children all over Japan to fold cranes in her honor and campaign for world peace. Now, people all over the world fold garlands of origami cranes as a prayer for peace and healing.

Inspired by Sadako and her cranes, I kept folding cranes. I still had some packets of colorful origami paper that I had brought back from Japan. Whenever I went home to visit Mum and when I had spare time in London, I sat folding the angular little birds out of yellow, blue, red, pink, orange and green paper. To begin each crane, I laid the paper square on the table, colored-side down, and folded it in half diagonally and then in half again, so that now I had small right triangle. I lifted one of the corners and then pressed it down toward the bottom left corner, squashing the paper out to each side to make a square. Then I turned the paper over and repeated the maneuver on the other side. I had made the Bird Base, an origami base I had learned nearly twenty years before. I was surprised at how well my hands seemed to remember the order and directions of each fold from when I was a child. I continued folding, opening up each of the sides to create a long diamond form containing the sections that would become the wings, head and tail. After carefully folding those parts, I brought up the head section on one side, and the tail on the other. With one final fold, I formed the head and then pulled the wings outward to each side so that the bird's back puffed out into three-dimensional form.

As I had when I was a child, I found the precision and symmetry of the forms—and the rhythmic repetition of the folds—very calming. Now, as I faced the sadness and fear of losing my mother, the folding helped to focus my mind and sooth my spirits a little. When I reached one hundred cranes, I decided to stop. I could tell I wouldn't make it to a thousand, so I mounted the completed cranes on a little mobile, which I hung in Mum's bedroom for her to see, a mini version of the colorful garlands that I'd seen at the Hiroshima Peace Park and at other memorials. It was pretty and cheerful, but it seemed like such a small offering for someone who had given me so much—from life itself, to the clothes she had skillfully sewn for me, to the plates full of snacks she lovingly prepared for my siblings and me every day after school. She may not have been as impressive professionally as Dad was, with all his college classes and publications, but she had utterly devoted herself to her family and to giving us a stable, loving home. It was her *ikigai*, and over the many years she had cared for us, she had taught me some of my most valuable life skills—how to be kind, friendly and considerate to others, to be frugal, to seek moderation in life and to sew. She had selflessly given her three children enough love, sustenance and security to see us into adulthood. And, in the past few months and years, she had demonstrated how handle pain and discomfort with grace. In return, all she wanted was to see us grow up safely into kind, competent adults. I hoped she thought I was doing that. I hoped she could see that I was finding my way and that she didn't need to worry about me now.

Sadly, as in the case of Sadako, my paper cranes didn't help stop the progression of the leukemia. Mum weakened over the weeks and was bedridden at home for her final days, fading a little every day, though she was lucid and loving until she finally lost consciousness. She died on November 26, 1993—her fifty-first birthday. We all agreed this was very in keeping with her character. She was a neat, tidy woman, so naturally, her life span would be neat too. We held a memorial for her in the Old Library of Emmanuel College, a beautiful, old, wood-paneled room made available to us by Professor Brewer, the Japanophile Master of the college, who had become a friend. Many close friends and relatives gathered there to express their love for Mum, and I was able to witness the impact that a kind, selfless life can have on so many others. I was aware that I was not that kind of person—not yet anyway. I was still very much focused on myself and building my own life. Later, when I became a mother, I understood much better how she moved in the world and I've tried to emulate her on many occasions.

After the memorial, I returned to London and wrote my final essay for the Arts of India course. I chose to write about the influence of

Persian painting on Indian Mughal miniature painting. Although I had terrible difficulty concentrating on my research and writing, the topic of Persian painting helped keep me spiritually close to Mum for a couple more weeks. Over the course of the next academic year, I threw myself deep into learning about Asian art and became more and more convinced that this was my passion and my path. After Indian art, the next term was devoted to the arts of China, during which we studied everything from ancient burial ceramics and bronzes, to Song-dynasty paintings, to Ming-dynasty porcelain, exquisite imperial silk robes and, of course, Chinese porcelains. I almost shook with excitement when we were let into the basement of the British Museum and given several Shang bronzes that were well over three thousand years old to hold in our gloved and eager hands. The advanced technological skill of the people who made them made me reconsider the concept of "primitive" cultures. My mind was blown during a lecture by a Sotheby's expert in Chinese ceramics, who explained how to distinguish genuine Chinese porcelain from fakes by examining the tone and texture of the cobalt blue pigment, the whiteness of the porcelain clay and the quality and style of the painted lines. He ended his talk by telling us that what he just revealed would be no longer be true in a couple of years' time, because forgers attend lectures like these to learn how to make better forgeries!

During the final module, the Arts of Japan and Korea, I was giddy with excitement much of the time. The lectures about Japan's Buddhist temples and the styles of their buildings and sculptures had me scrawling pictures in my notebooks more furiously than ever. I wondered at the dramatic difference between the more traditional Japanese Tosa-school painting of the Imperial Court—with rich applications of mineral pigments and slender outlines—and the Chinese-style Kano-school painting—often monochrome, with dynamic, calligraphic lines—that was embraced by the military rulers. I was amazed at the many different styles of lacquerware created in Japan, and was fascinated to learn that Japanese lacquer became so admired in Europe that soon all lacquerware was known as "japon," the way fine porcelain was called "china." Of course, I shared many of these discoveries on the phone with Dad when I called home, hoping that they would cheer him up a little. It was painful not to be able to share them with Mum too.

About halfway through the Japanese art course, I was almost over-whelmed by whole complex world of the tea ceremony and all the various art forms that evolved along with tea culture—from architecture, interior design, flower arrangement and, of course, ceramics. When I started studying Japanese ceramics, I could barely contain myself. I had fallen in love with many types of ceramics while living in Japan. Now I was learning there were so many more—from the ornate Jomon ware of the Neolithic period to black raku tea bowls to the earth-toned and rough-textured Shigaraki ware jars, and all the porcelains too! I hungrily gobbled up the contents of all the classes, visits, and handling sessions, as if loading up my plate at a buffet dinner, but as the course drew to a close, I knew I wanted to learn much more. I needed more than a term to study all of this. I would have to earn a master's degree. With that realization, I also began to understand how truly complex life is. Just at the point in my life when I was discovering its purpose and direction, I'd lost one of my main anchors, my mother.

Two decades later, as an independent Asian art historian and curator in Los Angeles, I curated several exhibitions of origami art, and the largest of these exhibitions included tiny cranes folded by Sadako Sasaki. For the opening of one of the exhibitions at the Japanese American National Museum, Sadako's brother, Masahiro, came from Japan to present one of her tiny origami cranes as a gift to the museum. I felt deeply honored to meet this man who was carrying his sister's legacy of peace and hope around the world. When I shook his hand and looked into his kind eyes, a complex array of feelings of love, loss and hope, on both a personal and global scale, boiled up inside me and I found myself unable to hold back my tears. I bowed and thanked him for his gift to the museum—an object that was so tiny, yet so deeply meaningful.

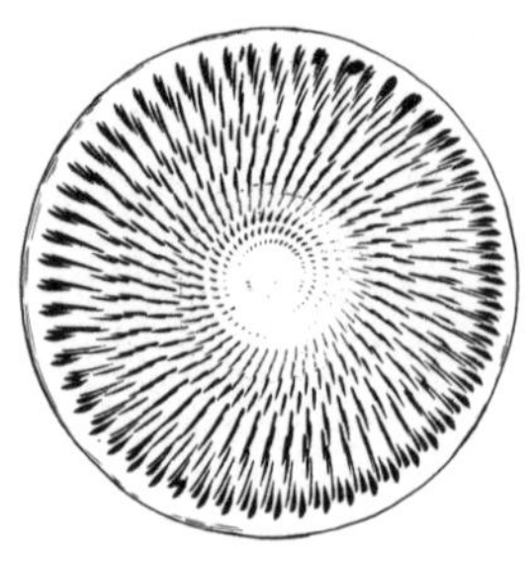

CHAPTER 5

The Ceramic Dish

When I first lived in Japan, one of the expressions that surprised me the most was "*shikata ga nai*." Meaning literally "no way of doing it," the expression is used whenever someone feels that a situation is beyond their control, so there is no point in worrying or stressing about it. It can't be helped. You drive to your favorite restaurant, but it's closed, so "*Shikata ga nai*." You planned a party outside, but it's raining so "*Shikata ga nai*." When I was hearing these words in my early twenties, I considered them rather defeatist and wondered if perhaps the Japanese were inclined to give up too easily. Surely there were "*shikata*," or ways to do these things; it was just a question of figuring them out.

The more I came to know the Japanese and saw how much effort and creativity they put into their lives, their work and dealing with catastrophic environmental challenges like landslides, floods, earthquakes and heavy rains, the clearer it became to me that the Japanese are not quitters or defeatist at all. They make significant efforts when the stakes are high, but for the smaller stuff, they often just throw up their hands, utter, "*Shikata ga nai*," and let it go.

———◆———

I stood at the edge of the narrow country road gazing out over the dark tiled rooftops of the houses and pottery studios that lined the roadside and the corrugated metal roofs and brick chimneys of the kilns that crawled up the sides of the wooded hills. To my right, wooden planks had been set out in rows next to the studios, and large ceramic dishes coated in white slip (kaolin clay slurry) had been lined up along them and left to dry in the heat of the afternoon sun. Every few seconds, I heard a heavy thud, the sound of a *kara-usu*, or Chinese pestle, filling with water from the river and then thumping down rhythmically onto the ground to pound the local mountain clay into soft powder.

It was almost magical to be back in the ceramics village of Onta, as it had been one of my favorite places to visit when I lived in Hita, the city where I had worked after graduating from college. This time, I had just finished my diploma course, and was convinced that Japanese art was my passion and my path, so I had applied to the School of Oriental and African Studies (SOAS) at London University to enroll in a master's course in Asian art and archaeology. I had been accepted, and I had amazingly received a scholarship! So, in order to gather as much information as possible about Japanese art over the summer, I had used the last of my savings and flown to Japan. I was back in Hita staying with friends, teaching English to support myself, and visiting places nearby that had fascinating artistic traditions, like Buddhist temples and ceramics centers like Onta.

Onta was in the hills about a twenty-minute drive from Hita. While Hita was a rural city with a very slow pace, unlike Japan's larger metropolises, Onta was a tiny village—a hamlet even—and it had the air of being frozen in time. Not surprisingly, the place was a popular tourist attraction. The village had strict rules about how it ran its operations so that it could remain true to its traditions and sustainable. There were four potting families, the Sakamotos, Kurokis, Yanases and Kobukuros, and a total of ten households, from which only two potters could be throwing pots at any one time—typically a father and son—so as not to overtax the clay deposits in the nearby hills. Other family members—often the wives—would also work the clay, mixing and sifting it to prepare it for the men to throw on the wheel. And the wheel was typically a kick wheel, one powered by the leg muscles of the potters, rather than electricity. When I had visited before, I had marveled at how the potters could move so energetically with their lower bodies yet keep their torsos completely still as they took a blob of rusty red clay and smoothly opened it out with their hands to form a perfect bowl or a cup. In particular, I had been lucky enough to watch Shigeki Sakamoto, one of the senior potters, at work. He was a very lively character with a cheeky smile and a wiry physique, who always wore a white vest and held a cigarette in his hand when he wasn't working the clay.

The most unique features of Onta are the large wooden pestles, mentioned earlier, that pulverize the clay using the power of the local river's running water. These *kara-usu* are essentially large wooden seesaws, with a pestle pointing downward at one end and at the other end, a receptacle for water that lowers into the river. As the river flows down the mountain, it fills the receptacle, but once full, the water tips out causing the pestle to slam down hard onto the clay. The rhythmic pounding of the *kara-usu* is heard continuously throughout the mountain hamlet, serving as the ceramic community's heartbeat—one that has been echoing through this enchanting village for nearly four hundred years.

Because I was captivated by Japanese ceramics, I had already decided that I would focus on ceramics for my master's dissertation, and it was very likely that I would write about Onta ware, or *Onta-yaki*. So much about the tradition was intriguing. I had been told years before that the potters from Onta had come from another ceramics community called Koishiwara over the mountains in Fukuoka Prefecture in 1705. The potters who had originally settled in Koishiwara in the late sixteenth century were Korean, so today's Koishiwara and Onta potters were descended from Korean immigrants. What nobody told me when I lived in Hita (and worked for the Japanese government) was that the original Korean potters had not come willingly to Japan but had been kidnapped by Japanese generals who were sent by the shogun Hideyoshi to Korea during his failed attempt to invade China in the late sixteenth century. I'd learned during my diploma course that, because there was money to be made in tea ceremony ceramics at that time, the Japanese generals had abducted Korean potters, brought them to Japan, and forced them to set up kilns in their domains. The wares from many of these kilns—like Hagi and Karatsu ware—are among the most admired ceramics in Japan.

The ceramics of Onta and Koishiwara were not made for the tea ceremony, but were "folk wares," or everyday wares used by ordinary people, but they were beautifully decorated. The Korean potters had brought to Koishiwara several decorative techniques and styles that had been used in Korean folk ceramics, and many are still used in Onta and Koishiwara today. Because the clay they used—both in Korea and in Kyushu—was dark in color because of its high iron content, the potters coated the vessels with a white slip, or liquid clay, to create a lighter-colored backdrop for adding decoration. The potters of Onta and Koishiwara are masters of slip decoration, either brushing it on with bold strokes (*hakeme*), combing patterns into the wet slip (*kushime*) or using a sharp, flexible blade to nick rows of tiny, dark marks (the color of the clay beneath) into the slip—a technique known as chattering, or "flying blade" (*tobikanna*).

I also visited Koishiwara that summer, and in both places, I bought myself quite a few ceramic souvenirs. Because these wares are for daily use, they are considered folk art, or "mingei," and so are relatively affordable, unlike ceramics made for use in the tea ceremony, which are traditionally very expensive. When I had lived in Hita, I had bought a few teacups and bowls of Onta-yaki, which I loved, used daily and brought home with me. On this visit, I treated myself to an Onta-yaki dish. It was coated with white slip and decorated with the *tobikanna* pattern. The simple spiraling pattern of dark, rhythmic notches cut through a cream-colored slip was a perfect two-tone background for any kind of food. Even though the dish was considered local folk ware in Hita, and so was actually affordable for someone like me, it would be rare and even exotic on any table outside Japan.

After a summer spent visiting friends, talking to Onta potters, taking slides and collecting articles and other material about Onta, I returned to London, ready to begin my master's course at SOAS. I had a very well laid plan and chose my classes strategically. My main subject would be Japanese art, and because so many of the Japanese ceramics I was interested in seemed to have their roots in Korean ceramics, I decided to study Korean language too, in case I needed to do future research in Korean. My third class was a Chinese ceramics course held at the Percival David Foundation of Chinese Art (PDF), a small museum near SOAS, housing a collection of one thousand seven hundred Chinese ceramic pieces, many formerly owned by emperors and given to the University of London in 1950. (The collection was donated to the British Museum in 2024).

Unfortunately, the college's Japanese art professor was on sabbatical that year, and the substitute professor was not an expert in ceramics or any of the areas of Japanese art in which I was particularly interested. However, I enjoyed the Korean language class, and even started going out with one of the other students in that class, Steve, who had studied Chinese and lived in Beijing for a year. It was fun to share and compare our experience with all three East Asian languages and our recollections of living in very different East Asian cultures. My third course, the Chinese ceramics course, was one of the best classes I have ever taken and the highlight of my master's coursework. It was taught by Rosemary Scott, or "Romie," as we all called her, who was the director of the PDF at the time. She overflowed with knowledge and passion for her subject—and with good reason. The Chinese ceramics in the collection were the finest examples of most types anywhere in the world. The collector, Sir Percival, was in China in the 1920s and acquired many of the ceramics that had been sold off by members of the Imperial Household Department during the late Qing dynasty. Many of the pieces rival examples on display at the National Palace Museum in Taiwan—pieces that were smuggled out of China when the Communists took over the country and destroyed much of China's imperial heritage. To sit in a class and learn about rare imperial Song-dynasty celadon glazes and then actually handle an example of the wares was literally breathtaking. To be able to look closely at the details of a Ming-dynasty porcelain chicken cup on the table in front of me made me feel more deeply connected to the little cup's creator and user than I would have ever felt looking through protective glass.

We learned from Romie not just about the ceramics themselves, but also about Chinese history, trade and imperial culture. She explained the popularity of certain motifs under the Mongols (who established the Yuan dynasty) and the trade between China and the Middle East—not only in ceramics but in cobalt, the mineral oxide that was used as a blue pigment underglaze on so many Chinese porcelains. She told us stories about the collecting habits of the Qianlong Emperor, who

Romie referred to as an "imperial vandal" for his habit of inscribing poems and stamping his seal on many of the ceramics and paintings in his collection. Her teaching style was informative but also warm and full of humor. Though armed with a rich vocabulary of descriptors, which she generously used for the ceramics, she wasn't afraid to call a design of rabbits "cute," a word not usually used in art history textbooks. I decided I wanted to teach like her in the future and observed her style carefully. When I give lectures today, I occasionally use the word "cute" in her honor!

Romie also introduced us to some of the ceramic wares used by the ordinary people, including a type called Cizhou ware, a "folk ceramic" that was characterized by a dark clay body covered by white slip, which became part of the ware's decorative scheme. Though less glamorous than the celadons and porcelains, this particular ware attracted my attention as it seemed there might be a connection with these ceramics and the Japanese wares that I was planning on exploring. I wrote my first paper for the class on the subject, and I started to see a topic emerging for my dissertation. Because Romie was so knowledgeable about East Asian ceramics, I shared my observations with her and asked her if she would supervise my dissertation/thesis at the end of the year, even though it was in Japanese art. She generously agreed, and I was thrilled. I would be able to research a subject I found fascinating with the help of an outstanding expert and teacher. Everything was going according to plan.

Until it wasn't. In the spring term, I was in the kitchen of the house where I was renting a room preparing for dinner when the phone rang. One of the other students answered it and called me over. "It's your dad," she said.

A familiar sense of dread chilled my body. Dad didn't usually call me. I called him each week to check in on him. It had been a year since leukemia had taken Mum, and since then, Alan had been in remission and had been doing well. He had graduated from his college and begun a job working in advertising. So what could it be? I leaned against the wall and said hello anxiously. Dad's voice spoke back to me. He sounded exhausted.

"Hi, Meher. It's about Alan. We just got the results of his blood test. His leukemia is back."

I clutched the phone hard and felt myself sliding down the wall until I was sitting in a heap on the floor next to the fridge. My questions poured out with my tears. "How?" "When?" "What are we going to do?" and "Why?" We had already been robbed of one family member because of this horrible disease, so why were we dealing with it again? We had all thought—or hoped at least—that we'd paid the ultimate price and that Alan would be okay now. But, apparently losing Mum to leukemia didn't mean Alan was safe. It was too awful. Poor Alan. Poor Dad. Poor all of us.

For the next few months, our small family started wobbling again. Alan went back into hospital in Cambridge, with Dad looking after him from home, this time without Mum as part of the team. Roshan and I traveled back and forth from London to visit Alan and lend Dad moral support. When Alan had first become ill, the doctors had told us that if he relapsed, one possible treatment would be a bone marrow transplant. If either Roshan or I were a tissue-type match, they could extract his bone marrow and replace it with our cancer-free marrow and potentially cure him. This seemed hard to believe—or even understand—but Roshan and I had both given a sample of our bone marrow tissue to be tested. I had been disappointed to learn that I was not a match and therefore would not be able to help, but fortunately Roshan was a match. Her bone marrow could now be used to hopefully save his life.

Most of the details of the rest of my master's degree coursework are a blur. I went to classes, I learned some Korean, submitted papers on Japanese art and enjoyed my classes in Chinese ceramics, but I have no recollection of my master's exams that summer. I know I took them and did quite well, but they have completely disappeared from my memory. They all happened around the same time that my sister was hospitalized so that doctors could extract a liter and a half of her bone marrow. Both she and my brother were in hospital at the same time, lying in beds and connected to various tubes. Dad and I did a lot of anxious pacing around. Alan's bone marrow had been removed to make way for the donor material, and Roshan's extracted bone-marrow stem cells were being intravenously transplanted into his body. Over the next few weeks, as Roshan recovered her strength and grew more marrow, the doctors monitored Alan to make sure that the "grafted" bone marrow didn't reject its new "host," that is, his own body. There were many scary moments, including several occasions when Alan felt that he was experiencing storms in his head. If he survived the transplant and it worked, it would be likely that his leukemia would be cured, but this wasn't guaranteed.

Amidst this whirlwind, I was supposed to begin writing my master's dissertation and finish it over the summer. I had identified a research topic—one I was excited about and which Romie also found intriguing. When I was studying Chinese Cizhou wares with her, I noticed that many techniques used to decorate these popular slip-decorated wares in thirteenth and fourteenth China were also used on Korean Bunjeong "folk" wares in the fifteenth and sixteenth centuries. Then these techniques were brought to Japan by the kidnapped Korean potters who employed them at ceramics centers like Onta and Koishiwara. However, I had noticed in my studies that one technique—the *tobikanna* chattering technique used on the dish I had just bought—appeared in Cizhou wares and on Onta and Koishiwara wares, but it wasn't part of the Korean potters' repertoire. I decided I wanted to find out why it had skipped this geographical step and not appeared in the Korean wares. In preparation for my research, I presented a lecture on the topic to my fellow students and some local Asian ceramics enthusiasts, using slides I had taken on my last trip to Japan. This was my first art history lecture.

On the very first day of my dissertation research, I gathered together the various articles I had found in Japan over the summer and some texts I had found since and headed for the art history section of the SOAS library to start my research. I loved working in this library. Though not as elegant as the oak-paneled library at Emmanuel College, this rather drab-looking, modern space was filled with books containing the knowledge I wanted in my brain. I now knew what I wanted to do and learn, and even the presence of classmates next to me at the large reading table wasn't a distraction. Rather, I could sit here reading or writing about some fascinating aspect of Japanese art and even forget for a while that there was anything wrong in my world.

I found a good spot in the library and sat down with all of my texts piled on the table around me ready to begin my investigation into the mysteries of the *tobikanna* technique. I began reading through a Japanese newspaper article about Onta pottery that I had picked up in Hita the previous summer. Using my dictionary, I was able to understand that in the 1930s, an Asian ceramics collector—a doctor from some other part of Japan—had visited Onta and spoken with some of the potters in the village. He had admired the chattering technique in Chinese Cizhou wares and asked one of the Onta potters to try it out on his wares. The potter gave it a try, and everyone liked the pattern created with the new technique. All the Onta potters started using it as part of their decorative repertoire, and then this *tobikanna* technique caught on in Koishiwara too. That was it. End of story.

I sat with my head in my hands and stared down at my feet under the table. I had solved my *tobikanna* mystery in the first hours of my research. Though part of me was pleased to have found my answer so quickly, the simplicity of the explanation meant that I no longer had a subject for my dissertation! I groaned with disappointment. I had gathered all these materials, taken all those slides, come up with my topic, and was hoping to make an exciting discovery that could perhaps be published and contribute to the field of Japanese ceramics. But there was no discovery to be made. Now what was I supposed to do? What a waste of all that time and energy. Now, I'd have to find another topic, but I didn't have much time. Deflated and anxious, I packed up all my papers and books and headed home, my head spinning as I tried to figure out how to proceed.

I called home and talked to Dad. I told him about my predicament, but the conversation quickly turned to Alan and how his day had been. Not too bad apparently. That was a relief. Soon my despair about my dissertation began to subside. As students, we had often talked about having an "essay crisis," but, unfortunately, I knew what a real crisis was. Faced with the much more horrendous reality of my brother's health situation, I had acquired a sense of perspective. My brother's situation was a real crisis, something worth worrying about. My dissertation "crisis" wasn't really a crisis. It was frustrating, but it was just a bump in the road, something that could be figured out. It fell into the *"shikata ga nai"* category of things in my life—things that just aren't worth getting that worked up about.

When I spoke to Romie, she reassured me that such moments are common in the world of research. She brainstormed with me to come up with another subject for my dissertation. It wasn't focused on Japanese folk ceramics, the topic I was hoping to explore deeply. The subject was the evolving cultural significance of the tea bowl in Japan. It was much more sociological and philosophical and relatively easy to pull together with books and articles available in the college library. Over the summer, in the library and on train rides between London and Cambridge, I read about the development of the tea ceremony, the many types of Chinese and Korean tea bowls that were used and admired by tea masters, and the birth of Japan's most admired tea wares. I discovered that there were legends attached to certain tea bowls, and that some were even given personal names. I found the topic fascinating.

Back in Cambridge, my brother's condition began to stabilize, and his donated bone marrow began working for him, building him a whole new immune system, one which we were told would not allow him to relapse into leukemia again. Secure in the knowledge that he was safe, I allowed myself to enjoy my research and relish crafting my dissertation into a solid-enough piece of writing. And somehow, I passed my master's with distinction. More importantly, I learned not to panic when research falters and to save my energy and emotion for real worries.

To this day, I still use my Onta ceramics, including the dish I had recently acquired. With its dramatic *tobikanna* patterns that spiral rhythmically around a central point, the dish is more than just a beautiful ceramic object that is part of a four-hundred-year-old Japanese tradition with fascinating ties to older Chinese and Korean ceramics. To me, it will always serve as a reminder of a valuable lesson about what is really important in life.

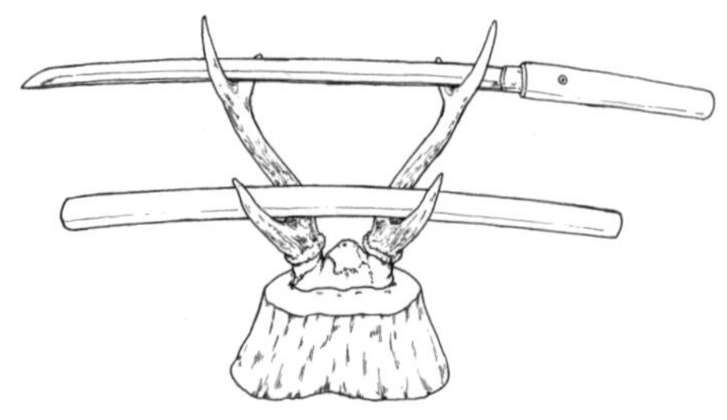

CHAPTER 6

The Sword

"*Naseba naru, nasaneba naranu, nanigoto mo…*" This Japanese saying translates literally as, "Try and you will succeed; don't try and you will not succeed—this is true of all things." It is extracted from a poem written by the feudal lord Uesugi Harunori (1751–1822), who governed Yonezawa Domain, in Dewa Province (modern Yamagata Prefecture). Also known by his pen name, Yōzan, Uesugi is known for the stringent reforms he established to improve the finances and education in his domain. He wrote the poem to his vassals to encourage self-discipline. The full poem ends with the line "If you don't succeed, you have only yourself to blame."

Loosely, the saying is the equivalent of "Where there's a will, there's a way," but it goes further than these words of encouragement, as it also stresses the consequences of not trying. To me, this proverb sums up the double-edged sword that is the Japanese spirit. Their philosophy of self-discipline is so intense that their intolerance of failure can often be devastating, but it can give rise to some of the world's greatest artistic, technical and cultural accomplishments.

———◆———

"Irasshai! Irasshai!"

Takeshi welcomed us warmly in Japanese. He had slid open the front door of his house and stepped out in wooden geta shoes to meet us. He was wearing his formal black martial arts ensemble, which was used for special occasions, his black hair was slicked back, and he was grinning widely. He looked as imposing as ever as he guided us through the front entrance and into his old, wooden home.

I had first met Takeshi the weekend I arrived in Hita, the city in Japan where I had worked for two years. It was the weekend of the local Gion Festival, one similar to the spectacular festival I had seen in Kyoto when I was a student. It was extremely hot and humid, and Takeshi was dressed only in white shorts, a headband and straw sandals, and he was pulling a heavy festival float through the streets with a group of other men from the neighborhood. He made quite an impression with his taut physique, slicked-back black hair, high cheekbones and mischievous twinkle in his eyes. He was one of the most beautiful men I had ever met, but he was much older and married, with three young children. He was introduced to me as Mr. Shigeishi by his cousin Mr. Shigeyama, the barber who was one of the people in charge of the neighborhood's festival float.

A couple of months later, as part of my work in Hita, I had visited an elementary school, and he was the parent who picked me up to take me to the school. After the visit, he took me out for tea as a thank you for visiting with his son Futoshi's class and insisted I call him Takeshi. That afternoon, he introduced me to Mr. Anai, the ceramic artist, who offered to become my ceramics teacher. I didn't have a car to drive to Mr. Anai's house, and without hesitation, Takeshi offered to drive me to my weekly pottery classes on Thursday evenings, keen for me to learn as much as possible about Japanese culture while in Hita. As with many other people I met in Hita, he was also very curious and keen to learn more about the outside world.

Takeshi worked as a post office chief in a small local post office, but his passion lay in martial arts. He had competed nationally in martial arts when he was younger. In recent years, he had become very serious about Shōrinji Kenpō, a Japanese martial art adapted from Shaolin kung fu—a type of Chinese temple boxing that combines self-defense training, mental training and health training. Even while working as a post office chief, he practiced his martial arts, training regularly both physically and mentally so that his martial art informed all aspects of his life—his dedication to his work, his philosophy toward his community, and his attitude to mental and physical health. He was also interested in teaching this foreigner what he considered to be the most important aspects of Japanese culture. He believed deeply in self-discipline and taught me the previously mentioned proverb, writing "*Naseba naru...*" down on a piece of paper so that I wouldn't forget it.

He was one of the people I had admired most during my stay in Hita.

Now, three years after leaving my job in Hita, I was back again looking for inspiration and direction. I had a master's degree in Japanese art history, which is what I wanted, but was now trying to figure out what to do with it. There seemed to be only three jobs in British museums for Japanese art historians, and they were all capably filled. Very few art dealers, galleries or auction houses were looking for Asian art specialists. I had been trying hard to find work, but it was not looking promising. I was starting to despair, and living in London was expensive. So I headed back to Hita in the late autumn after graduating. Again, I offered my services to friends and acquaintances as a private English teacher to cover my expenses, while I tried to figure things out. Though Takeshi didn't seem pleased that I was back in Hita again, he sent his son Futoshi, now fourteen years old, to me for English lessons. A lovely, sweet-tempered boy, Futoshi didn't seem at all interested in his father's beloved martial arts. However, Takeshi still wanted him to be armed with as many skills as possible so he could succeed in life—and that included learning the English language.

A few weeks into my stay in Hita, I was joined for a couple of weeks by my boyfriend, Steve, who I had met in Korean class during my master's coursework. Because of our similar interests in East Asian languages and cultures, I was hopeful about our relationship, but he didn't seem as keen as I was to become serious. He was spending a few months on a Chinese language scholarship at a university in Taiwan and decided to visit me during his winter break. While he was in Hita, I received an invitation from Takeshi and his wife to have dinner at their home as a thank you for teaching Futoshi. Because Steve practiced a form of Chinese martial arts, I had already told him about Takeshi. He was eager to meet him and learn more about Japanese traditions.

Standing in the doorway, Takeshi held out his hand to shake Steve's hand. Steve responded awkwardly, shaking Takeshi's hand and bowing at the same time, trying to get it right. I could tell he was intimidated by Takeshi. A slim, strawberry-blond Englishman with fine features and freckles, Steve was also a martial artist, but he was not at Takeshi's level. Takeshi was some twenty years his senior and clearly lived and breathed his practice. Steve was like me, still trying to figure himself out and find his direction in life.

We passed through the front door into the entryway, took off our shoes and stepped up onto the tatami mat floor. Takeshi's good friend Tomi was already there and was grinning in our direction. Tomi did not share Takeshi's finely sculpted features, but I always enjoyed looking at his face too. It was broad with slightly protruding eyes and lips that were seemingly made of rubber because he was always contorting them into different shapes when he spoke. A postmaster in a rural village in the mountains, Tomi was one of the wittiest people I had met while living in Japan, and Takeshi often invited him to join us at my favorite *yakitori* restaurant after my ceramics classes. We spent many evenings either arguing about politics and philosophy or laughing hysterically at Tomi's comical descriptions of the village where he lived and worked. His charming tales of foxes and raccoons (*tanuki*) trying to withdraw cash from ATMs using dried leaves would regularly have me in tears, particularly because I had studied Japanese folklore and understood the references to these two trickster animals. Tomi came right over and gave me a warm hug. It had been years since I had seen him last, and I looked forward to laughing with him again.

Then Takeshi's wife emerged from the kitchen. She was a petite woman with shoulder-length, lightly permed black hair, casual slacks, a blouse and an apron. Though she was not glamorous, her features were very delicate and pretty in a modest, unassuming way. I don't think I ever knew her by any other name than "Mrs. Shigeishi." I rarely socialized with her when I lived in Hita, as she was always at home looking after the family. But whenever I met her, she was always warm and friendly, with a very gentle, reserved manner.

"Meher-san. It's so nice to see you again," she greeted me in Japanese, bowing. "I'm so pleased you could come to our home. Thank you so much for teaching English to Futoshi." I bowed back to her, thanked her for inviting us to her home, and told her how much I was enjoying teaching their son.

She directed us into the main room and to a low, black-lacquered table on the tatami-mat floor. Takeshi took his place on one side and placed Tomi to his right. Steve and I were seated together across from him and his wife was on his left, the end closest to the kitchen. The table was almost entirely covered with various plates of tantalizing food.

"This is quite a spread," said Steve, eyes opening widely. "I don't think I've ever seen such a feast!" Steve was not used to people making such a fuss over him. His family didn't have much money, and his time abroad had been in China, before the country became wealthy, so his experience living in Asia had been quite different from my years in Japan, spent at a time when the Japanese economy was booming. While I had lived in Japan, I had become used to extravagant meals served by generous friends, but this was even more spectacular. There were tiny dishes full of rice, deep-fried vegetables and tempura shrimp, all surrounding a huge, round, red platter containing every type of sushi I knew, and sashimi in various shades of pink, yellow and white. On a separate dish were skewers of chicken—*yakitori*—a nod to our favorite yakitori restaurant *Ikko*, where we used to gather regularly. And because their home was in the countryside, there was a colorful selection of pickles and fresh vegetables.

"*Dozo*. Please eat," said Takeshi's wife, as she started moving around the table, pouring each of us beer. She then sat back a few feet away from the table, poised to fetch us anything we might need from the kitchen. She had assumed the role of waitress, rather than a member of the party, as Japanese wives often did. I picked up my chopsticks, said "*Itadakimasu*" with a slight bow, and started to dive into the beautifully prepared feast, savoring the delicate flavors and rich textures of every mouthful. As we all tucked into the food, I explained that Steve had a serious interest in martial artists, particularly Chinese styles, so Steve and Takeshi briefly discussed Shorinji Kempo, with me translating as best I could. Then Steve asked me about Takeshi's job. As I too had been, Steve was curious why a martial artist was running a post office. I translated Steve's question to Takeshi.

"I am a post office chief because my father was a post office chief," he replied straightforwardly.

He went on to tell Steve, just as he had once told me a few years earlier, that his father had also inherited the position, so this was something his family had done for one hundred years. In the Meiji period, he explained, when the Japanese national government was Westernizing and modernizing Japan, social systems like the post office were made the responsibility of local samurai families who had enough property, wealth and education to be able to run them well. As the eldest son in his family, Takeshi had grown up knowing he would inherit the position, even when he trained and worked as an electrical engineer, wiring large buildings in the nearest big city, Fukuoka. Then, when his father retired, he came back to Hita to take over the job and serve his community. "My family are samurai. The verb *samurau* means 'to serve.'"

Steve seemed as impressed as I had been when he had explained his situation to me. I had understood that the post office job wasn't Takeshi's passion, but he brought his energy and self-discipline to his work nonetheless, running his office well and helping the local community. He seemed to know everyone in the city, and he played an active role in both his home and work communities, volunteering at various organizations and schools, and in the many local festivals. He served his community and family well—a true samurai.

Steve then turned his focus to his food and Tomi seized the chance to ask me what I'd been doing in the past couple of years. I explained that I'd earned my master's degree in Japanese art history and had really loved studying Japanese art, but I was now trying to figure out how to find a job with my new qualifications. I explained that there weren't very many opportunities for a Japanese art historian in London, so I had come back to Hita to study, practice my Japanese and figure things out. Takeshi frowned and remarked slightly sternly that Hita didn't seem to be the best place to be figuring out how to get a job in Japanese art history in England. I looked down at my plate and nodded, ashamed. I knew he was right. Because I had enjoyed my time in Hita so much, I had kept coming back here for answers and support, but deep down I knew it was time for me to move on and build my career in my part of the world.

Sensing the mood sinking, Tomi quickly laughed and said, "That's right! You don't want to get stuck in Hita with all of us country bumpkins!" He raised his beer glass and made a toast.

"To country bumpkins!"

We all lifted our glasses, grateful for Tomi's humor at that moment, and he went on to regale us with his colorful, comical observations about the world. With me scrambling to translate for Steve, we all joined in with our own humorous anecdotes. More beer was served, and then we took turns pouring each other sake into tiny porcelain cups, and the conversation began sliding deeper and deeper into silliness, until Tomi and Takeshi had boozy-red faces and were wiping hysterical tears from their eyes. Steve too seemed to have forgotten his nerves, and although he only understood half of what was being said, was chuckling along with his new friends. Even Takeshi's wife had been infected by the lightness of the gathering and was clutching a small glass of beer in her hand, rosy-cheeked and giggling behind a raised hand. As I watched all these familiar, kind faces, I felt the warm sake flowing through me, I somehow didn't feel so worried about my future.

Then Steve asked Takeshi about the sword. I hadn't actually noticed it, but now I glanced over in the direction Steve was looking and saw a samurai sword on display on a shelf on the far side of the room. It was a long, curved sword, or *katana*, the type that would have been worn attached to a samurai's belt alongside a shorter sword, as a pair of lethal weapons that also served as a sign of the samurai's high social status. The sword was encased in a simple wooden sheath, and it rested on a stand made of deer antlers, in front of a hanging scroll—clearly on display as an object of importance. Despite its function as an implement used for killing, the sword was a remarkably elegant object. Takeshi sprung up and crossed the room. Suddenly he had transformed from a tipsy, red-faced dinner host into a serious martial arts master. He gently lifted the sword from its stand and carried it carefully back to his place at the table.

"Our family were samurai, and only samurai could wear swords. The sword was not just a weapon. It was the heart and soul of the samurai."

He held up the sword so that we could admire its elegant curve, even inside its sheath.

"Japan's swordsmiths were the best in the world, so the blades are very sharp and can cut through anything."

"Can you show us the blade?" I ventured.

"Yes, but when you look at a blade like this, you mustn't let your breath touch it."

Takeshi laid the sword down on the tatami. He took a white cotton handkerchief out of his sleeve and held it in his mouth to stop any air or moisture escaping from his mouth. Although we were several feet away, we all held our breath too as he slowly picked up the sword again and drew the blade slowly out of the darkness of its sheath. He held it up for us to admire. The long curve was perfectly balanced, giving the blade an eerie lightness. The temper mark along the edge of the blade side of the sword caught the light and shimmered like a ghostly snake slithering over its cool steel surface. I found myself momentarily paralyzed by its deadly beauty.

After a minute or so, Takeshi respectfully slid the blade back into the safety of its sheath and we all breathed again. I looked over at Steve who reached for his beer and took a swig, as if to bring himself back to reality. It took a lot to move Steve, and I knew this moment had. Then, I turned to look at Takeshi. He was holding the sword out with both hands. He almost whispered across the table to me in Japanese, "Steve-san *ni ageru.*" I'll give it to him.

"What?" I replied, thinking I hadn't understood him correctly.

"I'll give him the sword."

"No, no, no, no..." The words just burst out of my mouth. I couldn't believe he wanted to give his sword, something so precious, to someone he had just met. Steve was nudging me. "What's he saying?"

I explained quickly that he was offering him the sword, but that I refused it because it didn't seem right to accept such a treasure as a gift. Steve's eyes were huge. "God, no!" he agreed with me. "I can't take that!" He turned to Takeshi and stammered in very broken Japanese,

"*Domo arigato. Iie. Iie.*" Thank you, no, no.

Takeshi nodded, seeming to understand that Steve meant no offense. He stood up and returned the sword to its place on the shelf. The lively gathering gradually started to wind down, and Steve and I started to make our way back to standing position, reeling a little from the blend of beer and sake and the shock of the offer of Takeshi's sword. Takeshi and his wife accompanied us all back to the front entrance, where we recovered our shoes and fumbled around trying to put them back on again. Takeshi's wife was handing Steve a shoe horn, and I could hear her saying a few words of English to him, "Come back to Japan!" I could hear Steve thanking her profusely for the dinner as he worked his feet back into his shoes. Takeshi stood on the step beside me as I awkwardly forced my feet into my shoes. I stood up again with my shoes back on and looked up at him. He had that serious look in his eyes again and was frowning slightly. I was worried that he was going to give me another lecture.

But then his stern face broke into a wide smile and his eyes twinkled warmly. In a low but firm voice, he whispered, "*Naseba naru.*"

PART II

Becoming a Curator

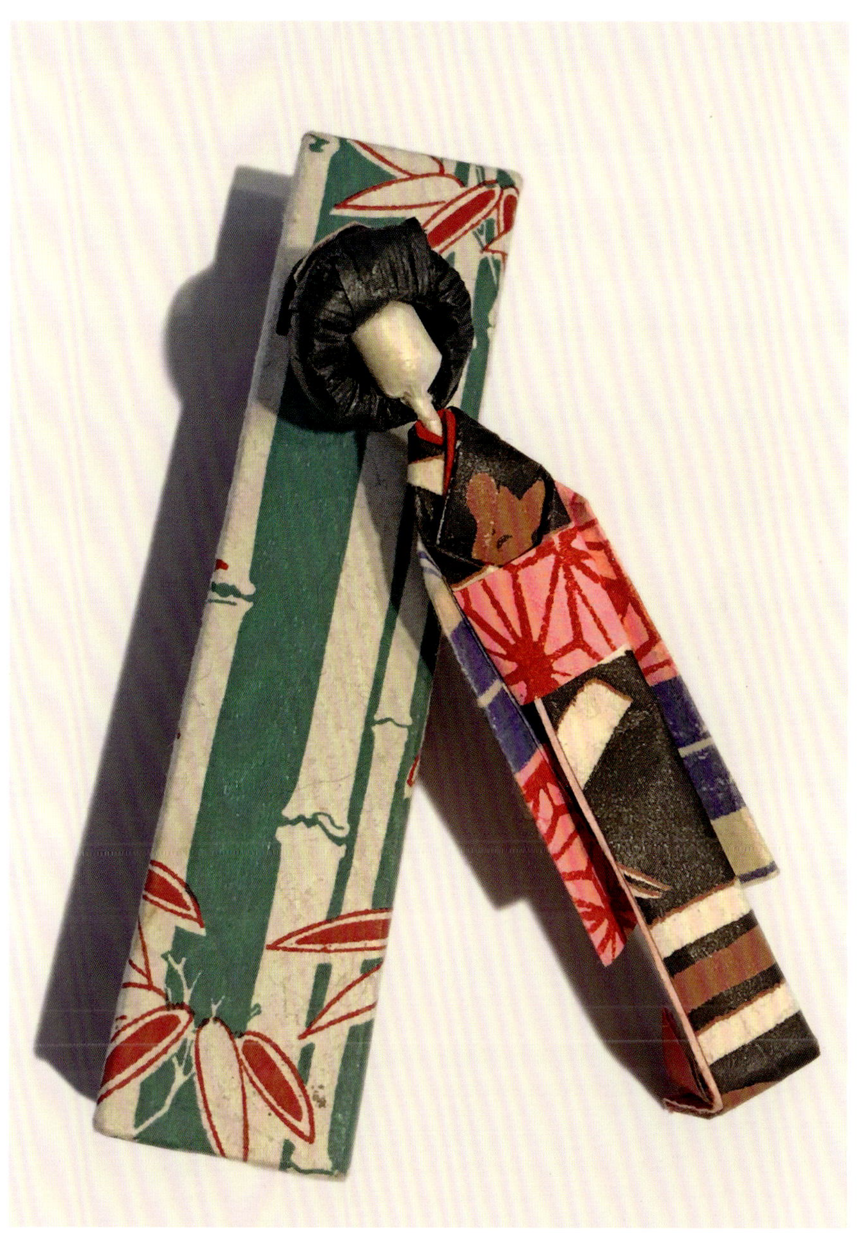

Chiyogami Doll, c.1975, printed, decorative handmade paper (*chiyogami*),
4" H × 1" W; Photo by the author

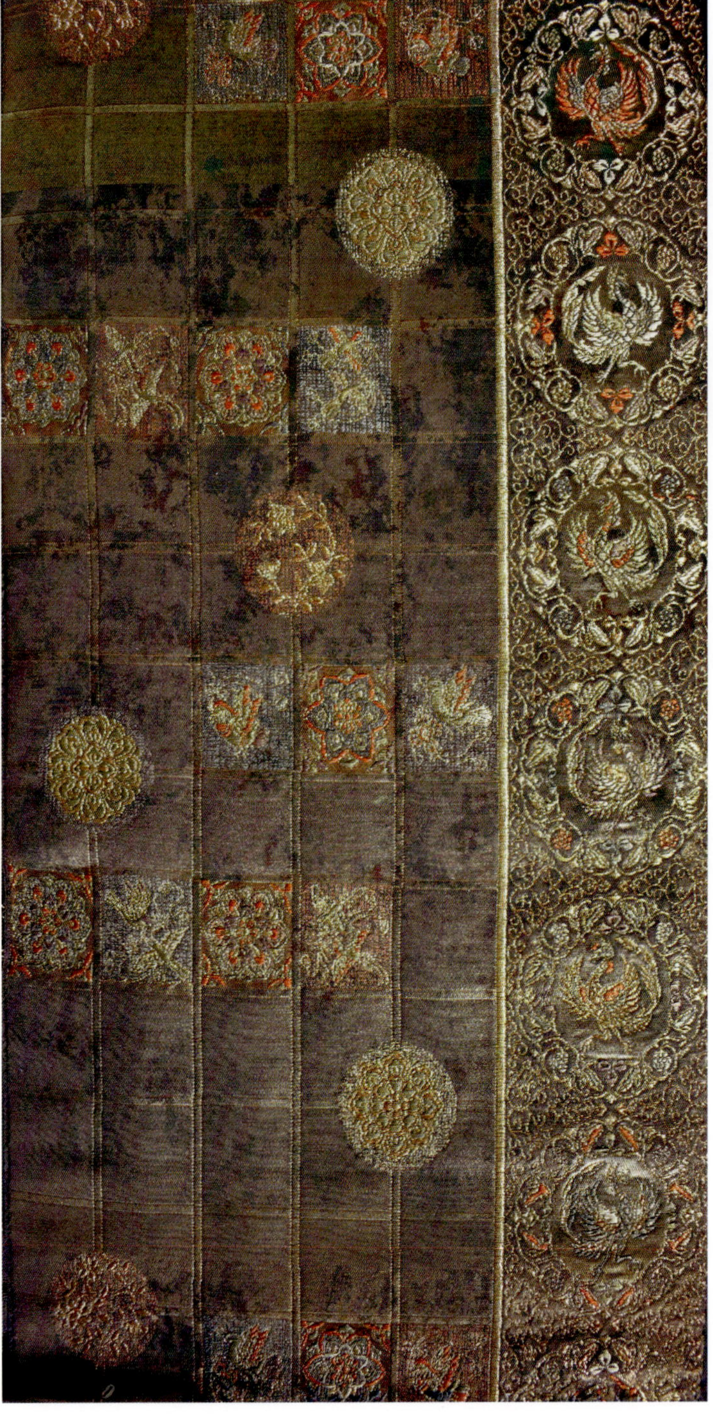

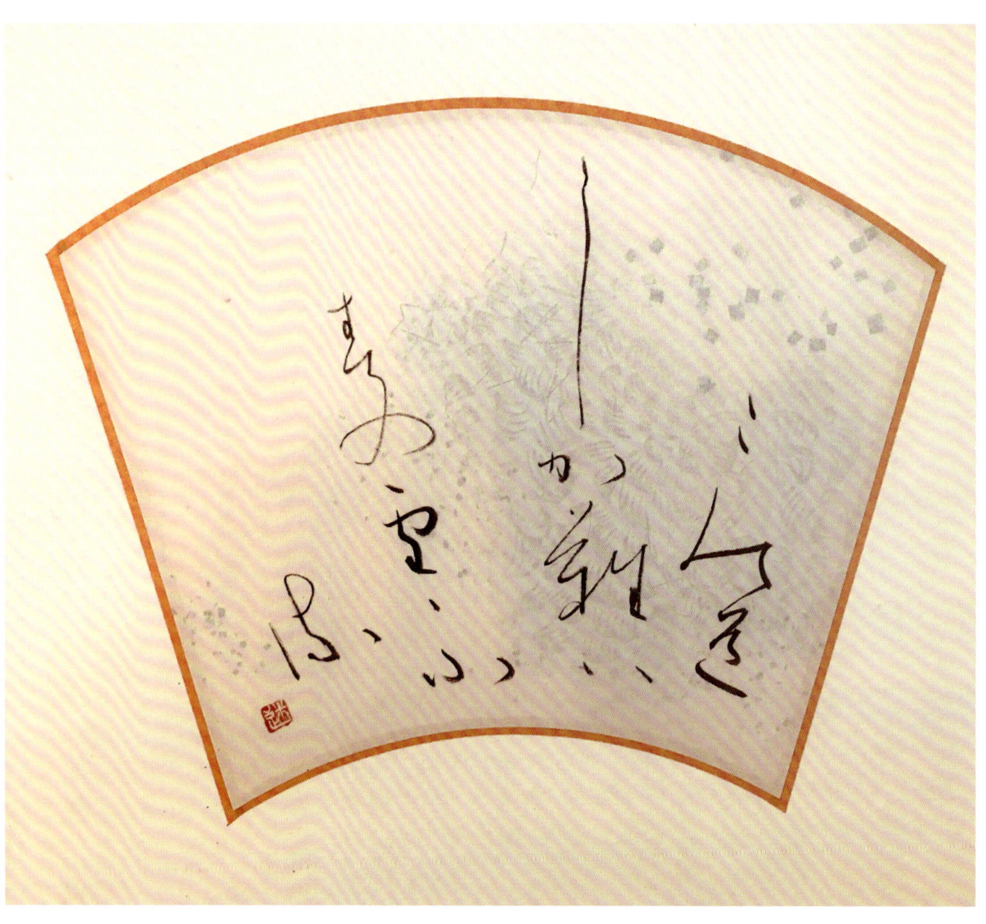

Calligraphy by the Author, 1992, ink on fan-shaped handmade paper, 1¾" H × 2½" W; Photo by the author

Obi Sample, c.1988, silk brocade with gold-wrapped threads, 25" L × 12½" W; Photo by the author

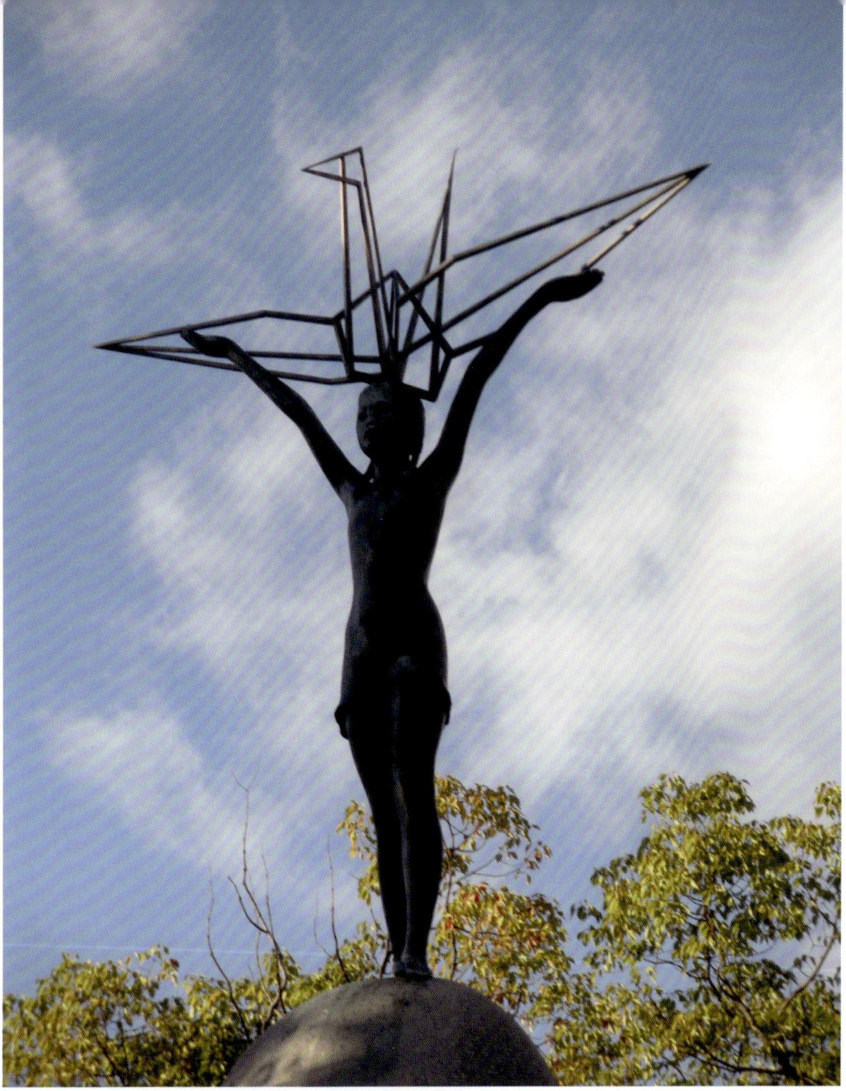

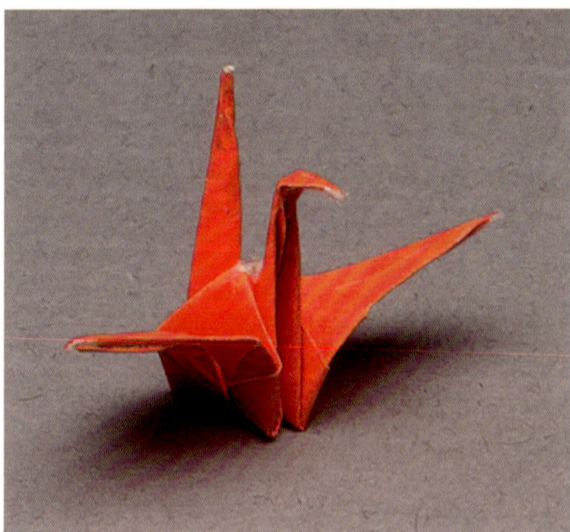

Statue of Sadako Sasaki, by Kazuo Kikuchi (1908–1985), bronze, Children's Peace Memorial, Hiroshima; Photo by the author

Origami Crane by Sadako Sasaki, 1955, paper, ⅔" × ⅔"; Photo courtesy of the Japanese American National Museum (gift of the Sadako Legacy [the Sasaki Family], 2016.1.1)

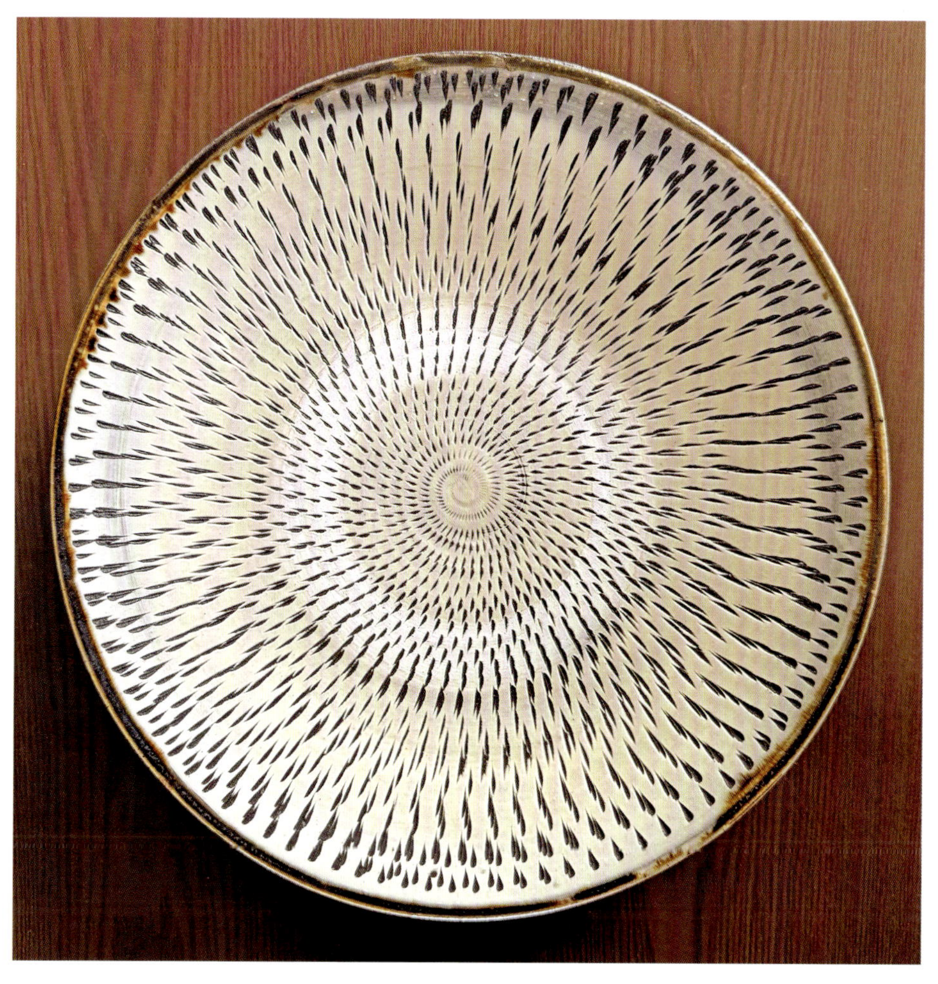

Onta-ware Dish, twenty-first century, white slip with *tobikanna* pattern on clay, 11½" D; Image of replacement dish (original dish lost); Photo by Futoshi Shigeishi

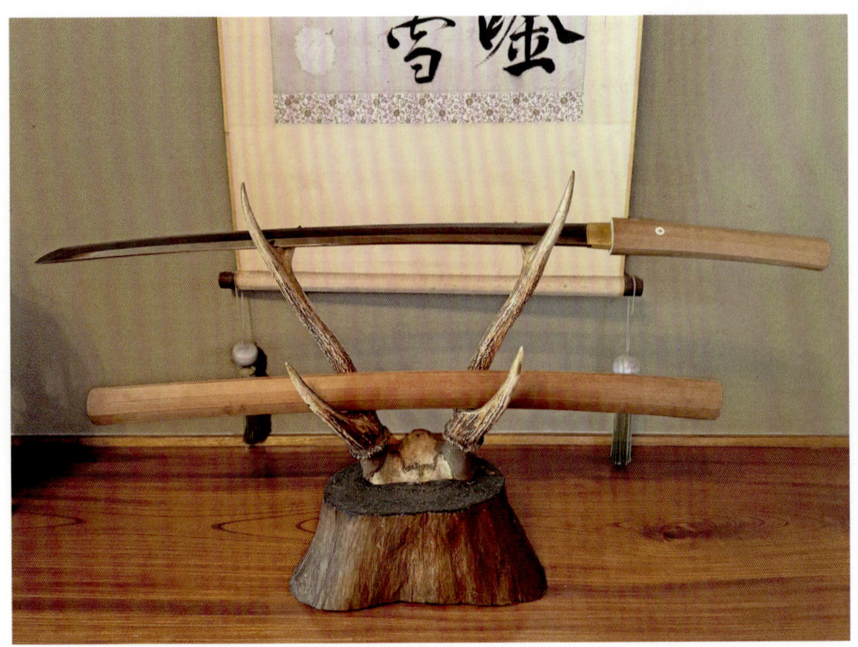

Sword, early twentieth century, *tamahagane* steel, 34½" L; Courtesy of Takeshi Shigeishi, Photo by Futoshi Shigeishi

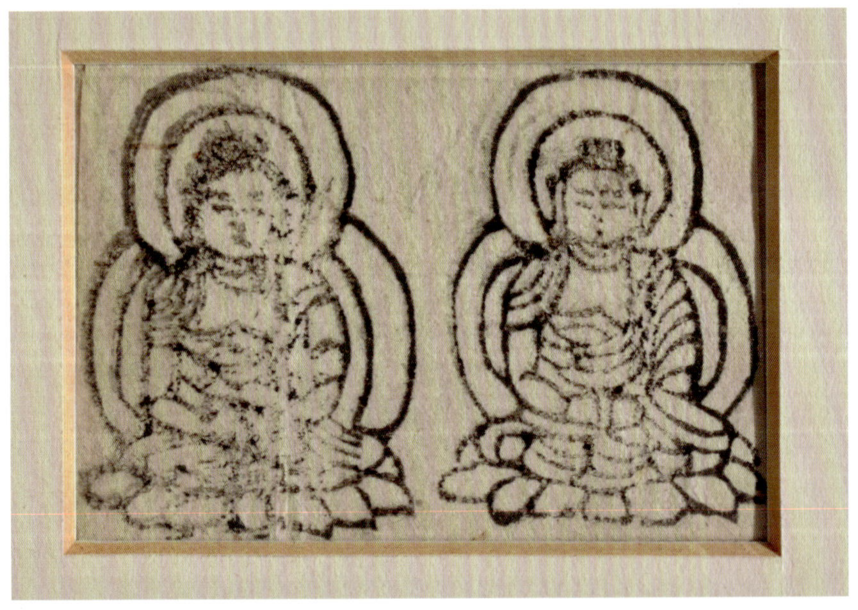

Seated Buddhas, eleventh to twelfth century, ink printed on paper, 1¾" H × 2½" W; Photo by the author

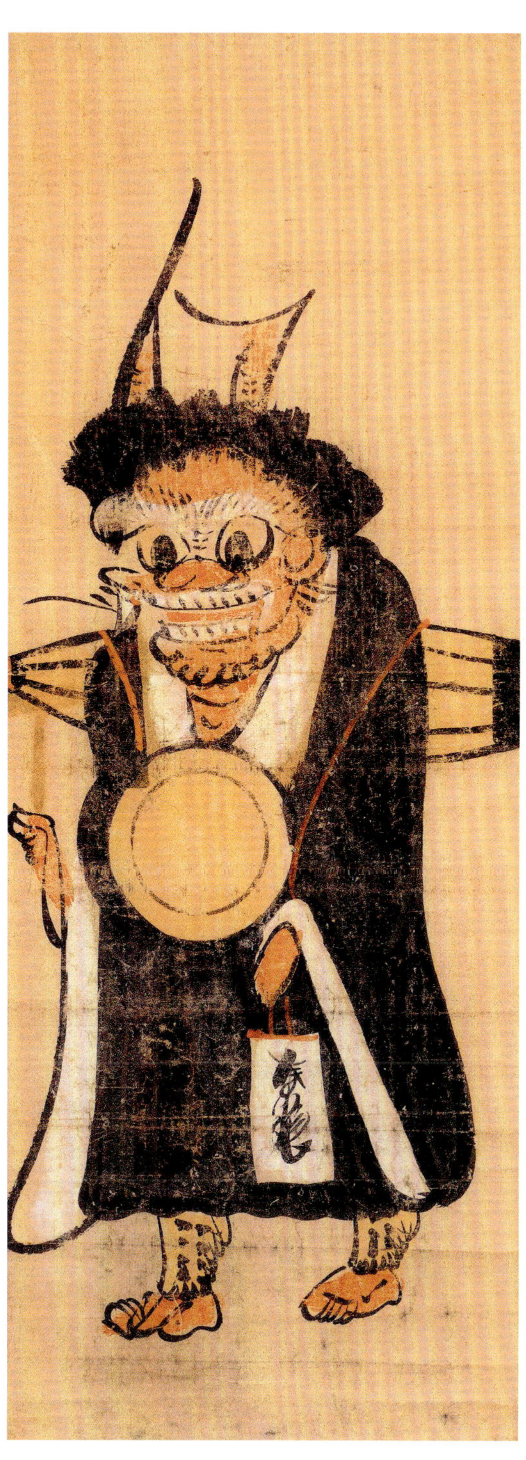

Otsu-e Painting of a Praying Demon, eighteenth century, ink and colors on paper, 15" H × 10¼" W; Photo courtesy of USC Pacific Asia Museum, Pasadena, CA (museum purchase, 1997.56.13)

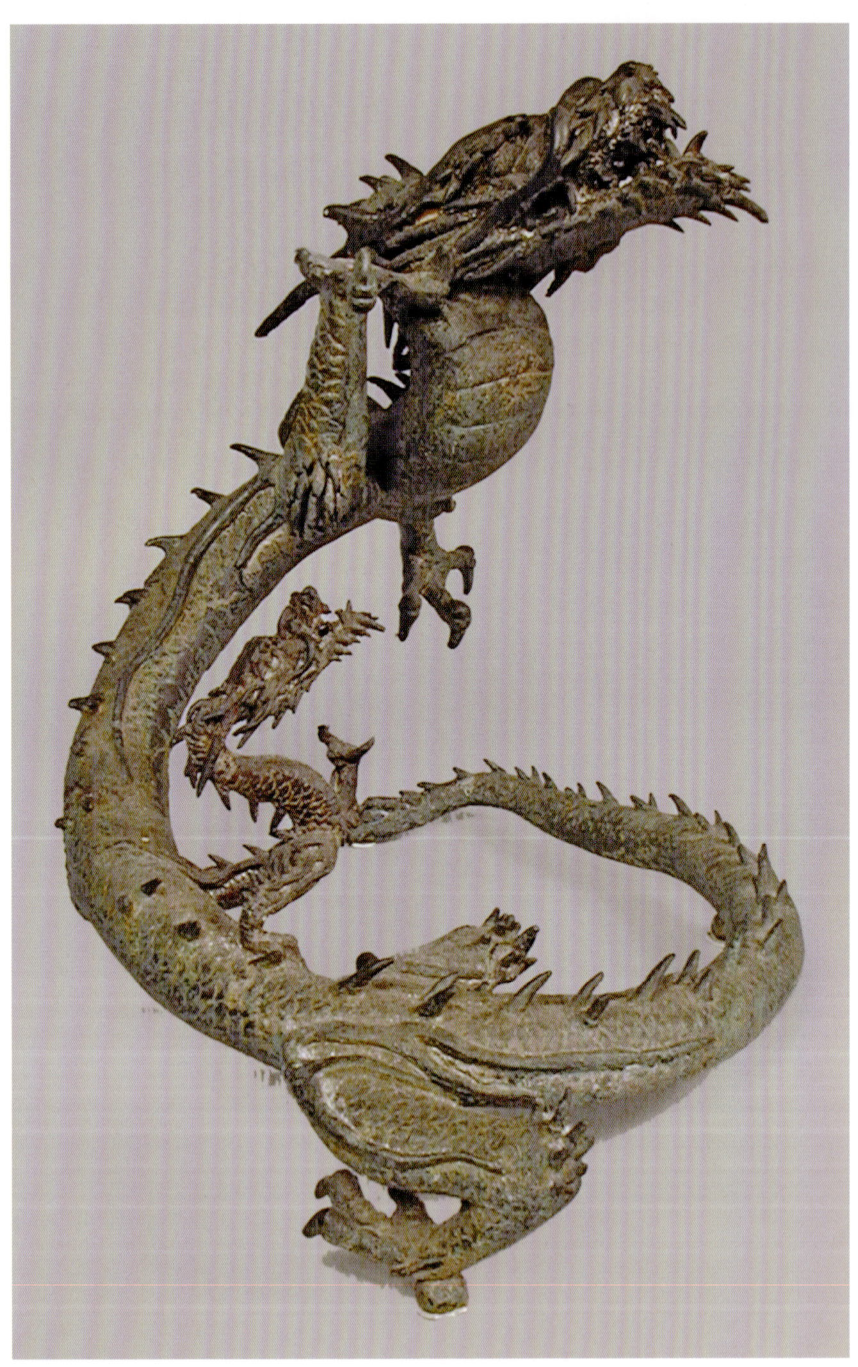

Dragon Figure, c.1900, bronze, 14" H × 15" W × 12" D; Photo courtesy of USC Pacific Asia Museum, Pasadena, CA (gift of Walt and Maylo Long, 2000.35.2)

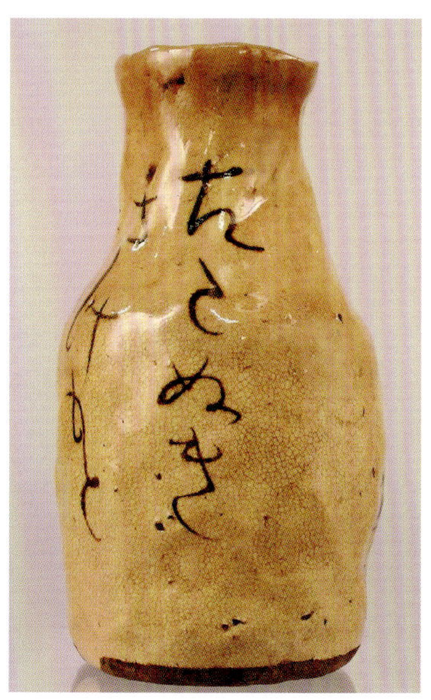

LEFT:

Sake Bottle by Otagaki Rengetsu (1791–1875), nineteenth century, glazed stoneware with underglaze iron oxide pigment, 4¾" H × 2¾" D; Photo courtesy of USC Pacific Asia Museum, Pasadena, CA (gift of James D. and Veronica H. Roorda, 2005.32.1ab)

BELOW:

Temple Ceiling Panel Depicting the Bodhisattva Kannon, fifteenth century, pigments on wood panel, each panel 16¾" H × 16⅜" W × ⅝" D; Photo courtesy of USC Pacific Asia Museum, Pasadena, CA (gift of an anonymous donor, 2004.19.1)

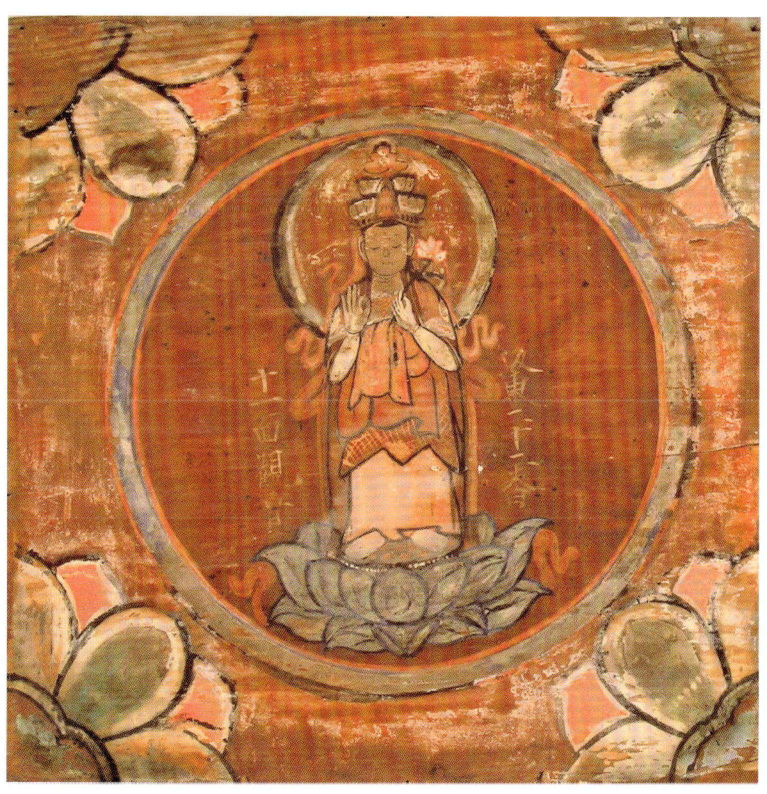

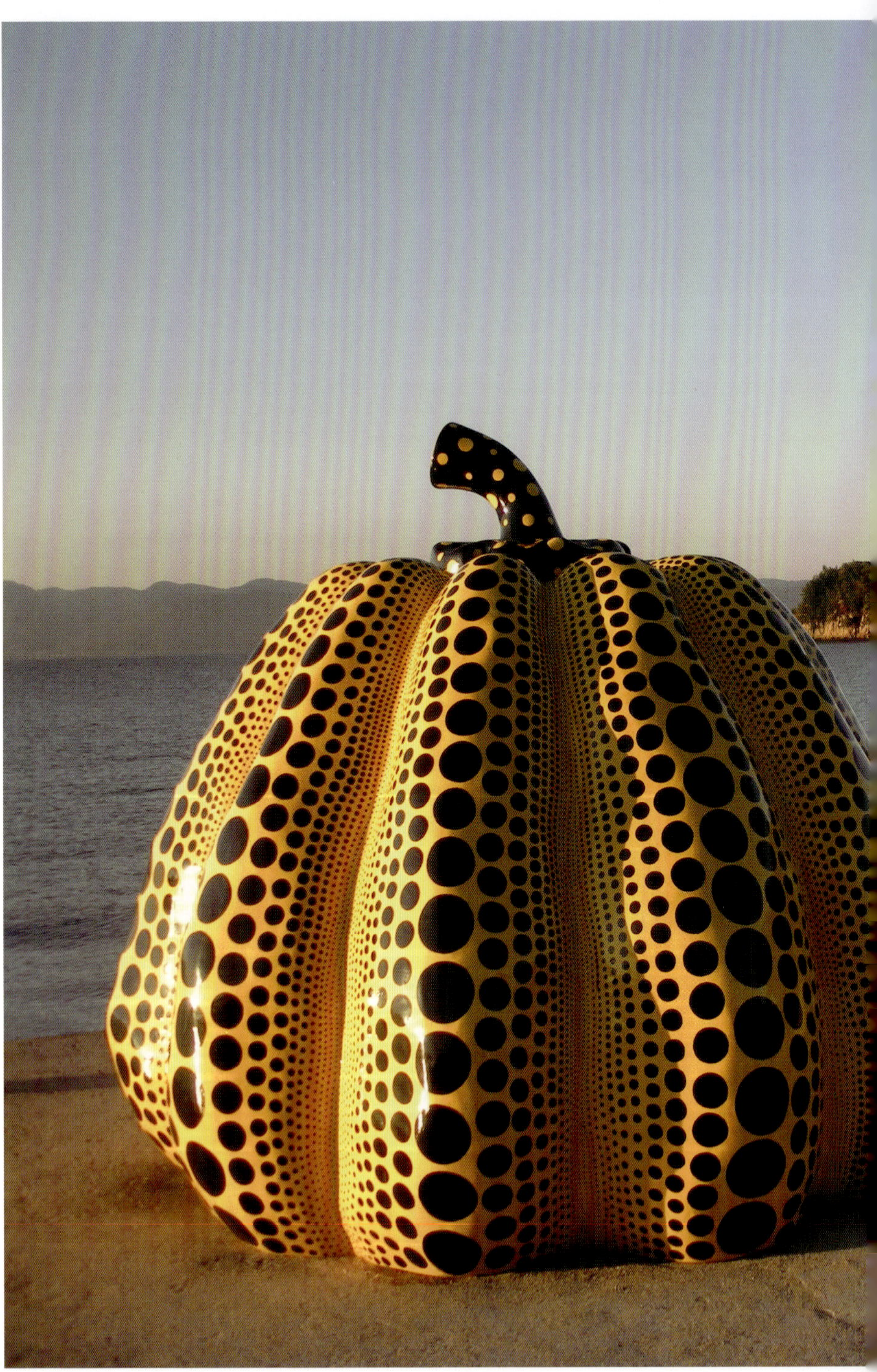

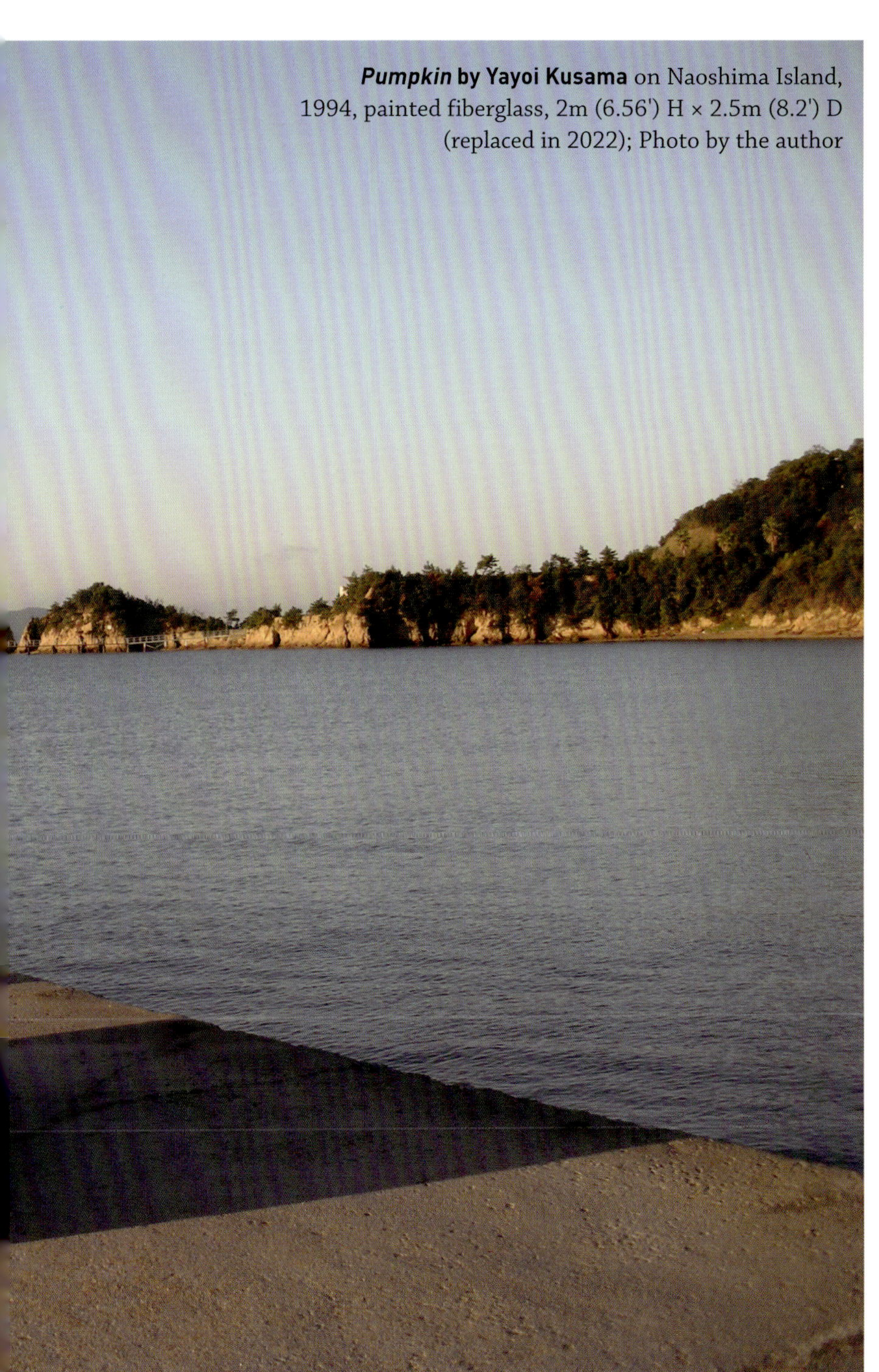

***Pumpkin* by Yayoi Kusama** on Naoshima Island, 1994, painted fiberglass, 2m (6.56') H × 2.5m (8.2') D (replaced in 2022); Photo by the author

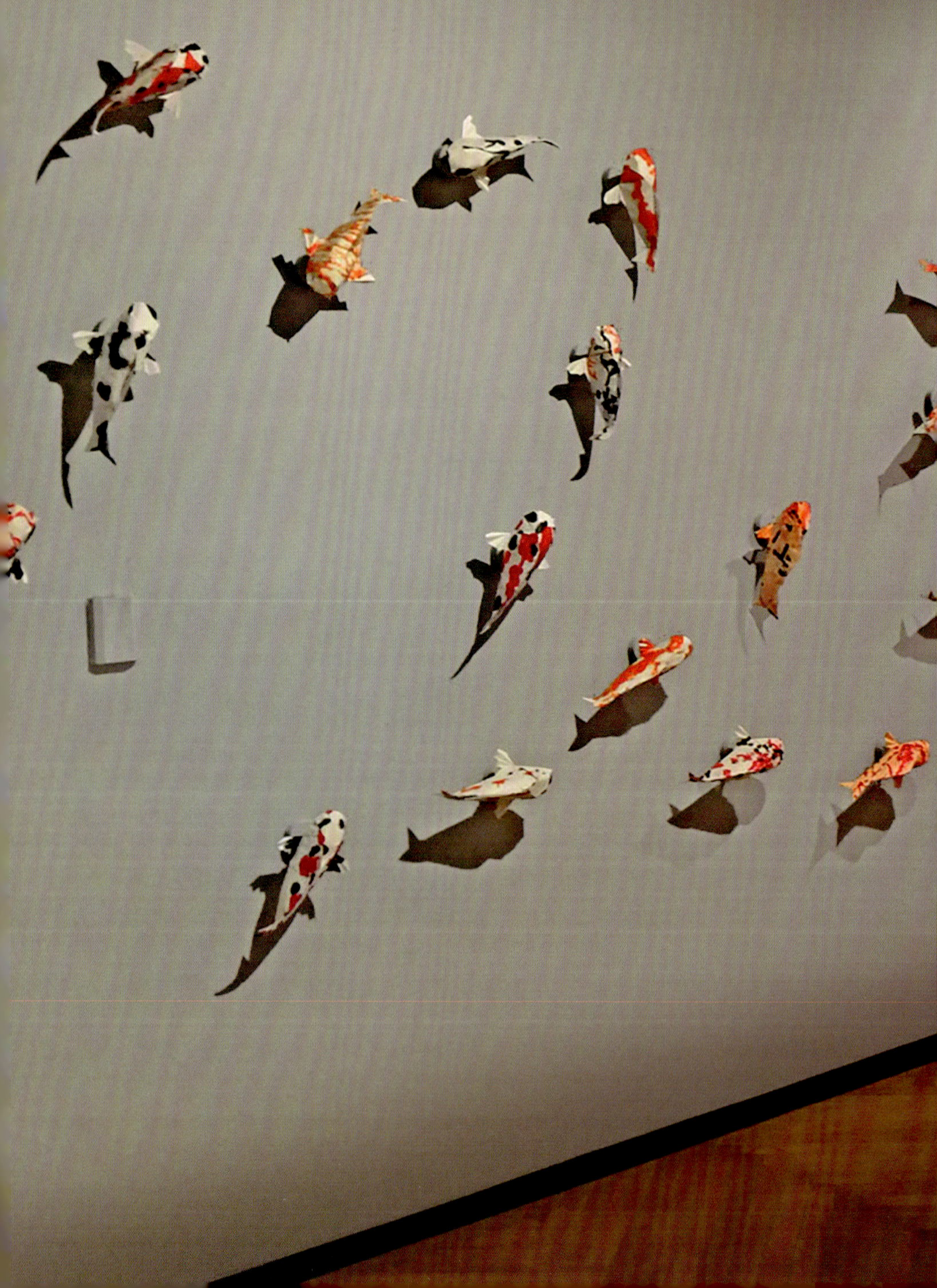

Vertical Pond II by **Robert J. Lang**, 2014, installation of sixty origami koi folded from uncut sheets of Origamidō paper (35' W × 10' H) at the Clay Center for the Arts & Sciences of West Virginia, Charleston, WV; Photo courtesy of the artist

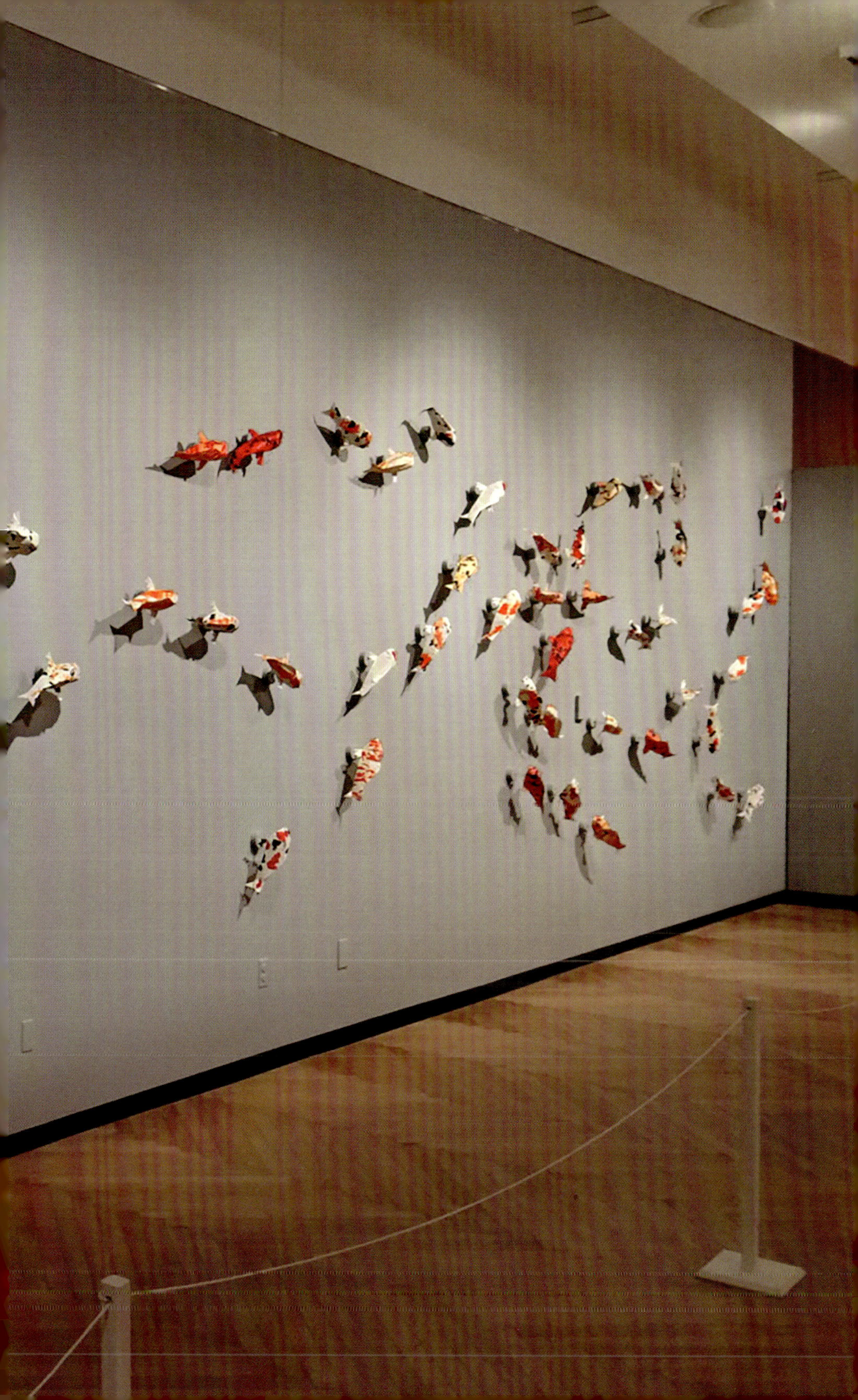

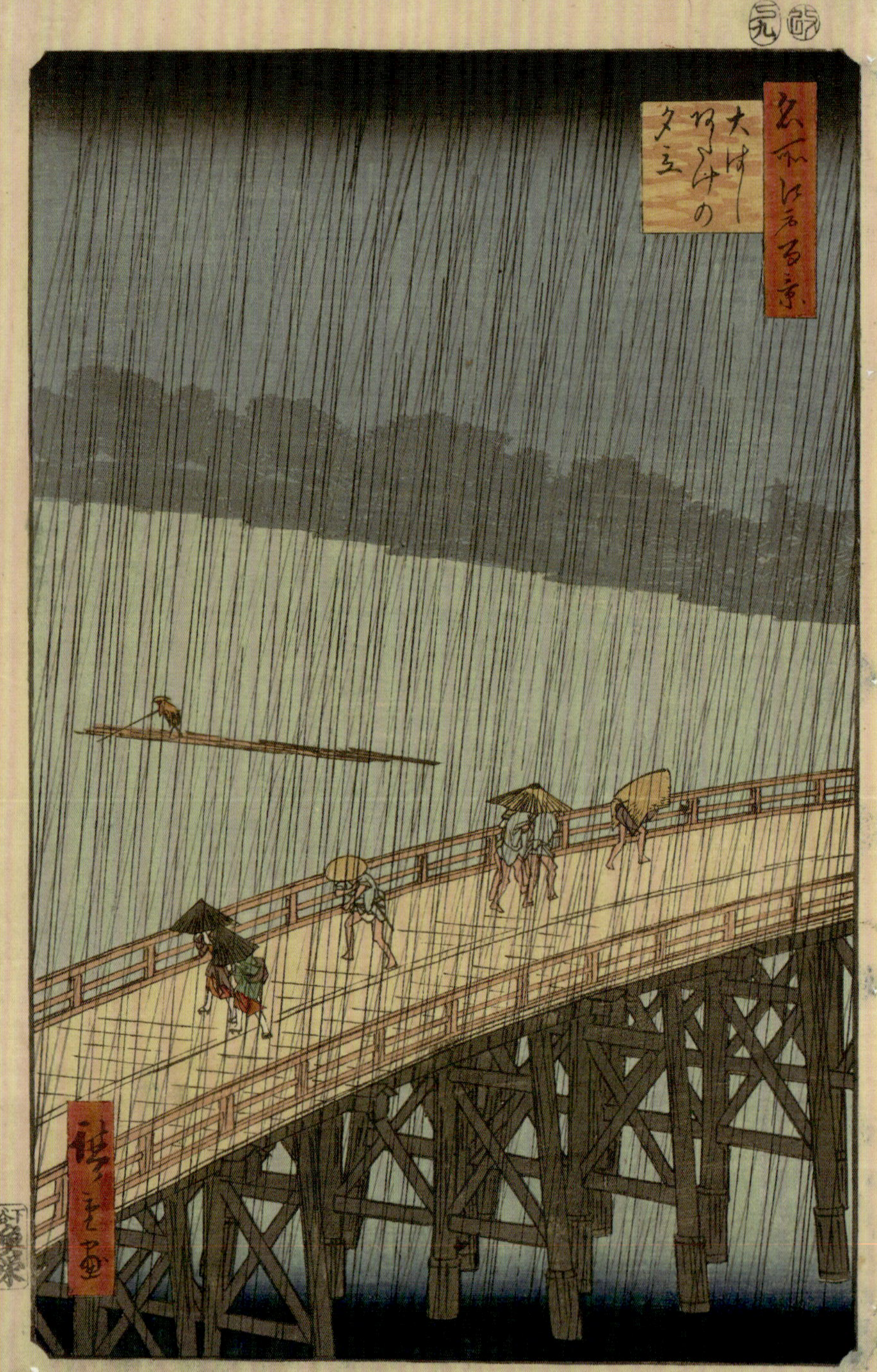

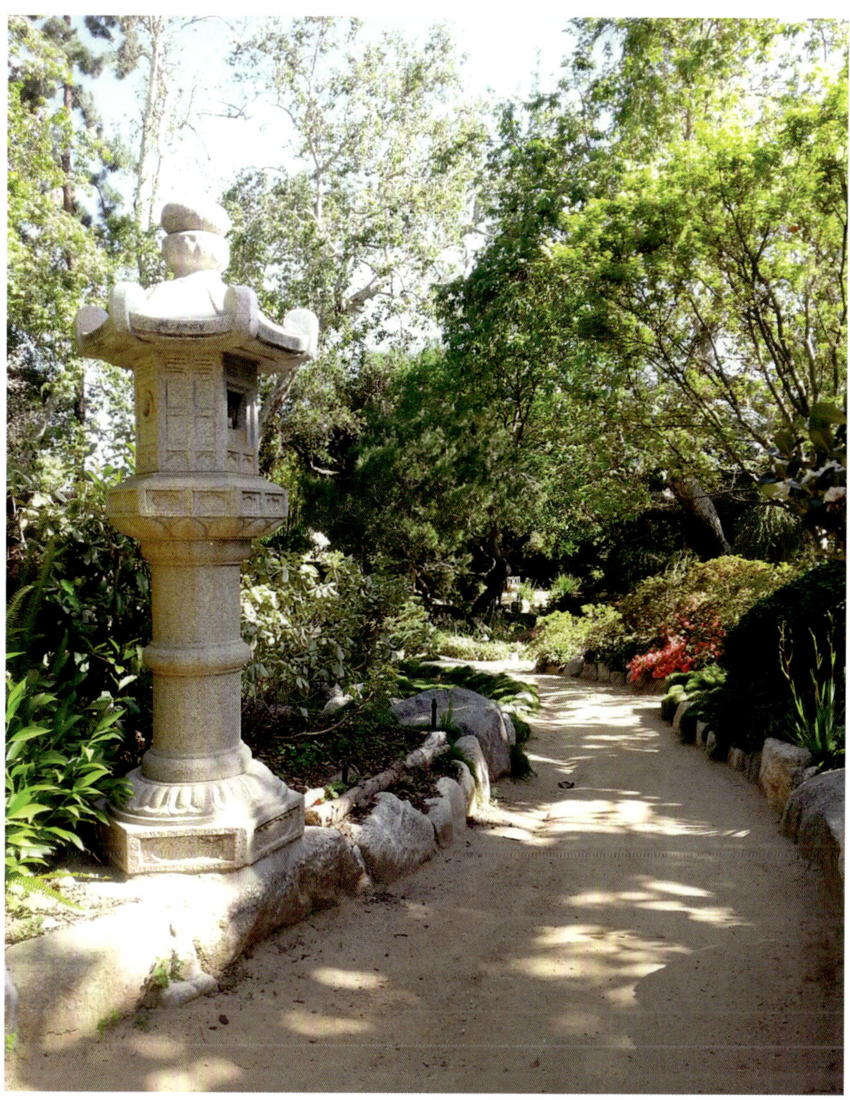

Storrier Stearns Japanese Garden by Kinzuchi Fujii, c.1940, restored by Takeo Uesugi in c.2015; Courtesy of the Storrier Stearns Japanese Garden, photo by the author

***Sudden Shower over Shin-Ohashi Bridge and Atake* by Utagawa Hiroshige**, 1857, full-color woodblock print, ink and colors on paper, 13.31" H × 8.69" W; Photo courtesy of the Ruth Chandler Williamson Gallery, Scripps College, Claremont, CA (gift of Mrs. James W. Johnson, 2019)

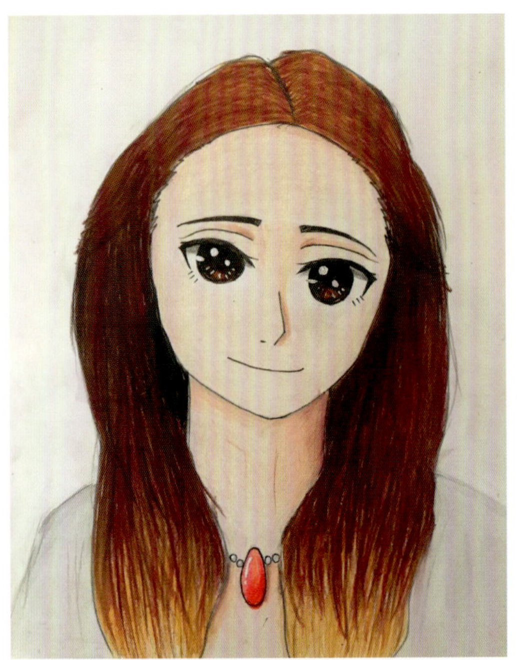

Portrait of the Author by Theo Marsh, 2022, ink and colored pencils on paper, 8½" H × 11" W; Photo by the author

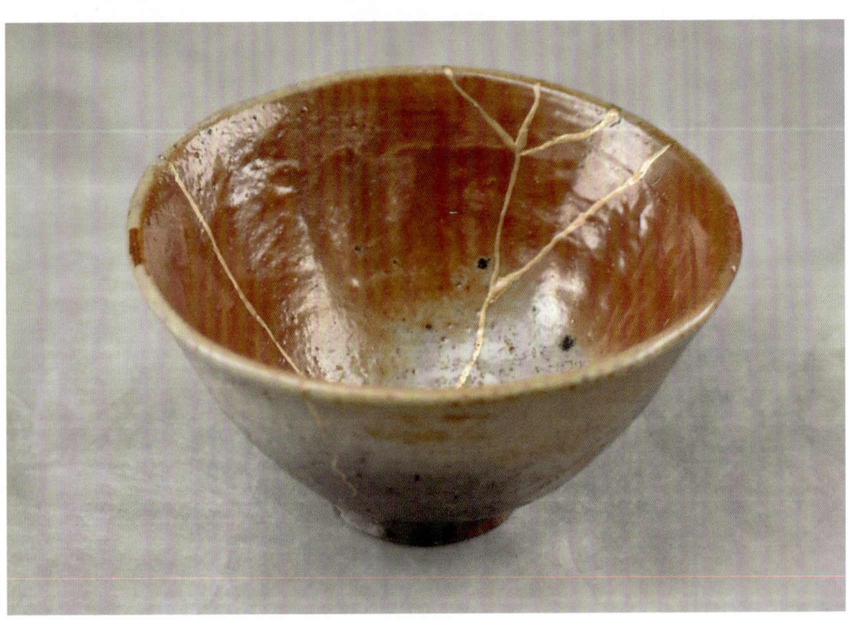

Tea Bowl with Kintsugi Repair, bowl made by the author in 1992, repaired by Shingo Murayama in 2024, glazed ceramic, lacquer and gold powder, 2" H × 5⅜" D; Photo by the author

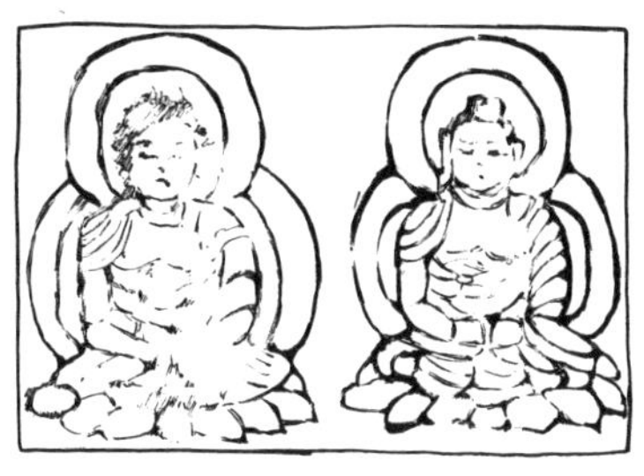

CHAPTER 7

The Buddhist Print

The English word "impression" has layered meaning. The noun refers to a mark produced by pressure—both on paper and on one's mind. It derives from Old French and Latin roots from as early as the thirteenth century and originally seems to have been more mental and emotional in meaning, becoming associated with the processes of stamping and printing a little later in the sixteenth century. The Japanese word for "impression," *inshō*, has a similar layered meaning. The two-character word comes from the Chinese *yìnxiàng*, written 印象. It too refers to a feeling about or response to a person, place, idea or thing and is also connected to the act of pressing something into or onto a surface to make a mark.

The first character, read *in*, means to stamp or print and is used in the word *inkan* (印鑑), the stamp or seals that the Japanese still use today to sign important documents. The character *shō* can mean "a phenomenon," but, strangely, the Chinese character actually means "elephant." I am still trying to find out why the character for elephant is part of such a word, but perhaps these huge creatures cannot help but make a great impression on both physical surfaces and on minds. And in all of these cultures, we know how important impressions can be!

——◆——

I sat looking around the small room I'd been renting in North London for the past couple of years wondering if the money, effort and time I'd invested in my postgraduate diploma and master's degree were going to pay off. I was twenty-eight years old and was patching together odd jobs, editing, teaching English and assisting on the postgraduate diploma course. I didn't earn enough to rent a proper flat of my own, so I was still living like a student—and a poor one at that! My boyfriend Steve was even worse off financially, and it was becoming clear to me that our interests were not actually that similar and we were not on the same path. But, what I was really worried about was that I was starting to lose sight of my path. I knew I wanted to work as a Japanese art historian, but the way to that career was very unclear. Some of my friends were starting to settle down in steady jobs, steady relationships, and were able to live in nice flats. Even though I was approaching the age of thirty, I wasn't feeling terribly grown-up. I didn't even have a private bathroom!

Then, I received a call from an art dealer called Sam Fogg. He was looking for a recent Japanese art master's student to research a collection of Japanese Buddhist prints that he had just acquired, and he had been given my name by one of the Asian art professors at SOAS. I was thrilled to hear from him. Sam was, and still is, one of London's most respected and successful art dealers, best known for dealing in Medieval European manuscripts and art. Although I had done well on my master's program, I was aware that there were very few full-time jobs in Japanese art. I had used up all my savings to pay for my studies and trips back to Japan, so I was getting worried that I wouldn't ever find work in the Asian art world. The phone call gave me some much-needed hope.

Sam welcomed me to his large townhouse in Islington in north London. It was full of boxes scattered all over the floors and piles of books and documents on every surface. He was a tall, elegant man, but his shirt was also a little rumpled and his grayish-brown hair slightly tousled.

"I'm in the middle of moving house, so am packing all of this up. Please forgive the mess," he said, clearly a little embarrassed to be interviewing a prospective researcher amidst such chaos.

"The prints are over here."

He walked briskly into what had been the dining room and indicated a stack of sheets of paper on the dining table. I sifted through them one at a time, image after image on paper of different sizes printed in black outlines of seated Buddhas, standing deities of various types and groups of figures. Beside the stack, were a few scrolls. He unrolled them one at a time and showed me more images of deities, Buddhist priests and what looked like mandalas, colored with dazzling mineral pigments. My eyes were wide at the artistic feast before me. I might have been holding my breath the whole time as I looked through them.

"Some of them look like paintings, but they are actually all prints," he explained, clearly very enthusiastic about the material in front of us.

"Wow!" I exclaimed. "These are amazing! Some seem old and really important too."

"I think so too!" replied Sam. "But, so far, you're the only other person who has shown any interest in them!"

I could hardly contain my excitement. Buddhist art, and Japanese Buddhist art in particular, had been one of my favorite subjects during the Asian art diploma course. Although I hadn't been able to study the area as part of my master's course, I had been studying Japanese Buddhism and its arts and iconography on my own as much as I could, in books and museum exhibitions and at temples when I was back in Japan. I recognized some of the figures. Others were new to me, but with time, I was hopeful that I would be able to identify the deities.

Sam explained that he had recently been in Los Angeles and had found out that the Philosophical Research Society near Hollywood was selling some of its collection of manuscripts and other spiritual material, mostly Asian. It had been his last day in the city, and although he usually didn't purchase Asian collections, he had rushed over to take a look. He had been given an hour to look through the collection, choose what he wanted and name a price, and had found mainly Chinese and Japanese religious material, including Buddhist sutras and other texts and paintings that he knew he would be able to find buyers for. He had also found this unusual collection of Buddhist and Shinto prints from Japan.

"I think these prints are rare and extremely interesting," he went on. "I want to document them in a catalog and sell them as a complete collection. Would you be interested in researching them for me?"

"Yes!" I almost shouted. "I'd love to!"

A week later, I was reunited with the prints in the basement office of Sam's gallery near Piccadilly. The office was rather dark and lined with old wood-paneled bookshelves full of art books, mostly on the subject of medieval European art. Sam had also bought a few English-language books on Japanese Buddhist prints as well as some other Buddhist material, so I started reading through them and soon realized that some of these prints were almost 1,000 years old. My research revealed that printing began in Japan in the Buddhist temples that had been established in and around the early capitals of Nara and Kyoto. As early as the sixth century CE, priests from China and Korea had brought texts and statues from the Asian mainland to Japan to encourage the Japanese emperor to convert to Buddhism. Although the Japanese imperial family retained its powerful connection to native *kami*—the deities long believed to inhabit and control many aspects of nature—the Court and much of the population eventually came to embrace Buddhism as well, because the two spiritual traditions—Buddhism and the indigenous belief system later known as Shinto—were largely able to co-exist harmoniously.

Through my research over the following weeks, I learned from Sam's books on Buddhist prints that woodblock printing was invented in China around 600 CE to mass-produce sacred Buddhist texts. The technology was introduced with Buddhism to Japan sometime in the seventh century and was used in early Buddhist temples to print Buddhist texts as a way of spreading Buddhist teachings. Japan's earliest surviving printed texts are the small, printed Buddhist charms, called *darani*, commissioned by Empress Shōtoku in 764 to thank the Buddha for suppressing a rebellion and to ensure the future protection of her realm. Millions of these charms were quickly and inexpensively printed using wooden blocks, placed inside one million small wooden pagodas, known in Japanese as the *hyakumantō*, and sent to Buddhist temples around the country. The Empress kept one hundred thousand charm-filled pagodas in the capital, in Nara's ten main temples as protection. Today, only the Hōryū-ji, a temple near Nara, still possesses its original pagodas and charms, examples of one of the world's most colossal early printing projects. Sam had acquired of one of these pagodas in this collection—a very exciting object for me to see up close!

To find out more about Buddhist printed images, I headed back to the SOAS library and pulled out all the books I could find on the subject. I discovered that Japanese woodblock printed images came after printed texts, the earliest surviving printed Buddhist images dating to the Heian period (794–1185). These were printed Buddhas, or *shubutsu* ("rubbed Buddhas"), made by carving a block with multiple small images of Buddhist deities, inking the block, and then transferring the image to paper. Creating an image of the Buddha is considered good action, or *karma*, and woodblock printing made it easy for lay practitioners to make multiple images and build up merit, creating good impressions, as it were.

Among the printed Buddha's in Sam's collection were some of the oldest examples of these *shubutsu*, including fragments of several sheets of one hundred Buddhas printed in the eleventh or twelfth century at the Jōruri Temple near Nara. These sheets of Buddhas were made by carving a row of ten Buddhas into a horizontal block which was then inked and transferred onto a sheet of paper by laying the paper onto the block and rubbing the back of the paper. Practitioners could print row after row of these rubbed Buddhas (also called *suri-botoke*) onto sheets of paper to accumulate spiritual merit relatively quickly and easily. Then, once printed, bundles of these sheets were placed inside a large statue of the Buddha Amida (Sanskrit: Amitabha) at the Jōruri Temple near Nara, in an offering that not only further increased the merit of the donor but added to the spiritual power of the statue of the Buddha, since it now contained thousands more Buddhas. Apparently, after these sheets had been extracted from the Buddha in the Meiji period (1868–1912), some of them were acquired by dealers, and they found their way to different collections around the world—including the one that Sam had acquired.

Part of my research also included identifying the various deities in the hundreds of printed images in Sam's collection. In the SOAS library, I sifted through Japanese language books on Buddhist iconography, scanning the pages to find images that matched those in the prints. The images of major deities, like certain Buddhas and bodhisattvas (beings who postpone their enlightenment to save others), were relatively easy to identify, but some took much more investigation. I realized that being a Japanese art historian felt like being an art detective, in this case trying to figure out the identity of the more mysterious characters in this collection of prints. The most challenging were the strange-looking animals associated with specific mountain temples and the portraits of priests who were not named in the inscription and could only be identified by their clothing and the objects they held.

I was lucky enough to find a couple of Japanese Buddhist iconographic guides, which included many of these esoteric figures, but I still needed to figure out how to translate their names into English! With each new discovery and every gap in my research filled, I felt more invigorated and satisfied. Once I had finally completed the task of identifying the subjects, I organized the images into sections by iconography, starting with the main deities, Buddhas and bodhisattvas, followed by lesser deities and guardians, and then fantastic creatures and historical figures such as Buddhist teachers and finally mandalas—the colorful geometric diagrams depicting the realms of enlightened beings. Once I had organized all my findings, we began putting together a catalog of the collection for publication—a thrilling climax to this project. The catalog would have a cover and pages with words and pictures—an actual book! It was hard to believe that I was getting paid to do this amazing work and I'd have a book of my own too!

When the catalog came out, I was ecstatic to see it. The cover looked very handsome, featuring a fifteenth-century image of multiple impressions of the Buddhist deity Jizo—printed in black ink separated by red lines on white paper—set against a rich, blue background. Sam told me he was impressed by how quickly I had been able to work and was very pleased with the catalog. As I leafed through the pages, I felt pride swelling up inside me. This was my first book. I had written a book! It wasn't a big book, and probably not one that many people would read, but it was still a book! Though light to hold, it felt weighty with significance. I couldn't wait to show it to Dad. He would understand how I felt, having published quite a few books himself. Sure enough, when I hopped on a train to Cambridge and held out a copy for him to see, he beamed with pride and said, "How old are you? Thirty? I hadn't yet published my first book when I was your age. Well done!" My jaw dropped at this realization. My father was a brilliant and well-respected scholar, and I didn't see myself at his level at all. He had a PhD after all, and I just had a master's degree. With those words of encouragement from Dad, I felt myself grow a few inches intellectually and I hugged him hard. Maybe I was more like him than I had thought. Maybe I would be some sort of writer and teacher like him. Maybe I had landed on my feet after all.

Once I had finished the Buddhist prints catalog, however, that was the end of my project for Sam. He hired me for bits and pieces of research on some of the other Japanese and Chinese material he had bought in Los Angeles while the catalog was being designed and then printed, but eventually the work that I could do for him just dried up, and I had to look for other work to support myself. Over the next few months, I took on some rather random jobs, including editing a Korean PhD student's dissertation, and giving English conversation classes to six charming young Japanese ballet dancers who were spending a year training at a dance school in London. I enjoyed my time with these interesting people and was grateful for the work, but as the weeks and months went by, I became increasingly anxious about how I was going to continue my career in Japanese art history. Although I had hit the jackpot with my first job with Sam, it was only a very short-term jackpot, and it didn't seem to be leading me to another art history job in London.

I began to worry that if I wanted to work in the field of Japanese art history, I might have to pursue a career as an academic, and that would mean earning a PhD. Going deeper into the academic world didn't really appeal to me, as I didn't fancy spending four years researching a single topic that might not be of interest to anyone else. The process seemed very isolating, and although I loved research, I didn't think I would have the patience to stick with something so specific for so long, with very few people to talk with about it. But I seemed out of options, so I made an appointment with the Japanese art professor at SOAS, who was back from his sabbatical, to discuss the possibility of a PhD with him. I showed him my catalog and asked him if he thought a PhD in Japanese Buddhist prints might be viable. He looked through the catalog and thought about it for a few minutes and then suggested that, indeed, he could supervise me if I were to focus on Buddhist prints from the Edo period, because this was the period that he specialized in. I thanked him and began thinking hard about going back for one more long round of academic training.

I decided to go back to Japan, this time to meet the scholars there who specialized in Buddhist prints and get their advice. There were two: Mr. Keiichi Uchida at the Machida Museum of Graphic Arts in Tokyo, and Professor Junichi Kikutake at Kyushu University. Because I was an individual without a university or museum behind me, I armed myself with copies of my shiny new catalog and some youthful optimism, hoping to gauge from them whether I should continue my research. I headed first to Machida, a small city in Tokyo. Arriving at the museum, which focuses exclusively on printed works, I asked to see Mr. Uchida, the curator specializing in Japanese Buddhist prints and who had published a couple of the books on the subject that I had used at Sam's office. A serious, thoughtful man probably in his early forties, Mr. Uchida greeted me and led me to the museum café, where he ordered us some coffee and cakes and we sat down. The museum had been built recently and was very tastefully designed. The café had large windows looking out onto a park, and the tables and chairs were designed with a modern elegance. I explained my interest in pursuing research in Japanese Buddhist prints and handed him a copy of the catalog as a gift.

Mr. Uchida told me how surprised he was that a young, foreign woman was so interested in his rather esoteric artistic specialty. He leafed through the pages, nodding knowingly at the various images and headings on each page, impressed by the quality and range of the print collection and with the amount of information I had managed to unearth in London. But at one page he stopped. He pointed at the image of three Buddhist deities called Kannon that was supposedly from the Hōryūji Temple and dated to the Heian period. "This one is a modern fake," he explained. "There is only one of these and it is in the temple. Ones like these were copied by dealers and sold as the real thing." I was both shocked and fascinated at the same time. I felt bad that we had published it as a genuine print, but I was surprised that there was such a thing as a fake Buddhist print. Why would someone go to the trouble of faking one of these? I took this to be a good sign. They must be important, valuable and worthy of more research.

Handing me a couple of the museum's catalogs as a gift, Mr. Uchida wished me well with my research into the subject and told me to contact him if I had any questions. As a final gesture of kindness, he offered to call Professor Kikutake at Kyushu University, who he knew and looked up to as a senior scholar in the field, to introduce me to him. I bowed very gratefully at this, knowing that it would help me get at appointment with the Professor. Sure enough, the following week, when I was in Kyushu, I called to arrange a meeting with Professor Kikutake, and he had already heard about me from his colleague. He was currently the leading expert in the field of Japanese Buddhist prints, and his books had been particularly helpful to me in my research. I was a little nervous to meet such an illustrious scholar. When I met with him in his office, which was jam-packed with books and stacks of journals and papers, he was very curious to see what I was working on. I nervously gave him a copy of my catalog, and he looked through it carefully, as Mr. Uchida had, nodding his head and muttering "hmmm" to himself when he reached certain pages. As he was looking through the catalog, I looked around his crowded office and my eyes rested on a small, framed print on the wall. Two seated Buddhas, each less than two inches (five centimeters) in height, were printed in slender, broken black lines that had faded with time. The Buddhas were seated on lotus thrones next to each other, each surrounded by double halos and gazing forward. I recognized them immediately.

"Are these from the Jōruri Temple?" I asked.

Professor Kikutake let out a gasp. "Yes!" he exclaimed, his eyes lighting up. "And you are the first person who has come into this office who has known what they are!" He seemed genuinely excited that I had recognized the print.

Surprised and a little proud, I smiled shyly and told him how intrigued I had been to learn that sheets of these small Buddha images had been printed in such large numbers and then placed inside Buddhist statues. It was such an interesting use of a printed image. He nodded and went on to share with me some of his thoughts about the importance of these prints in early Buddhist practice and his surprise that very few Japanese scholars had really looked into the subject. I told him that I was considering researching Edo Buddhist prints for a PhD. He seemed pleased and said that he thought that this would be a good subject to study more deeply, though, he added, he personally found the earlier prints far more interesting. I agreed.

After I felt I had taken up enough of his time, I thanked him for sharing his knowledge with me and looking through my catalog. He smiled kindly and told me to be in touch if I had more questions. I explained that I would and rose from my chair, ready to take my leave. Just then, Professor Kikutake suddenly jumped out of his chair, walked around his desk and reached for the framed print on the wall.

"Here," he said. "I want to give you this print!"

This time I gasped. The print was a thousand years old and was no doubt one of his personal treasures. When I tried to refuse, he insisted. "It will help you with your research, and you can use it to tell more people about these very important Buddhist prints."

I thanked him profusely and left the university, even more determined to succeed as a Japanese art historian and share information on Buddhist prints and other aspects of Japanese art with the rest of the world.

I returned to the UK and my small rented room and began seriously contemplating whether or not to apply for a PhD at SOAS to study Edo-period Buddhist prints. From what I had learned in Japan, the subject needed more exploration and could probably sustain my interest for several years. Then, with a PhD, I could hopefully find a teaching position at a university. However, it would mean being a poor student for several more years. I was already in my late twenties and didn't relish the prospect of four more years of poverty. I was ready to be a professional, and I wanted to be able to support myself. One day, as I was deliberating this tough choice, I received a phone call that demonstrated to me just how important printed words and images can be in spreading information and affecting change. The call was from Robert Sawers, a Japanese art dealer, who was a colleague of Sam Fogg's in London. He had sent a copy of the Buddhist prints catalog to David Kamansky, the director of the Pacific Asia Museum (now USC [University of Southern California] Pacific Asia Museum) in Pasadena, California, who was looking to hire an Asian art curator. He apparently needed someone who knew about Buddhist art and ceramics in particular, because these were some of the museum's collecting strengths. David was coming to London in a few weeks, and Robert wanted to invite me to tea to meet David and discuss the possibility of my working for his museum. Wow!

I put on a simple and what I hoped was an elegant dark blue dress and made my way to Robert and his wife Mia's flat, which was beautifully decorated with a mix of Japanese paintings and European objects and furnishings. David was already there sitting on a couch with a copy of my catalog on his lap. He was around fifty years old, with thinning dark hair, wearing a tweed jacket and a tie. When he saw me, he reached out for a cane that was resting on the side of the couch and used it to push himself up out of his seat and onto his feet. Leaning on the cane, he walked unsteadily toward me and introduced himself, adding, "I'm sorry I can't shake your hand. I had a stroke and can only use one arm. It's very nice to meet you." Impressed that he was able to walk and talk at all after a stroke, I smiled and replied that I was also happy to meet him.

Over the next hour or so, we all chatted amicably, moving quickly from the topic of London weather to Asian art, my time in Japan, the various Asian art professors we knew in London and the work I'd been doing on Asian material for Sam. David had a twinkle in his eye and a sharp wit, and I did my best to be witty back as I shared my experiences and aspirations with him. He complimented me on the print catalog, saying he thought I wrote well and seemed to have organized the prints in a very clear manner. He asked if I was interested in curating art. He explained that, for years, he had served as the museum's executive director and senior curator, and that he needed a full-time curator to take on more of the curatorial work. I had no experience curating at that point but explained that I really liked gathering and organizing information, a skill that I'd perhaps inherited from my father, and that I would love the opportunity to work in a museum, learn more about art and share the knowledge with others.

"Well then, why don't you come to Pasadena and see the museum?"

I'm sure I sat there for a few seconds with my mouth open. It seemed that I had made it through this first part of the interview, and now he was offering to fly me out to California to meet the museum's board members and get their approval. I replied that I'd be thrilled to see the museum and said I'd wait to hear more from him. I said goodbye to David and my hosts and left their flat feeling extremely light on my feet. As I made my way to the nearest Tube station, I reflected on what was happening to me. I had been lucky enough to be hired by a kind, supportive dealer such as Sam Fogg on a dream research project and had worked hard to understand, organize and write about

Buddhist prints and their history for his catalog. Not only had it been an incredibly stimulating first job as a Japanese art historian, but it also allowed me to make a strong impression on several key people who were active in the field I hoped to enter—thanks to a beautifully printed catalog that came out at just the right moment in my career. I realized on a deep level that, far more than simple word of mouth, having something printed—or impressed—on paper can shape our lives in such unexpected ways, even shifting the whole course of our careers and lives. Like those people long ago who achieved spiritual merit by printing images of the Buddha on paper, I had attained professional merit by studying the prints, writing about them and having my words printed in turn. And now my printed words were potentially launching my career as a Japanese art historian.

Today, more than twenty-five years later and six thousand miles away, the two printed Buddhas—impressed a millennium ago in a Japanese temple and given to me by a kind professor—hang on my wall by my bed, a daily reminder of the power of good karma and first impressions.

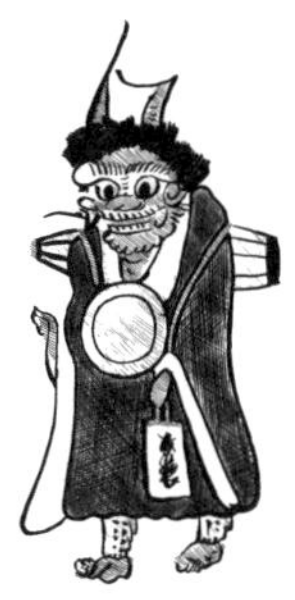

CHAPTER 8

The Folk Painting

The word *mingei*, meaning "folk art," was coined in the mid-1920s by the Japanese philosopher Yanagi Sōetsu (1889–1961), who was inspired by the works of unnamed craftsmen to start the Japanese folk art movement. He formed the term *mingei* by blending together the words *minshū* (民衆), meaning "common people," and *kōgei* (工藝), meaning "craft." Now, almost one hundred years later, *mingei* is a widely admired aspect of Japanese art, and its name has been adopted by galleries and museums in Japan and abroad—including the Mingei International Museum in San Diego, an organization born of the founder's love for Japan's *mingei* but exhibiting folk art from around the world.

In fact, many Japanese words relating to art were only coined as Japanese equivalents for existing European terms in the late nineteenth century, when the country began absorbing Western politics and culture. Until then, the Japanese didn't even have a general word for "art"—only names for individual art forms like sculptures, paintings, prints, hanging scrolls or folding screens. So, to translate the broader European concept of art, Japanese scholars coined the word *bijutsu* (美術), combining the characters for "beautiful" and "skills." Japan's long history of borrowing new words and the continuous coining of new words for foreign concepts have made the Japanese language one of the richest and most dynamic aspects of Japanese culture.

After what seemed like weeks of cloudy, drizzly or rainy weather in London, teary farewells to friends, family and boyfriend, a long, tiring flight across half of the world, and a week with dear family friends in Northern California, I stepped off the plane at LAX, ready to begin my new life in Pasadena, California. Exiting the airport terminal, I was struck by how sunny and bright it was and by the vivid blue of the sky—on the second of January! David Kamansky, the director of Pacific Asia Museum—the man who had hired me and brought me to this dazzling place—had come to pick me up in his golden-brown Mercedes. He drove me along busy freeways, past unfamiliar buildings and neighborhoods and row upon row of palm trees to Pasadena, a city I had visited six months earlier for my official interview at the museum. Since then, as I awaited my work visa, I'd been questioning the reality of my memory of the museum—a Chinese palace filled with art in a perpetually sunny land.

The facade of the two-story building, with its camel-colored stucco walls, celadon window frames and deep red arched door, had instantly charmed me. It was crowned by a two-tiered, greenish-blue-tiled roof, with eaves that curl upward to make the roof appear light. The Chinese also made them like that, David explained, so that dragons would have a place to land. Passing through a shady breezeway, I stepped into an almost magical courtyard garden with a koi pond and large limestone *taihu* rocks riddled with holes that gave them the appearance of ancient faces. In the far-right corner, a delicate Chinese magnolia tree had sprouted a few pink buds, and a slender ginkgo tree reached its straight trunk upward into the sky. The building itself was built in the 1920s, David continued, for Grace Nicholson, a dynamic, art-loving woman with a passion for native-American basketry and Asian art. Nicholson had housed her Asian antiques downstairs and her own home and a guest suite upstairs. After she died in the late 1940s, he explained, the building housed the Pasadena Art Institute, which later changed its name to the Pasadena Art Museum and went on to host many exciting contemporary art exhibitions, including the famous 1963 retrospective exhibition of Marcel Duchamp. During this exhibition, David recounted with a cheeky grin, the French artist, then seventy-six and fully clothed in a suit, had famously played chess with the naked Eve Babitz. A few years later, in 1970, the Pasadena Art Museum left the building to become part of the new Norton Simon Museum a few blocks away, and a group of Asian art enthusiasts gained permission from the City of Pasadena to turn the building into an Asian art museum. And this is where I found myself now. (Much later, in 2013, the museum became part of the University of Southern California and was renamed USC Pacific Asia Museum.)

I was set to become the curator of East Asian art. When David offered the job at the end of my earlier visit, it had taken me no time at all to decide to accept it. This was a dream job for me—working in Asian art in an idyllic setting. I would be using my training, learning even more on the job, and sharing my knowledge with others, which was exactly what I wanted to do. It meant moving six thousand miles away to a new country on my own and leaving my family, friends, and boyfriend behind. There was one day when I sat alone on the living room floor sorting through personal belongings deciding what to keep and what to toss, when the enormity of my move hit me, and I broke down sobbing. I would be all alone in a whole new country without any friends or family! Was I really going to be able to do this? Then I remembered that I had done that before when I moved to Japan, and I had been fine. I knew I would be okay in California too. I did feel awful leaving Dad, even though he was genuinely excited for me and wouldn't be alone. He had met Jacqui, a Chinese woman, in Hong Kong and they were now very close, even discussing the possibility of marrying. They would come and visit me, he promised. Roshan and Alan were both doing well. Roshan was working as a journalist in London, enjoying her life in the big city. Alan was in better health, had begun a career as a photographer, and was himself traveling to different parts of the world. I promised them and my friends too that I would return to the UK regularly and invited them to come and visit me. It was California after all—who wouldn't want to visit? As for Steve, he was sad but not devastated. Our relationship was not moving forward, and this was my chance to move on. Other than that one shaky moment, I had been completely thrilled to be embarking on a new international adventure.

Now that I had arrived in Pasadena, I was keen to get to work. I was intimidated by the responsibility of being the museum's first full-time curator, but the museum's community, in particular the docents, welcomed me wholeheartedly. I think it helped that I was British, as this seemed to make me appear more exotic, cultured and even intelligent! The docents were a formidable group of volunteer guides—mostly retired women, many of whom had been teachers or lawyers, who had a passion for art and art education. With their encouragement, I threw myself into my work. I had acquired some experience writing about Asian art and had handled actual Asian works of art at Sam's gallery, but I had no previous experience organizing artworks into an exhibition. I was excited to learn. Because museums have an ongoing schedule of exhibitions, there is always an exhibition on view, and at least one more being prepared in house at any one time. Almost as soon as I sat down at my new desk, I found myself working with the museum staff—particularly David and the collections manager—to prepare the upcoming exhibition. By jumping in and watching and learning from my colleagues—a bit like leaping onto a train that is already moving—I came to understand the process of curating an exhibition.

First, I would have to identify a subject or theme and articulate it clearly so that the rest of the staff could understand it and buy in. Then, I would have to create an exhibition narrative and develop the basic structure and flow. Next, I would select the objects, build a checklist and fill out the structure, deciding which objects to use from the museum's collection and which to borrow. Finally, I would write the text—the main text panels introducing the exhibition and its various sections, and the individual object labels. Developing the exhibition content was the fun part because it involved research, creativity and organizational skills. The more challenging part was figuring out the logistics of making it happen, by building a budget and identifying organizations that might fund the exhibition and writing grants, and then constructing the physical exhibition itself. These parts were done as a team with the rest of the staff; the collections team figured out loan logistics and cost, the development team sent out grants, and the installation team designed and constructed the exhibitions. Developing an exhibition could take a year or even longer, but I was excited to conceptualize and curate an exhibition of my own, because it was the reason I'd left my life in the UK behind. I was keen to not only learn more about the art and share it with others, but also to add my contribution to the world of art.

For the first few months of my time in Pasadena, I spent almost all of my time working, both at the museum and at home. Fortunately, I was able to rent a lovely apartment just a ten-minute walk from the museum, and once I had furnished it, it became a comfortable space in which to do my research. I soon made a good friend, Lynn, a clinical psychologist and neurologist who lived in the same apartment building. She quickly became someone with whom I could share my joy at my new life in this sunny place, as well as my anxieties about living alone far from family and about my drive to succeed professionally. One evening, she stopped by when I was having a particularly challenging time understanding the art of New Guinea, about which I had to write labels for an upcoming exhibition. I ranted at her for a good half hour about yam masks and how I had no training about New Guinea and didn't really get what they were all about. She stood laughing at me then and still laughs today about that moment in my curatorial training. I was learning that curators at museums that represent multiple cultures often have to interpret the art of cultures they don't know well. I couldn't wait to work on an exhibition of Japanese art and be back in my comfort zone again.

After several months, David suggested I curate an exhibition on Otsu-e, or "Pictures from Otsu." Otsu-e were colorful and inexpensive folk paintings made in the city of Otsu-e near Kyoto and sold to travelers passing through. The earliest versions date back to the seventeenth century, when they were roughly painted images of Buddhist deities sold at Buddhist temple markets. But later, most Otsu-e had secular themes and were painted as "tourist souvenirs." Most featured characters that could be spotted along the road connecting Kyoto with Edo (Tokyo), the Tōkaidō, or "Eastern Sea Road," like haughty samurai and beautiful maidens, as well as folk gods, demons, mythical creatures and comical animals. Many included moralistic phrases, cautioning against bad or careless behavior.

I was enamored with Japanese folk art, or *mingei*, including the ceramics of Onta and the Buddhist prints I had recently worked on, so I was thrilled at the idea of focusing on Otsu-e for an exhibition. I had done some research on a collection of Otsu-e for Sam Fogg and found the paintings, their humor and place in Japanese culture fascinating. In fact, in a brave moment during my interview with David, I had asked him if Pacific Asia Museum might be interested in the collection and was delighted when he arranged for a group of museum supporters to purchase them and bring them to the museum with me. It was these paintings that were to be the content of my first exhibition.

David and I decided that I would need to do more than read books about Otsu-e. I would need to visit Otsu and talk to experts there. So, he sent me back to Japan in the autumn of my first year in California. I flew to Tokyo, took the bullet train to Kyoto and then a local train another seven or eight miles to Otsu. The moment I stepped off the train in Otsu, the tradition of Otsu-e came to life. All around the station were large-size pictures of the Wisteria Maiden, a young woman in a kimono holding a branch with cascading wisteria blossoms. And right in front of me, larger than life was my favorite character—the Praying Demon, or *Oni no Nenbutsu*, a hairy demon, or *oni*, with one crooked horn, huge teeth and bulging eyes dressed as a Buddhist priest. I loved the comical appearance of this character, at once fearsome and likable, and the many different interpretations of his motives. He carries an umbrella on his back, a gong around his neck, a striker in one hand and a Buddhist subscription list (Japanese: *hōgachō*) in the other. His mouth is open reciting the *nenbutsu*, a chant believed to help Buddhists attain salvation in paradise. In my research about him, I'd discovered that he could be seen as a warning against wolves in sheep's clothing, but he could also suggest that even the most wicked beings can be saved by the Buddha's teachings. To see a ten-foot tall version of him was both astonishing and wonderful.

A souvenir shop also caught my eye. All over one wall were hung small paintings depicting these characters and many others including lucky gods wrestling, a blind man with a dog, and a demon climbing into a bathtub—all very comical and cartoon-like. In particular, an image of a cat feeding a mouse a chili pepper reminded of Tom and Jerry. In the image, the cat also offers the mouse some sake, supposedly to cool down its burning mouth, but in fact, he is trying to make the mouse drunk and easier to catch—a warning that people aren't always what they seem. Below these paintings was a glass showcase full of sake bottles, plates and cups, as well as dolls, clay bells and postcards, all similarly decorated with Otsu-e characters, offering a modern twist on the tradition, which had been restricted to paintings on paper. It was fascinating to see how this town celebrated its local artistic tradition and adapted it to modern travelers. Otsu-e had always been tourist souvenirs, after all.

After I checked into my hotel, I made my way to Lake Biwa, the largest freshwater lake in Japan that is known for its beauty and connection to the country's literature. Not only has it been celebrated in poetry and prose for over a thousand years, but Lady Murasaki Shikibu, the noblewoman who wrote *The Tale of Genji* in the eleventh century (the world's first novel), is said to have written it in a temple on Lake Biwa. The lake itself is the main reason for visiting the town of Otsu, and indeed it was lovely to behold, surrounded by mountains completely covered in trees, many of which were beginning to take on their rich autumn hues. In the harbor in front of me, numerous small boats tied to posts bobbed on the water, presumably waiting for their owners to take them for a weekend jaunt, while in the distance, large passenger boats sat moored in front of a row of hotels that lined the coastline. I tried to imagine what the lake would look like without the modern hotels and large boats, in the time when visitors arrived on foot and stayed in small wooden inns lit with oil lamps.

In a building beside the lake, I saw a sign for an Otsu-e exhibition, so I went inside. In a large, open room that seemed to be some sort of community center, I was welcomed by a group of older people, possibly retirees. Excited to host a foreigner in the hall, they explained that this was an exhibition by amateur Otsu-e artists, members of one of several such groups based in the city. On the walls all around the room were paintings of various Otsu-e characters in the traditional colors I was used to, but painted with varying degrees of skill. Though simple in design and drawn with bold brush strokes, the characters had to be drawn quickly and confidently; otherwise, they would seem stiff, as a few of these did. Nevertheless, I was amazed to see how many community members were embracing this local painting tradition. There were even tables set up and covered with newspaper, where a couple of middle-aged women were trying their hand at painting the Wisteria Maiden.

The next morning, I had an appointment with the Otsu-e artist Takahashi Shōzan IV, so I made my way to his home and studio—an old building with a tile roof, a sliding wooden door and plant pots clustered on either side to form a miniature garden. Above the door was a huge sign reading 大津絵—Otsu-e. A slim man of small stature with long, dark, thinning hair and black-rimmed glasses, Shōzan was the fourth generation in a line of Otsu-e artists who have been producing Otsu-e since the late nineteenth century and have carried it into the twenty-first century. Born in 1932, Shōzan was already in his late sixties when I met him in 1999, but he exuded youthful energy and enthusiasm and was keen to share all he knew about Otsu-e with me. In his studio full of antique wooden furniture, old paintings, pigments and brushes, he explained to me more deeply the background of the various characters in the paintings and shared with me how to tell the age of an Otsu-e painting by the colors of the pigment and the size of the paper. When I asked him if he would like to come to Pasadena to give some painting demonstrations during the exhibition, he clapped his hands, clearly delighted at the prospect of sharing his art with a new audience outside of Japan.

When I returned to California, I began thinking about how I wanted to present the exhibition, and what I wanted to say about Otsu-e in the exhibition and the accompanying catalog. I knew that I would want to introduce the history of the tradition, how the paintings were made and who they were made for. I would explain the main characters depicted and how they became so popular throughout Japan that they reverberated throughout the Japanese art world at the time.

In my research, I had noticed that most literature about Otsu-e stated that the tradition had concluded with the end of the Edo period and the advent of the railroad in the Meiji period (1868–1912). This resulted in fewer people traveling on foot through Otsu or stopping in the town for the night, and apparently the market for the paintings dried up. This statement seemed to have first been made by the great proponent and scholar of Japanese folk art, or *mingei*, Yanagi Sōetsu, so other scholars echoed it in their writings. However, when I visited Otsu, I saw all sorts of products—not only paintings but also cakes, plates and sake bottles and cups—decorated with Otsu-e characters and sold to tourists, not only in the railway station but at many other shops. The tradition still seemed very much alive to me.

Also, the artist Shōzan had told me that his great-great-grandfather, Takahashi Shōzan I, began creating Otsu-e in the Meiji period, just when the tradition had seemed to be declining. He painted the various Otsu-e characters with the same lively brushwork as the Edo-period artists had, and continued to sell them to Otsu's tourists. He then passed on his skills to his son, who continued to keep the tradition alive. Shōzan IV and a couple of other artists were still creating these paintings and selling them to tourists one hundred years on, so I couldn't help wondering if it was correct to say, as Yanagi did, that the tradition had ended. These paintings had been through many transitions and phases in their long history.

In the seventeenth century, they were primarily cheap Buddhist paintings for lower-class devotees. In the eighteenth century, they became more secular in tone and larger and longer in format. Ten major characters became dominant, and they were sold as souvenirs to travelers. By the nineteenth century, the format became smaller, and the images were accompanied by moralistic inscriptions, also directed at travelers. At that time, the paintings and their characters were so well known that major artists also incorporated characters like the Praying Demon into their paintings and prints.

It seemed to me that Otsu-e quite regularly went through various incarnations, changing to meet the current market demands, probably because of efforts by artists in Otsu to keep the tradition alive. So, surely, the efforts by Takahashi Shōzan I and other artists in the Meiji period, after the advent of the railroad, had sparked another evolution of this painting tradition. Even though, unlike traditional Otsu-e artists, he and his successors now signed their work, they had succeeded in keeping the tradition going well into the twentieth century for new generations of travelers, including those arriving by rail!

So, I decided to challenge Yanagi Sōetsu's assertion that the tradition of Otsu-e had died out in the late nineteenth century. As a young Japanese art curator, I was nervous about sticking my neck out like this and contradicting an important figure like Yanagi—the founder of the Japanese Mingei Movement, the author of many books and magazines on the subject and the founder of the Mingei Museum in Tokyo—and in writing too, particularly because I had recently become very aware of the power of the printed word! I had, and still have, tremendous respect for Yanagi's contribution to the world of folk art. If it weren't for him, there might not have been as much interest in folk painting like Otsu-e or many other *mingei* art forms in the first place. However, it also seemed important to respect the intent of the artists who were working hard to keep this folk tradition going. As a curator, I believed I needed to point this out and contribute to the broader historical art conversation about this art form. So, in the exhibition text and the catalog, I made the somewhat nerve-wracking choice to go beyond merely presenting Otsu-e in the traditional manner as a dead art form, but to reshape the narrative about these artworks. I asserted that Otsu-e was still alive today.

The opening night of *Gods and Goblins: Japanese Folk Paintings from Otsu* was a lot of fun. David and I smashed open the wooden lid of a large barrel of sake together—a Japanese celebratory tradition—and we welcomed a large number of guests into the exhibition. We had made exhibition banners and hung them in several parts of Los Angeles, in the hope that the cartoon-like images would draw people from "Hollywood" to come and see these whimsical Japanese paintings. As visitors entered the first gallery, they were virtually transported to the traditional town of Otsu with a mock-up of an Edo-period shop selling Otsu-e, created by the exhibition installation team based on an image in a Japanese woodblock print. In this wooden building, Otsu-e were hanging on the walls and lying on the tatami floor as if for sale. Then, they were able to see prints and photographs depicting the town of Otsu through the ages. In the second gallery, the later Otsu-e of the eighteenth and nineteenth centuries were displayed, with descriptions of each of the characters and translations of the moralistic phrases written beside them. In a walled-off area in the center, we showed examples of paintings and woodblock prints by famous artists of the same period who had incorporated Otsu-e characters into their work, as a sort of homage to this popular folk painting tradition. And at the very end of the exhibition, we created a mock-up of the station shop I had seen at Otsu with the types of souvenirs sold to modern visitors to Otsu, showing that the tradition is still alive today.

The high point of the exhibition for me was Takahashi Shōzan IV's visit to Pasadena to give demonstrations of Otsu-e painting. Though he had rarely left Japan, he happily got onto a plane with his son (who will eventually become Takahashi Shōzan V) and daughter-in-law and spent a week with us teaching workshops and talking about the tradition to which he had devoted his life. He seemed extremely happy to be sharing this tradition with people in such a faraway place, and made several large paintings of demons dressed as priests or getting into the bath, delighting audience members of all ages. Guests at the exhibition and at Shōzan's demonstrations were very taken by this whimsical folk painting tradition and all of its delightful characters, and many congratulated me on doing a nice job with my first major exhibition. I was thrilled. The only thing that would have made it a better opening for me would have been having my family there to see it.

I was eventually able to show them the catalog, though. The beautifully designed volume was funded by generous donations from several of the museum supporters and Sam Fogg, who was thrilled that the museum was featuring the collection in an exhibition. The catalog contained my essays about the painting tradition, including photos from my visit to Otsu and pictures of Shōzan IV and his creations, as well as extremely valuable translations of the most common inscriptions found on the paintings provided by Dr. Kendall Brown and his wife Kuniko Brown. Unlike the exhibition, which typically—and heartbreakingly for a curator—only lasts three months, a catalog lives on, so the statement I made as an art historian about Otsu-e also endures. When I traveled back to Cambridge and showed the publication to my father, he was impressed by this and particularly by this statement, proclaiming, "Good for you! That means you're a serious curator now!" I beamed with satisfaction at the thought that maybe I was indeed growing as a curator and at last doing what I had set out to do.

Despite my concerns, in the more than twenty years since the exhibition opened and the catalog came out, I haven't heard a single comment about my statement about Otsu-e still being alive as a tradition, either in support of it or against it. In fact, if I think about Yanagi Sōetsu and the kind of man he was, I wonder if he might actually have approved of my statement were he alive today. As a dynamic proponent of Japan's traditional crafts, he would surely acknowledge the efforts of Shōzan IV and the other active Otsu artists to help Otsu-e survive into yet another century, to be enjoyed by tourists and art collectors alike. After all, Yanagi believed in the importance of folk art, or *mingei*, the value of the artists who make it, and the need to preserve it. And he himself challenged existing ideas and concepts. In fact, he was radical enough in his thinking that when there wasn't a good word to describe the type of art he loved—folk art—he invented one!

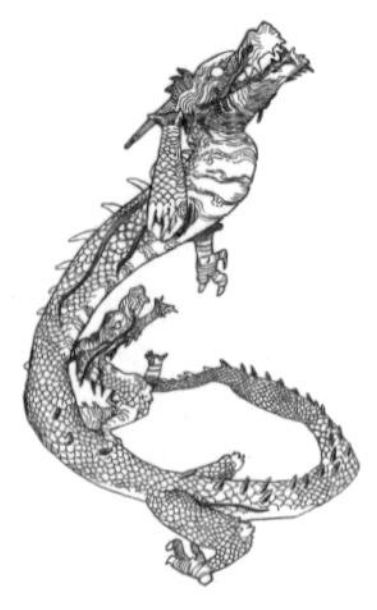

CHAPTER 9

The Bronze Dragon

In Japan, dragons are known as *tatsu* or *ryū*, the Japanese translation of the Chinese word *lóng*. These powerful beings feature in many Japanese myths and legends, often as water gods or rulers of the sea, since they were believed to inhabit the sea and the clouds. For centuries, Japan's military rulers used them as symbols of power, displaying paintings of them in their castles, and decorating their swords and personal items with them. The word "dragon" is written with several different *kanji*: the old form 龍 (read *ryū, ryō, tatsu*), the simpler and more widely used form 竜 (also read *ryū, ryō, tatsu*), and another form 辰 (read *shin, tatsu, toki, hi*), only used for the dragon in the Chinese zodiac, as in the Year of the Dragon, or 辰年 (*tatsu doshi*).

Not surprisingly, there are many expressions in Japanese that refer to dragons. One noteworthy one is *shōryū no ikioi* (昇竜の勢い), meaning unstoppable momentum like a rising dragon. In myths and many paintings, dragons are depicted rising upward into the clouds, often representing an ascent to spiritual wisdom or godly status. The expression is often used when talking about a person, organization, or sports team that is achieving continuous success.

———◆———

Toward the end of the year 2000 (the Year of the Dragon), almost three years after I started working at Pacific Asia Museum and at the age of thirty-four, I was starting to feel like I knew what I was doing as a curator. I had curated two major exhibitions and two smaller ones, and people seemed to like them. But I spent most of my time working, and much of my social life was connected to the museum. So, when I received invitation from a friend to go to the fortieth birthday party of one of his friends, I happily accepted. It was in Hollywood. I had only recently started driving, so I wasn't thrilled that I would have to drive so far to get to it—it would take me over half an hour to get there from Pasadena—but I would be going with a girlfriend, so that would make it easier. Then, at the last minute, my girlfriend canceled because she was feeling under the weather. Not thrilled about going to a party on my own, I considered staying at home, but I was craving social interaction that wasn't related to the museum. Just the night before, after several months of hard work, we had opened three new Chinese ceramic galleries at Pacific Asia Museum. Because the installation had been well received, I was feeling positive and brave, so I took a deep breath, got into my rickety white 1985 Chevy Sprint and headed for Hollywood.

I had written down the directions and gone over them before I set off, but I managed to take the wrong off-ramp from the 101 Freeway and ended up getting lost. I considered giving up and going home, but I somehow managed to find my way back to the freeway and tried again. This time, I exited at the right place and made my way to the Hollywood neighborhood where the party was taking place. Now to find parking—another stressful aspect of car culture in LA. I drove round and around the nearby streets, becoming increasingly flustered and less in a mood to party. I was just about to give up and head home when someone pulled away from the curb. I quickly squeezed into the spot before another driver could grab it. I made my way to the address on my piece of paper, through a gate that was propped open with a brick and into a very modern condominium complex. One door was open, and upbeat music and voices spilled out. I stepped inside and was greeted by a slim man with a shaved head, a goatee, a bright orange shirt and a dazzling smile. He looked like he owned the place, so I guessed, "Are you the birthday boy? Are you David?"

He answered that he was and invited me in. We small-talked for a couple of minutes, and then I told him Peter had invited me, so he led me to Peter and then disappeared off into the party. For the next hour or so, I stood talking to Peter, looking at all the people around us, and admiring the artwork on David's walls. I was having a pleasant time, but at times I wondered if it had been worth coming here just to small-talk in someone else's home. Then, David reappeared and asked me if I'd like to dance. I said I would, and we headed into the living room area, which he'd transformed into a small but hopping dance floor.

"So how do you know Peter?" he asked me, shouting into my ear to be heard over the music. "He's my sister's friend," I explained, shouting back. "She knew him before he moved out here. She introduced me to him because he's British and she thought I would appreciate having a British friend here."

"So you're British. I could tell you have an accent, I but wasn't sure what it was. What brought you here?"

"I'm an Asian art curator and am working at Pacific Asia Museum in Pasadena."

"Wow! That's interesting and very different. I'm a lawyer, a Public Defender with Los Angeles County. I don't meet many art curators."

We danced and talked through song after song, and it soon became clear that we were making a connection. I was now feeling very pleased that I'd made the annoying drive across the city and hoped that we might be able to see each other again and talk to each other in a quieter place. When the party wound down, David offered to escort me to my car and said he'd like to see me again soon. We met a few days later, and again a few days after that. Soon, he wanted to visit Pacific Asia Museum, see where I worked and check out the new Chinese Ceramics galleries. Though he wasn't part of my art world, his intelligence, kindness and commitment to justice for the underprivileged were very attractive qualities to me. The world he inhabited seemed much grittier and more real in many ways than the beautiful, shiny art world I lived in, where often my biggest problem at work was how I was going to fit so many artworks into such a small space. Some of his clients were wrongly accused of crimes, and he had to make sure they weren't sent to prison unjustly, while others did commit the crimes they were accused of, but he had to make sure they got a fair sentence. Very different and very noble work. I soon shared with him that I wasn't sure if my work was really useful to others, but hoped that seeing art from other cultures helps people understand those cultures better. Surely that improves global relations and ultimately contributes to world peace, I told him. David said he thought so too.

David and I became a couple, and soon we were doing everything together. He was coming to every museum opening and fundraiser, and we even traveled to Southeast Asia together for a vacation. I went to some of his fundraisers, which were not as glamorous and full of well-dressed wealthy people as the museum events were. Family members of people who had been sentenced to life in prison for their "third strike" of stealing a DVD and other minor offenses were joining together to raise money to change the law. (The California "Three Strikes Law" has since been amended.) We met each other's friends and socialized together. At one point, my sister Roshan visited from England, and she and one of David's friends, Jeff, fell for each other. She had to return to England, but their interest deepened across the distance, and within a year, she decided to move here, too. A couple of years after we met, David and I decided to get married, and Roshan and Jeff did, too. Life was becoming full of not just work, but also family building and a strong sense of forward momentum.

Also in 2000, the Year of the Dragon, around the time that David and I met, the other David in my life—the museum's director, David Kamansky (from here on, "David K")—received a phone call from a collector saying he was interested in donating some of his art collection to Pacific Asia Museum. Phone calls like this were common occurrences and were generally very welcome to museums like ours, which didn't have a budget for purchasing art. In rare cases, the whole collection was outstanding, and we would keep all the artworks, but more often, there were only one or two items we wanted to accept for the collection. This collection would likely be the latter, David K explained. The collector was an eighty-five-year-old veteran who lived in Hemet, a town about ninety miles east of Pasadena. Since the 1960s, Hemet had become known for its large community of mobile homes and retirement communities.

"The collector is a man called Walter Long, and he lives in a mobile home," David K added. "He says he has a collection of dragons he wants to give us while he's still alive. I doubt he'll have much that's museum quality, but you never know. Hopefully it will be worth the long drive."

David K and I set off in his gold Mercedes, a much more comfortable ride than my little old car. He spent a lot of time in his car, driving from his home in Long Beach, about 25 miles from Pasadena, but easily an hour's drive with heavy traffic. He also regularly visited collectors who lived in Beverly Hills, Bel Air, Brentwood and Malibu, so the trek to Hemet was nothing for him. Even after nearly three years living in the Los Angeles area, I still wasn't used to so much driving and such long distances. What's more, my car didn't have air conditioning, so when it was over 80 degrees Fahrenheit outside, a lengthy drive was not pleasant. I often drove with my windows open, which was very loud and made playing music impossible. However, David K's Mercedes was a different experience, with air conditioning and even Bluetooth-to-cell-phone connectivity before that was common. It was a first-class driving experience. David was also a good conversationalist, sharing humorous stories about collectors, museum donors, or strange occurrences at the museum over the years. The trip took almost two hours of driving through often flat, dry scenery, but it went by quickly.

We pulled up in front of Mr. Long's mobile home and David K and I walked slowly up the ramp to his front door. David K was still walking with a cane because of the stroke he had suffered a few years earlier, and I stayed close by, just in case he lost his balance. Because Mr. Long was expecting us, the front door was open, so we shouted hello and rang the doorbell too, just in case. A few seconds later, an elderly man rolled around a corner toward us in a wheelchair.

"Well, hello there!" he shouted out. "Thank you so much for coming all the way out here from Pasadena!"

We answered back and introduced ourselves, thanking him for inviting us to his home.

Walter Long was a slim, fit-looking 85-year-old with white hair and a friendly smile. He was wearing a t-shirt and shorts, and I immediately noticed that on each of his thighs, he had a tattoo of a dragon. The colors were very vivid, so they looked quite newly done.

"Oh wow!" I exclaimed. "Your dragon tattoos are amazing! Did you just get them done?"

"Yes, I did. I'm planning on giving your museum my collection, but since I wanted to take a couple of dragons with me when I leave this world, I got these done!"

I liked this man already! He was clearly quite a character. He explained to us that when he was in the military, he had traveled extensively around Asia, and had picked up dragon souvenirs in most of the places he'd visited. He just loved all the different kinds of dragons he found fashioned from all sorts of materials—wood, jade and various types of metal.

"I'm sure you know that your name, 'Long,' means 'dragon' in Chinese." I remarked. "Does that have something to do with your love of dragons?"

"Oh yes," he replied. "Someone told me that years ago. I loved dragons anyway, but it probably made me feel more connected to them."

David K and I scanned the tables full of dragons of all shapes and sizes. Most were small and seemed like tourist souvenirs from China, Japan and Southeast Asia, but a couple of large bronze dragons stood out. They were so much bigger than all the others and beautifully detailed, probably Japanese. One dragon was rendered in very dark, shiny bronze crouching low to the ground as if about to attack its prey, its mouth open in a ferocious expression and three claws on each of its feet. The other dragon, much lighter in color and with a matte surface, was posed on its two hind legs and tail and appeared to be rising upward to the sky. It was holding a smaller baby dragon, so perhaps represented a dragon mother and baby. I thought this one was spectacular.

David K was clearly taken by them too and asked where he had acquired them. Mr. Long replied that he had actually found those at an Asian art dealer's shop here in California, and that they were his great treasures. He really thought they belonged in a museum. David K agreed wholeheartedly. He said they looked to be over a hundred years old. They were probably Meiji period and made by master Japanese metalsmiths for export to the West. These were the types of dragons made for display and sale at the international expos that were held around the world in the late nineteenth and early twentieth centuries. David K told him that he would be happy to give them a home at Pacific Asia Museum. He then added kindly that he didn't think that most of the other smaller pieces were quite museum quality, but if Mr. Long would like to donate them to one of the museum's fundraisers, they would probably find good homes among the museum's supporters and still help the museum. Mr. Long reassured us that this would be fine. We could take them all and accession the two large ones into the museum's collection. I gave him a donation form, and he filled out the paperwork with David K's help while I started packing up the dragons, wrapping them in paper and putting them into the boxes we had brought with us.

David K and I thanked Mr. Long and told him we would be in touch with a donation receipt letter soon. He thanked us again for coming and bid us and his beloved dragons farewell. David K and I then began our long drive back to Pasadena, chatting all the way about what an interesting fellow Mr. Long was and sharing ideas about the kind of exhibitions in which we might be able to display the two magnificent bronze dragons. We agreed that it seemed particularly auspicious that we had received this gift for the museum during the Year of the Dragon.

When I got home, I was excited to share my day with my other David. After dinner, I called him and told him about driving all the way out to the town of Hemet, meeting the wonderfully quirky Mr. Long who had dragons tattooed on his wrinkly thighs, and about the beautiful Japanese dragon sculptures we had received that I now was very excited to research. He told me that his day at work hadn't been anywhere near as exciting, but that he had helped his client get a fair sentence, so he was happy too. It was nice to have someone to share my day's art adventure with.

Shortly afterward, Mr. Long's two magnificent bronze dragons were accessioned into the museum's collection, as objects #2000.35.1 and #2000.35.2 in the museum's records. These museum accession numbers indicate that the objects were gifted to the museum in the year 2000, that they were the thirty-fifth donation of the year, and that they were the first and second objects donated as part of that donor's gift. The credit line that accompanies these dragons on their label whenever they are exhibited reads "Gift of Walt and Maylo Long." Sadly, most museum visitors don't read the object labels that curators work hard to write, let alone pay attention to the object's accession numbers and credit lines to see who donated the objects and when. Those who do take the time to read the labels for these two dragons—and know that the Chinese word for dragon is *lóng*—might smile when they make the connection. Even so, they will still have no idea what a likable and fascinating character Mr. Walt Long was and what a memorable acquisition adventure this Asian art curator had on a long drive to a trailer park on a warm day in 2000, the Year of the Dragon.

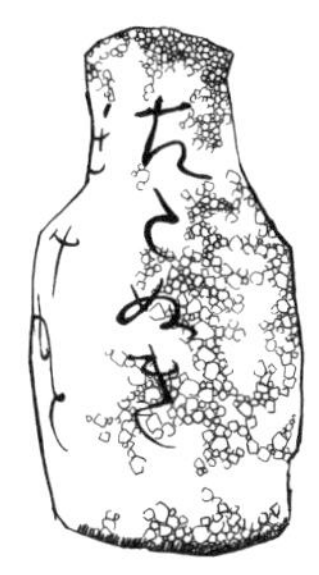

CHAPTER 10

The Sake Bottle

One of the jolliest words in Japanese is *"Kampai!"* (also written *"Kanpai"*), which means "Cheers!" The word comes from the Chinese word *"Ganbei,"* which is written with the two characters 乾杯, meaning "dry" and "cup," so the cheer literally encourages others to "drink their cup dry." In the case of Japanese rice wine, or sake, the cups are usually very small, and because sake is only as strong as wine, knocking back a small cup of sake isn't as intoxicating as slamming back tequila shots. And it is perfectly acceptable to simply sip one's sake.

For me, the word *"Kampai!"* has many happy associations, of various celebrations over the years—birthdays, New Year's celebrations, exhibition openings. Generally, in Japan, because you don't pour your drink for yourself, drinking is a very sociable experience. If your cup is empty, you offer to pour more for your neighbor, and then they reciprocate for you. So, drinking and toasting, *"Kampai!"* has always been a way of filling each other's empty cups and growing closer together.

———◆———

I had never seen so many ceramic sake bottles in one place before! Bottle after bottle, each in its own individual cubby, filled the shelves that lined the walls and extended across two rooms of the house. There was a bulbous one coated with shiny, iron-brown glaze, a flattened circular

111

one with a sandy-colored glaze and inlaid white floral designs, another dark brown one in the shape of a tea whisk, and a square one with a dark gray glaze decorated with autumn grass motifs. Some were clearly several hundred years old. I recognized a slender "crane's neck" bottle with a warm, rust-colored unglazed surface as Bizen ware from near Okayama, and there was a bottle from my beloved village of Onta, with a dark brown glaze and splash of turquoise blue. I smiled as I read the inscription written in underglaze cobalt blue pigment on a white porcelain bottle: "JAPANSCH ZAKY," Old Dutch for "Japanese Sake." The bottle was made in Arita in Kyushu for the Dutch, the first Europeans to trade in Japanese porcelain from the mid 1600s. Clearly, over the centuries, not only the Japanese enjoyed the country's rice wine!

The collection of sake bottles, or *tokkuri*, belonged to Dr. James Roorda, a retired physician with white hair and a warm smile who lived alone in a mid-century bungalow in Palos Verdes, about an hour's drive from Pasadena. His modest home was spacious and tastefully decorated with Japanese artworks—some lacquered vases, carved wooden masks and several hanging scrolls. I had met Dr. Roorda at a museum event, where he had told me he collected Japanese sake bottles and was interested in exhibiting them at the museum. Because he had heard that I also loved Japanese ceramics, he wondered if I'd like to see his collection. I had jumped at the chance, of course, but hadn't realized the breadth and depth of his collection.

"What's this one?" I asked, pointing to one with a white and copper-green and cobalt-blue glaze.

"Ah. That one's Aizu Hongo ware," he replied quickly. "It's from Fukushima Prefecture in northern Japan. The kilns there have been making ceramics for over four hundred years. This *tokkuri* is a nineteenth century example. Nice, isn't it?"

I nodded. I had never heard of this ware, and this indeed was a lovely bottle. In fact, all of the *tokkuri* on the shelves, were beautiful. Dr. Roorda had impeccable taste.

"They're all organized here too." He led me to a computer on a desk close to the shelves. "My daughter and my assistant have helped me to input information about the ceramics into a database on this computer."

Not only did he have a good eye, but clearly Dr. Roorda had amassed his collection very thoughtfully and with tremendous attention to detail over the years—not surprising, as he had been a successful doctor for many decades. As we talked, it became clear that he knew each piece very well. He was also extremely modest about his efforts and patient as I fired question after question at him. How had he started collecting *tokkuri*? Which was the first one he'd collected? Which was the oldest? He had answers for all my questions, and, on the rare occasion when he didn't remember a detail about a specific bottle, he looked on his computer. He was truly a gold mine of information and clearly loved these bottles. To him, ceramics seemed to be a portal into Japanese culture—something I had felt too. And he was delighted to share his knowledge and passion for his collection with me.

Collectors are critical members of a museum's community. For curators, they are fellow enthusiasts and experts on certain areas of art—and in many cases, they are not only sources of objects to borrow for exhibitions but also of valuable knowledge about the objects and artistic traditions that can't always be found in books. While working at Pacific Asia Museum, I curated about twenty exhibitions, drawing mostly from the museum's permanent collection, but I also often borrowed artworks from collectors. This usually meant visiting their homes to look through their collections, and these excursions were often very exciting and illuminating. In preparation for a Buddhist art exhibition, for example, I visited a collector who had an impressive collection of Buddhist sculptures displayed throughout his house. He kept one important Himalayan Buddha on a shelf in his office. Next to it was the Oscar he had won for Best Picture in the 1970s. As I was relatively new to Los Angeles at the time, I was very distracted by the Oscar. I had never seen a real one before. I even asked to hold it! In the end, I did borrow the Himalayan sculpture for the exhibition—and not the iconic Hollywood one. Another memorable visit was to the home of a couple who collected Japanese bamboo baskets and displayed them alongside their collection of modern abstract American paintings. Their unique juxtaposition worked surprisingly well, and the visit felt like another "only-in-LA" experience.

If a curator and museum are very lucky—or very strategic!—collectors can be persuaded not only to lend their works but to donate some or even all of their collection to the museum. In fact, it is quite common for museum collections to be made up more of donations from collectors than from purchases made using museum funds. That was certainly the case at Pacific Asia Museum, since David Kamansky, the director, had a talent for convincing collectors to gift their treasures to the museum, where they could be seen and enjoyed by visitors from all over the world, and could be displayed in educational exhibitions. Without a large purchasing budget, the museum relied on its strong community of collectors as a critical source of support, and they gave generously over the decades.

During my years at the museum, I couldn't help noticing that there are several distinct types of collectors, with quite different motivations for collecting art. There are what you could call the "Competitive Collectors," who seem to collect to impress or outdo others. I had lunch once with two (male) collectors, who both collected a certain type of sculpture. They seemed to be vying with each other to have the best example of a particular figure. The conversation ended with one of them actually saying, "Well, mine is larger." Some collectors—let's call them the "Social Collectors"—build a whole social identity for themselves through their collection, becoming the best-known collector of a particular type of object and gaining a social status and reputation that they may not have achieved otherwise. Others—the "Investor Collectors"—collect art as a financial investment, watching the art market to see which artist is "hot" and buying their works in the hope that they will keep getting hotter and more valuable. There are others still who are genuinely passionate about a particular type of art or artist and take the time to research deeply and widely, primarily as a means of educating themselves and others. I call these the "Scholar Collectors." They spend hours learning about the artworks, often ask curators for advice, and they share their collection and knowledge with fellow enthusiasts, hoping to contribute to the field or spark broader interest. As a curator, this last type has always been my favorite, as their collecting goal aligns with my curatorial one, namely, to learn, grow, and inspire others.

Dr. Roorda was most definitely a Scholar Collector. He had begun collecting Japanese ceramics years ago with his wife Veronica, and together they had enjoyed learning about Japan's many different types of ceramics, especially the *mingei* styles from various folk kilns. After she passed away and he retired from his work as a doctor, he focused on collecting sake bottles as a way to tell the story of the breadth of Japanese ceramics. With the help of his daughter, he dedicated his time and energy to growing the collection, organizing it digitally and sharing it with fellow enthusiasts, collectors, and curators from local museums.

"And what's this little one?" I asked Dr. Roorda, picking up a sandy-colored *tokkuri* that was only about six inches (fifteen centimeters) in height. It was rather lumpy in texture, as if it had been built by hand. Wrapping around the outside surface was a poem inscribed with vertical columns of cursive calligraphy in an iron-brown pigment under a slightly cracked transparent glaze. The calligraphy reminded me of the classes I had taken in Japan years before.

"That one's by Otagaki Rengetsu. She was a Buddhist nun who became a potter. She was also a calligrapher and poet and wrote her poetry on her ceramics. I can't read the Japanese, but I have a translation of it right here in the database."

He leaned over the keyboard and typed a few words into the database. An image of the small bottle appeared on the screen. He clicked on some text below, and a translation of the poem came up.

Furutanuki,
Sake motomuruya.
Ame no yo no
Sono tsurezure no
Susabi naruran.

Below it was the English translation:

Old badger,
asking for sake.
This is the pleasure
of leisure hours
on a rainy night.

"Wow!" I laughed. "That's so playful!"

The poem was written in highly refined calligraphy. I could tell from my time studying the art form in Japan. But traditional calligraphy was usually about love or flowers or seasonal change. The words in this beautifully written poem were whimsical and charming. My mind conjured up the comical image of a scruffy *tanuki* (an animal like a raccoon or badger that is a popular character in Japanese folklore) dressed in the robes of a Buddhist priest knocking on someone's door in the rain and begging for sake. What an extraordinary work of ceramic art—and poetry and calligraphy—the bottle was! And what a fascinating woman this nun-potter must have been! I was utterly enchanted and determined to learn more about her.

On my hour-long drive home from my visit to Dr. Roorda's home, I started thinking how I might be able to exhibit his sake bottles at Pacific Asia Museum. Even though I loved Japanese ceramics and would travel quite far out of my way to see them, a collection of ceramic sake bottles might not appeal to a wide audience. However, perhaps they could be part of a larger exhibition. Maybe one about sake. I knew of books and exhibitions about art relating to tea and the tea ceremony, but I had never heard of an exhibition about art relating to sake drinking. As I had seen at Dr. Roorda's home, there were hundreds of different styles of sake bottles. He had also shown me vessels in his collection made of lacquered wood and other materials used for storing, serving, and drinking sake in shrines and at weddings. I had noticed in the museum's collection and elsewhere quite a few paintings and prints that depicted people—and even gods —enjoying sake in various contexts, particularly during celebrations. Sake is also associated with the gods, or *kami*, of Japan and is served at weddings and other special occasions, so it has strong religious and cultural aspects that could be explored too. And it would be interesting to explain how it is made and sold. Sake had become really popular in Japanese restaurants in the Los Angeles area recently, so surely an exhibition exploring art relating to sake would have wide appeal. Dr. Roorda wholeheartedly agreed, and I began work on the exhibition. It would emphasize the role of the drink in life's celebrations, so would include the word *"Kampai!,"* or "Cheers!" in the title.

In the lead up to the exhibition, I had many reasons of my own to celebrate. I had moved into David's condominium in Hollywood, and we had been discussing the possibility of getting married. On a trip to Hong Kong to visit Dad and Jacqui, he had proposed to me on my birthday in a restaurant on Victoria Peak, and I had enthusiastically said yes! We had then traveled to Japan, and I took him to Hita to meet my friends there. When I had lived in Hita, they had taught me the expression "Christmas cake," which referred to a single woman after the age of 25 being unwanted like old Christmas cake. Since I was now 35, they were beyond delighted—and relieved—to meet David and hear our news! They treated us to celebratory dinners, toasting us with cup after cup of sake and many cheers of "*Kampai!*." We invited them to the wedding, and a group of them came to LA the following summer to join us in a beautiful garden setting to celebrate our marriage. A month after this, David and I then toasted my sister Roshan and Jeff as they in turn got married in a beautiful beach wedding. Plenty of cheers all around!

A few months after the weddings, the exhibition *Kampai!: The Arts of Japanese Sake* opened at Pacific Asia Museum accompanied, of course, by much toasting with sake! Hearing a whole courtyard full of guests shouting "*Kampai!*" at once after we smashed open another sake barrel was quite exhilarating. Borrowing from Dr. Roorda and other generous local collectors, the exhibition introduced the history of sake, how it is made, stored and served, and the rituals in which it plays a key role, such as New Year's celebrations and weddings. Our installation staff built a case to display over twenty of Dr. Roorda's *tokkuri* to show how regionally diverse their forms and decoration could be. Paintings and decorative objects depicted people, animals and gods drinking sake, including a couple of Otsu-e folk paintings that warned against the dangers of drinking too much, including the Tom-and-Jerry-like image of a cat offering sake to a mouse (mentioned in the previous chapter) in order to make it drunk and easier to catch!

As I had hoped, interest in the subject was strong and our visitor numbers were high. In fact, *Kampai!* was probably the most popular exhibition I ever curated at Pacific Asia Museum. We also organized a sake tasting event with an American expert from Japan. It sold out quickly, and the museum was packed with people excited to learn more about the drink and its significance in Japan—and to drink it too! The exhibition even got a mention in *TIME* magazine as the first of its kind! Most importantly for me, though, Dr. Roorda seemed happy with how it turned out. At the opening reception, he took me aside and explained to me that he would like to donate the little Rengetsu sake bottle, which he had lent to the sake exhibition, to the museum. I gasped. And not only bottle, he added, but all of the other Rengetsu ceramics and scrolls that he owned. I was close to tears at this news, so deeply was I moved and honored that he wanted his precious Rengetsu wares to become part of our collection. Ever since he had told me about Rengetsu, I had been in love with her work.

Soon after Dr. Roorda gifted his pieces to the museum, I proposed an exhibition of Rengetsu's calligraphy, ceramics and poetry at the museum. Over the next months, in the time I had between projects that were already scheduled, I tried to find out as much as I could about the artist. There was only one tiny book in English about her, which I devoured quickly. I reached out to Japanese art dealers, and some of them were able to share information in Japanese about her. Through them, I was also able to discover other collectors of her work, and they too shared with me what they knew. Gradually as I learned more about her personal life, and her unique, exquisite art, she became my favorite Japanese artist.

Rengetsu had been born in Kyoto in 1791 and was probably the illegitimate child of a courtesan and a noble. She began life with the name Nobu and was adopted by the samurai Otagaki Teruhisa and his wife and sent as a child to Kameoka Castle near Kyoto to serve as a lady-in-waiting. While there, she was trained in the traditional arts of calligraphy, poetry and dance. Nobu was apparently a woman of great beauty and married twice, bearing five children, all of whom died in childhood. At age 33, undoubtedly heartbroken by the loss of so many of her loved ones, she vowed never to marry again and joined her elderly father at the Chion'in Temple in Kyoto, where she became a nun. She took the name Rengetsu, which means "Lotus Moon."

After her father's death in 1832, Rengetsu was forced to leave the temple and find a way to support herself—a rare situation for a woman in Japan at this time. She decided to try to make a living as an artist and drew upon on her childhood training in *waka* poetry and *kana* calligraphy, the type I had studied in Japan. She learned from other potters in Kyoto how to hand build pottery and decorated her rough and rugged bowls, cups and other vessels with her poetry, either painted onto the surface or scored into the clay in delicate, feminine calligraphy. *Rengetsu-yaki*, or Rengetsu-ware, became so popular during her lifetime that it is said that every household in Kyoto owned some. She is best known for her tea wares, including bowls, or *chawan*, for the traditional tea ceremony (with powdered tea) as well as teapots and teacups for *sencha* tea (steeped leaf tea). She also made bottles, flasks and cups for sake, inscribed with verses reflecting a light-hearted mood, as in Dr. Roorda's lovely little bottle about the *tanuki* asking for sake. During her lifetime, demand was so high for her work that forgers soon began duplicating her wares, and, according to one legend, she actually helped some of them by writing her calligraphy on their bowls and cups!

It took several years for me to be able to realize the Rengetsu exhibition at Pacific Asia Museum. During those years, a lot of life happened, much of which deepened my appreciation of her life and work. While working full-time, I began writing *The Arts of Asia: Materials, Styles and Techniques* for Thames & Hudson, a book exploring Asian art through their materials and techniques. Researching all the materials and techniques, speaking to experts, and securing all four hundred images for it felt like an epic undertaking! It was the largest and most complex publication I had worked on to date and I was very excited and honored that the publisher had trusted me with such a project. Within days after I sent the book off, my sister, Roshan, gave birth to a beautiful baby girl, Kaia, and I felt my own heart growing with love and joy for both her and her new daughter, seeing her become a mother and handling the new responsibility so beautifully.

David and I had also been trying for a child, but the stress of my intense workload seemed to be getting in the way. It seemed that perhaps we might not be able to conceive, and I was preparing myself for the possibility that I might have to just be a wonderful auntie to Kaia. However, once I had submitted my manuscript to the publisher—and perhaps also after seeing Kaia being born—something seemed to be triggered inside me. One morning a few weeks later, I picked up a pregnancy test on the way to work and decided to try it out there. Alone in the museum bathroom before a team exhibition meeting, I waited for the results to appear. When I saw two lines materialize on the stick, I nearly fell over. I rushed to my desk and called David right away, whispering the news into the phone in the office I shared with two other colleagues, so that he could barely hear what I was saying.

I could hear David's voice cracking on the other end of the line and wished I could be with him to celebrate our miraculous moment in person. It was almost impossible for me to concentrate on the meeting. My mind was thousands of miles away.

Theo was born in September of 2005, the same month that *The Arts of Asia* came out. To me, they both seemed miraculous and gorgeous! The book made me very proud—a glossy coffee-table-type volume, with an elegant cover featuring a close-up shot of a vibrant red Chinese carved-lacquer vase on the front. But Theo made me giddy with love—with his thick head of dark hair and big, bright eyes. This little person seemed like a part of my own heart living outside of my body, and I now couldn't imagine my world without him. The emotionally overwhelming twin birth of a child and a book in the same month was an indicator that I was going to be torn between the two passions of my life, but hopefully I could find a way to make this work.

I began research on the Rengetsu exhibition in earnest after Theo was born, and this felt very right. Being a mother myself gave me a more profound understanding of what she had suffered through and how she needed to channel her pain into creating art, not only to support herself but to have a reason to want to live. I wanted the exhibition not only to introduce her art, but to tell her story. To supplement the Rengetsu pieces that Dr. Roorda had given the museum, I asked the various collectors of Rengetsu's work if they would lend some of their pieces to the exhibition. They were all very excited at the idea of an exhibition of Rengetsu's work and offered to lend me their precious bowls, pots, cups and other tea wares, as well as scrolls featuring her poetry. One remarkable collector who I particularly enjoyed getting to know was Grace Schireson, an American Zen Buddhist nun who lived, practiced and taught in Northern California. Tall, elegant and very erudite and witty, Grace had discovered Rengetsu's ceramics and poetry a few years before and was so inspired by the artist's simplicity and humility that she had collected several pieces of her work to help her in her own Buddhist practice, scholarship and teachings.

The exhibition opened in the museum's new Japanese gallery in early 2008. We exhibited several of Rengetsu's cups, bowls, bottles, other tea vessels and the sake bottle on pedestals inside the cases at the front so that visitors could see them up close. Behind them on the walls, we hung scrolls featuring her poetry. The gallery's lighting was low to protect the artworks, but the dimness and the size of the room created a sense of warmth and intimacy. I wrote labels describing her background, her tragedies and her evolution into an artist who not only supported herself through her work, but became recognized as an exceptional talent, at a time when few women were. We included translations of her poetry by Kuniko Brown, the Japanese art scholar who had translated the Otsu-e inscriptions a few years before, and visitors lingered reading the poems and gazing at her delicate artworks. One particularly poignant poem was inscribed on a hanging scroll over a printed image of chrysanthemums. The scroll had been offered to the museum by a Japanese dealer who I had told of my interest in Rengetsu. Even the dealer had been unable to read the inscription in highly cursive script. Kuniko deciphered it for us too:

> To my own children,
> Words remain to be said.
> The flowers of sincerity
> Bring back old memories
> In Sakurai Village.

I cried when I first read Kuniko's translation. Now that I was a new mother, the idea of losing one child was unimaginable, let alone losing five children, as Rengetsu had. This woman's ability to not only survive such painful losses, but to live on and create such deeply beautiful and unique art, seemed utterly remarkable. Her words as a mother were heart-breaking.

Although it was small, the exhibition *Lotus Moon: The Art of Otagaki Rengetsu* was probably the most powerful exhibition I have curated. It was so intimate and personal, and this is what I believed it had to be. Rengetsu's tragic but triumphant life story and her success as an older single female "mixed media" artist were extraordinary, but it was the Buddhist spirituality and warm-hearted humor in her poetry that caused many visitors to feel a personal connection to her. When inside the intimate space of the gallery, with its low lighting and close-up access to Rengetsu's hand-made ceramics, visitors slowed down and lingered in front of the pieces, contemplating not just the elegance of her work, but its humanity. A local ceramic artist was so awed by Rengetsu's work that she began inscribing her own poetry on her ceramics—in English, and in cheerful-looking cursive script—scored through the glaze. And a group of local *tanka* poets, mostly women, held several poetry sessions in the gallery. They created their own poetry inspired by Rengetsu and read it to each other in the gallery. The fact that this nineteenth-century female Japanese artist's work spoke to so many creative and thoughtful women in the United States in the early twenty-first century is a testament to the beauty, emotion and spirit of her artistic creations, which transcend time and place.

Dr. Roorda was also moved by the exhibition and pleased that his collection was the catalyst for the first exhibition of her work in the United States (there have been more since). When the exhibition opened, Theo was still a toddler, and Dr. Roorda presented him with a Japanese folk art toy from his collection, a sweet gift that I have held onto. Sadly, I lost touch with him after I left Pacific Asia Museum, and a few years ago, I learned that he had passed away. He donated most of the ceramics in his collection to the Los Angeles County Museum of Art, where they have been beautifully exhibited in groups over the years. Whenever I see them there, I reminisce about my visits to the home of this Scholar Collector who impacted my career so strongly and deeply. If he hadn't shared his sake bottle collection with me, I would not have curated two of my most meaningful exhibitions, and I may never have learned about the extraordinary art and resilience of Rengetsu. From time to time, I drink Japanese sake, and when I am pouring it from a ceramic *tokkuri* into a ceramic cup, I remember Dr. Roorda and raise a cup to him with a silent *Kampai!*

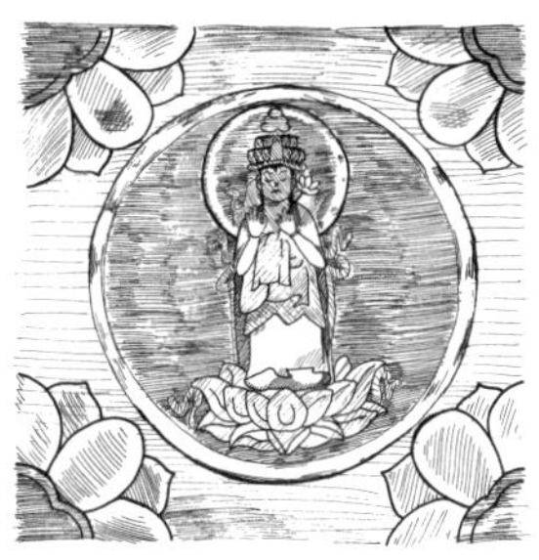

CHAPTER 11

The Temple Ceiling

The word *en* (縁) in Japanese means a connection, a mysterious force or agency that binds one person to another or to an object. The word is sometimes translated into English as "destiny" or "fate," because it is similar to these forces, which are also believed to bring people together mysteriously. The Japanese term has roots in Buddhist ideas about the relationship between cause and effect, in which an action, or *karma*, is believed to cause an effect, in this lifetime or a later one. Causes can be direct and indirect, just as a seed is the direct cause of a plant's growth, while sunshine and water are indirect causes. The word *en* is the Japanese translation of the Sanskrit term *pratyaya*, meaning indirect cause, so the bond may have an indirect cause one or many lifetimes ago. The Japanese have long believed that *en* plays a crucial role in people's relationships, and not just their initiation, but also their development, continuity and even termination.

Interestingly, the character 縁 can also mean "veranda," the walkway that runs around traditional Japanese buildings, neither inside nor outside. This architectural *en* is also mystical, created as an in-between space that connects the interior and exterior, both keeping them together and apart at the same time.

I stood in the museum's tiny Japanese Gallery, despairing, as I often did, that this rather sad little space was the "gallery" the museum dedicated to its Japanese art collection. It was roughly 10 feet by 10 feet, and clearly wasn't created to showcase art. It had doorways on three of its walls and a large window on the fourth. On the narrow walls between doorways, there was one large case containing a selection of ceramic plates and another large case featuring a random assortment of sculptures, lacquerware, masks and other objects. On the remaining walls in two small cases were about twenty miniature decorative toggles called *netsuke* and some *inro* containers and other lacquered items that were traditionally worn suspended from a kimono sash. The artworks themselves were wonderful, but the pitiful display really did little to show off the museum's impressive collection of Japanese art. There was no space to show its exquisite Edo-period paintings and drawings, its woodblock prints, textiles, lacquerware, ceramics and fine Buddhist sculptures. Japanese art was my specialty, so I felt compelled do something about this predicament, but I needed some help.

When I first became a curator at Pacific Asia Museum, I began to understand the importance of cultivating relationships with the museum's supporters, not only the collectors who might give their art, but also other supporters who might fund certain projects, from the purchase of artworks to the funding of education programs, exhibitions, catalogs and even gallery renovations. After a year or so, I had started to be comfortable asking supporters to help fund exhibitions and pitching art objects for purchase at our annual Collectors' Circle event, where the director, David K, and I proposed artworks for the Circle to purchase for the museum's collection. I was particularly keen to grow the museum's Japanese art collection, but the state of the current Japanese Gallery made it a little difficult to approach collectors. I dreamed of creating a larger, more attractive Japanese Gallery, but this could cost hundreds of thousands of dollars. I was not confident that I would ever be able to make such a large request of any of our supporters. So, for several years, I contented myself with curating temporary exhibitions of Japanese art in the changing exhibitions galleries.

A couple of years into my time at Pacific Asia Museum, I was attending a special dinner for high-level museum supporters at the Atheneum, a members' club of the California Institute of Technology, or Caltech, one of the most prestigious colleges in the country. The exteriors of the main college buildings were Spanish in style, with stucco walls and tiled roofs. But inside, the rooms were wood-paneled, like the elegant public rooms of my college at Cambridge, so I always felt comfortably nostalgic when I was there. I was seated across from Frank Mosher, a typically reserved man in his seventies with black-rimmed glasses and a full head of white hair, who had owned the Oriental Book Store in Pasadena for many years. I usually talked to his wife Toshie, a lovely Japanese woman who shared my enthusiasm for Japanese art, but this evening, over the main course, Frank became quite animated when I asked him how he and Toshie had met. He explained that they met in Kyoto when he was visiting the city as a tourist in the 1960s. She was his tour guide and he found her very pretty, he recounted, with a twinkle appearing in his dark eyes. It was raining that day, and he hadn't brought an umbrella, he continued, so he was delighted when she offered to share hers. It was a very romantic start to their courtship. They were married soon afterward and then decided to take some time to travel together.

Frank went on to tell me that one of the countries they visited was India. As he started to describe their travels throughout the country, I suddenly felt a chill.

"Was this in the mid 1960s?"

"Yes," replied Frank. "It was 1966."

"Oh my God! Did you by any chance know my dad, Tom McArthur?"

Frank looked straight into my eyes as if he was having the same realization as I was. "Yes, we met him and his wife Feri. She was pregnant."

"It's you!" I blurted out. "You're the couple from the houseboat in Kashmir!"

My heart was now racing. When we were children in Scotland and were being teased and bullied by our classmates for looking different, my father repeatedly reassured us that we were citizens of the world, and we would soon meet other children like us. To illustrate the point, he told us about another mixed couple who he and Mum had befriended in India when Mum was pregnant with me. The husband, Barry, was American and the wife, Rie, was Japanese. They had traveled in Kashmir together and shared a houseboat, where Rie performed the tea ceremony for them all. Over the years, Mum and Dad had lost touch with Barry and Rie, but the image of my parents drinking tea with this Japanese/American couple on this exotic houseboat in the Himalayas had spurred me on as a model of a truly globalized world.

Tears were welling up in my eyes, and I could feel my lower lip quiver. I pushed back my chair and jumped up. "I have to tell Toshie!"

I rushed over to where his wife was sitting and tapped her on the shoulder, trying to remain composed and polite even as I was bursting with emotion. "Excuse me, Toshie," I whispered to her as calmly as I could.

Toshie turned to look up at me, fondly, as she always did. A petite, elegant woman whose short black hair was always perfectly coiffed, Toshie had become involved with the museum as a trustee around the time I had joined the staff. We had taken an immediate liking to each other, often chatting about Japanese life and Japanese art. Born in Hiroshima, she was a young child when the atomic bomb had been dropped, and her memories of this horrendous event had motivated her to seek ways to bring the US and Japan closer together. Like me, she saw art as a means to connect people from different cultures.

I leaned over her and explained excitedly what Frank and I had just discovered. As I talked, her eyes opened wider, and she immediately got up out of her chair too.

"Oh my goodness!" she exclaimed. "So we met you before!"

Toshie was just as moved as I was, and we hugged. I was by now visibly crying, and all the other members of the dinner party were now looking over at us, wondering what was going on. Feeling sheepish about disrupting this elegant dinner, I shared the story with them as well. There were gasps from several people as they realized the extraordinary quality of the moment.

"This is Japanese *en*," Toshie added, holding onto my arm. "We met more than thirty years, and now we have found each other again. This means we must have a special relationship."

We all learned a new word that evening, and my friendship with Toshie immediately acquired a new depth.

Shortly after that evening, Toshie and I arranged to have lunch. Over our salads, I asked a question that had been puzzling me. Why had my parents called them "Barry" and "Rie" when their names were Frank and Toshie? Had they perhaps been forced to change their names for some reason? (I was thinking they might have been in an FBI witness-protection program and hoped they hadn't been in some sort of trouble.) She laughed and explained that "Barry" was Frank's nickname, one that he had inherited from his father who was a fan of John Barrymore! As for her name, the Japanese characters could be read "Toshie" or "Rie," so Frank had given her the nickname Rie—one that usually only he used. They had shared these names long ago with my parents. I was relieved.

"By the way," Toshie added, "We have found some pictures of us with your parents in Kashmir and we thought you would like them." Toshie took out an envelope containing several 35-mm slides that Frank had taken of my parents with them in Kashmir. One was of Mum sitting back on the houseboat smiling up at the camera. She looked young, glamorous and very relaxed. It was just possible to make out the bump of her swollen belly. That was me in there. There was now not an ounce of doubt that Toshie and Frank were the stars of my father's story. I smiled to see the image that I'd had in my mind for so long become a reality.

Toshie had been sad to learn that Mum had died so young. She clearly remembered her fondly and felt connected to me through her memory of Mum. Over the years, our friendship grew, and I came to see Toshie as my adopted Japanese mother, and she even told me on a few occasions that I was like a daughter for her. She and Frank had a son about my age. He didn't live close, so they didn't see each other very often, and I never met him. Toshie and I often met for lunch, and she was always interested in hearing my latest news. She was happy that David and I were doing so well and starting to plan a family ourselves. She also liked hearing my plans for Japanese art exhibitions at the museum. I enthusiastically shared my ideas for exhibitions about Japanese paintings of animals, a print show by Hiroshige and the sake exhibition, knowing not only that she understood what I was talking about, but she would also cheer me on! Having an *en* connection with Toshie made me feel like I could share anything with her.

One day after lunch, we came back to the museum and were walking through the permanent galleries on our way to look through a new temporary exhibition together. We stopped in the tiny Japanese gallery. Toshie looked around the undersized space.

"It's a shame that the gallery for Japanese art is so small," she remarked.

Immediately, I agreed and launched into a rant about how frustrated I was with it. I went on to describe my ideas for a dream gallery of Japanese art to her—a larger space, for sure, and one that would include Japanese architectural elements in it to show how art was traditionally displayed in Japan—perhaps even a *tokonoma*—an alcove in traditional Japanese buildings where scroll paintings were hung. If we designed it well, we could even have changing displays of Japanese art in it and showcase our collection better. She listened attentively as I talked excitedly about my vision and nodded gently with interest. When I finished, she said simply, "I think this would be a very good idea," and then we left the gallery and went on to see the exhibition.

A few days later, Toshie came to see me at the museum again and explained that she had discussed my idea with Frank and that they would like to support the creation of a new Japanese Gallery at the museum. Because she was from Hiroshima, and one of her personal goals in life was to help people in the US understand Japanese culture better, she believed that the gallery would be a perfect tool to that end. And, she wanted to support my idea because of our *en*—our special relationship. I couldn't believe what she was saying! I hadn't even asked her to fund my dream gallery; she had just offered. This would involve a couple hundred thousand dollars, at least! But Toshie explained that she and Frank were at a point in their lives where they wanted to support cultural projects that they believed in, and this was one of them. I was knocked sideways by their generosity. The moment felt very special, just like our whole relationship was.

I threw myself into the new Japanese Gallery project. We hired a very talented designer, Carol Porter, and planned to transform a medium-sized but rather drab gallery space into one which beautifully evoked a Japanese interior. Carol and I consulted with Toshie as we drafted designs that included a small tatami-mat area that would evoke a teahouse or other traditional interior space. We would display art in this space to show how the Japanese have traditionally displayed hanging scrolls and flower arrangements. The small Japanese-style area would be in one corner of the gallery and would have enough room for two tatami mats. One wall would function as a *tokonoma* alcove, where a painting could be hung, and on the other wall, a small window lined with Japanese paper would give the space the appearance of the interior of a small teahouse. A crooked wooden pillar called a *tokobashira*, which is traditionally positioned at one side of a *tokonoma*, would add to the humble, natural feel of the space. We planned to line the two full-length gallery walls diagonally across from the *tokonoma* with deep glass cases with sliding glass doors—like the ones I had seen in Japanese museums. This would allow us to display paintings and prints on the wall with other artworks in front of them. Unlike the current tiny display space for Japanese art, the new gallery would have enough space to mount small exhibitions using Japanese objects from the collection and beyond. Toshie was as excited as we were to see the space begin to transform.

The true highlight of the gallery, though, was a remarkable ceiling that had once belonged in a Japanese Buddhist temple. The ceiling was made up of forty wooden panels, thirty-nine of which feature Buddhist paintings. The ceiling was donated by Tom Grayson, another supporter of the museum who admired and collected Japanese art. He had been offered the panels by a Japanese dealer who had rescued them from a five-hundred-year-old temple that had been destroyed by a fire near Kyoto. Tom hadn't known what he would do with the panels, but he had a strong interest in Japanese Buddhist art and knew they were very special. After purchasing them, he had a frame fabricated so they could be mounted as a ceiling again, once he had found them a home. When David K and I visited Tom's house on one occasion, he showed us the ceiling and suggested he might donate it to Pacific Asia Museum. With the creation of the new Japanese Gallery, we had the perfect space to display it. Once Tom donated it to the museum, we began to incorporate it into the design.

I had never seen anything like this ceiling before. The thirty-nine original painted panels each feature an image of a Buddhist deity painted directly onto the wood using bold mineral pigments. Some of the images were smudged or faded, but some of them were quite well preserved. From my research into Buddhist iconography over the years, I could tell that the figures all represented the bodhisattva Kannon (Sanskrit: Avalokiteshvara), one of the most important deities in Buddhism. These compassionate deities postpone their own enlightenment in order to help other beings become enlightened. Kannon is the most beloved bodhisattva and is believed to assume thirty-three different forms in order to help ease people's suffering. In Japan, temples have been dedicated to the various forms of Kannon, for example, Eleven-headed Kannon (Jūichimen Kannon) or Thousand-armed Kannon (Senju Kannon), each representing different aspects of the deity. As I prepared to write the label for the ceiling, I looked through the digital images of each of these panels to figure out why so many different images of the deity in various forms might have been featured on the ceiling of the temple. Some of them had the names of a temple next to them. Why would such images be painted on a ceiling? I called a colleague, Hirokazu Kosaka, who is an artist, curator and Buddhist priest, and asked him for help solving this mystery.

I sent Hirokazu digital images of the panels, and he quickly called me to tell me he'd figured it out. The panels were related to specific Kannon temples along several major pilgrimage routes, and each panel had the image of the main sculpture of Kannon at one of the temples. There were three main routes, the Saikoku (West Country) route in the Kyoto-Osaka region (a total of thirty-three temples), and the Bandō route (thirty-three temples) and Chichibu route (thirty-four temples) in eastern Japan, near Tokyo. Each temple had a number, and visitors collected stamps or printed images of the main deity from each temple and assembled them in a scroll or album to accrue spiritual merit.

I knew about Kannon pilgrimage routes and that Japanese devotees of Kannon believe that visiting Kannon temples along specific pilgrimage routes will help them accrue spiritual merit. I had even been on a short version of one of these tours on one of my visits back to Hita. I had also seen some printed images from these pilgrimages when I had been working on the Buddhist print collection before coming to Pacific Asia Museum. But why were these images on a temple ceiling?

Hirokazu went on to explain that some of the images bore the numbers of temples on the Bandō route—for example "Bandō 6" (the Hasegawadera Temple) and "Bandō 17" (the Manganji Temple). Others were from the Saikoku route; others had lost their inscriptions entirely. He suggested that there had been more panels in the original temple ceiling, and that they represented at least two entire pilgrimage routes.

"This ceiling," he concluded, "was made for people who couldn't go on an actual pilgrimage. Maybe they couldn't afford to go, or they were disabled. Then they could come to this temple, stand in the hall and look up at the ceiling at each of the images. They would make a symbolic pilgrimage to all of the temples of the Bandō and Saikoku routes and make a connection with the deities of all the of temples from this one place."

"Wow! It's like a virtual pilgrimage!" I exclaimed. What an extraordinary idea—and a very compassionate one. It was a way for poor, disabled and elderly devotees to connect with and pay their respects to each of the painted figures of Kannon, and attain religious merit! I had already admired this ceiling before, but this made the Gallery very special. Not only could it be a space that could visually transport our visitors to a Japanese teahouse, but it could also give them a taste of being in a Japanese Buddhist temple, where they could learn about karma, and accruing spiritual merit, and even about the idea of spiritual connections, or *en*! I thanked Hirokazu for his brilliant detective work and got to work on writing the label for the ceiling while I could still remember everything he had said.

When the new Japanese Gallery opened in September of 2006, a year after Theo was born, the space was everything I had hoped it would be. I was not a large space, but it was a magical one. As I entered, on the left was the tatami-mat space, with a stunning autumn flower arrangement made by a professional ikebana teacher. Behind it, a scroll hung on the wall. It had a small window lined with paper, and the *tokobashira* was beautifully gnarled and rustic. The space reminded me of the small, intimate tearooms I'd seen in Kyoto. I looked up and gazed at the many painted images of Kannon, seemingly bestowing blessings on the space and adding an ancient sacred aura to the room. And all along the wall in front of me and wrapping around to the wall on the right side were floor-to-ceiling cases, in which I had arranged my first Japanese Gallery exhibition. This presentation was an introduction to Japanese aesthetics, a theme I felt was appropriate for this new, beautiful space. The spacious new cases held a wide variety of ceramic bowls and vases, and lacquerwares, and scrolls and framed prints hung on the walls at the rear of the cases. When I took Toshie and Frank through the gallery, I could see that they were happy with what we had accomplished and how we were now presenting Japanese art, and in particular the very special ceiling. Tom Grayson was also clearly moved when he visited the gallery and looked up and saw the ceiling the way it was supposed to be viewed. The space was not only beautiful, but also very spiritual—something we had not foreseen in the original plans for the gallery.

But as Buddhism teaches, change is inevitable. In order to avoid suffering, the Buddha taught that we shouldn't become too attached to any one person, thing, idea or place. A couple of years earlier, David K had retired as director but had stayed on as senior curator. About a year before the Japanese gallery opened, he announced that he would also be stepping down as senior curator. I was interested in the position, but despite my hard work at the museum for over eight years, I was not promoted to the position. I was told that the board wanted someone with experience at different museums for the position, and because I had no other museum experience, it was clear to me that I had gone as far as I could at Pacific Asia Museum. I was deeply disappointed, so I decided to leave—but on a high note. I worked my hardest on the Japanese Gallery, and though it pained me to leave this beautiful new space, I handed in my resignation just a week after its opening. I offered to work as an adjunct curator, and for several years, I curated exhibitions in the Japanese Gallery, including the Rengetsu exhibition in 2008, as well as two more exhibitions in the larger exhibition space. The arrangement worked well now that I had a young child with whom I wanted to spend more time.

After a few years, Toshie and I both became more involved with projects at other organizations and our lives gradually drifted away from Pacific Asia Museum. She and her husband devoted more time to the Huntington in San Marino near Pasadena and supported its Japanese and artistic cultural offerings, while I embarked on a free-lance career, developing exhibitions for other galleries. We continued to meet often for lunch, and she always asked me how my family was. She was very fond of Theo, and always sent him a generous birthday gift, perhaps because my own mother wasn't there to do that for him. She also checked in regularly about my father. Sadly, on each of my visits back to the UK, I had noticed that he was becoming more forgetful and confused. I shared my concerns with her that he might have some form of dementia. Because she had met Dad and knew what a sharp, brilliant mind he had, she was one of the few people in my life in California who understood how painful such a loss would be.

Several years after I left the museum, Toshie and I shared another very powerful moment of *en*. I had curated an origami exhibition at the Japanese American National Museum, and at the exhibition opening, the brother of Sadako Sasaki from Hiroshima presented one of Sadako's tiny origami cranes to the museum. Toshie, a survivor of the atomic bomb in Hiroshima and a member of the local Japanese American community, was there too. We were both deeply moved to meet him as he made his offering of peace in the United States, the very weekend that President Barack Obama was giving a speech at the Hiroshima Memorial Peace Park. Many tears were shed that evening. In fact, quite a few of them were shed by me during my curator's address to the museum supporters, government officials and friends and family who had gathered there for the occasion. So many important aspects of my life—both professional and personal—seemed to be converging in a single evening, and my curatorial work seemed to be taking on deeper meaning. As I tearfully remembered my mother and brother's battles with leukemia but also celebrated what seemed to be an important moment in my career, Toshie was there to share the moment with me, while also undoubtedly recalling many powerful and sad moments in her own life.

Perhaps one of the most important lessons I learned from Toshie was to truly accept Buddhist teachings about change and attachment. Just ten years after the construction of the museum's "permanent" Japanese Gallery, Pacific Asia Museum was under new management and directorship and made the decision to renovate all of its galleries, including the Japanese Gallery. When I heard this, I was shocked and very upset, not only because I was personally very attached to the space, but also because Toshie and Frank had given the museum a considerable amount of money to create it. I called Toshie to express my anger and apologies for not being able to stay at the museum and protect the gallery. But instead of being angry too, Toshie was surprisingly philosophical, saying simply that it was the museum's decision, and she understood that they had different plans now. But she did think it was a shame that the wonderful temple ceiling was going back into storage, where no one would see it. I was awed by her gracious attitude, and I tried to work on my own sadness and anger as best I could. Eventually, I managed to come to terms with the idea that by leaving the museum, I had given up any say in the gallery's future, and I shouldn't be angry at decisions made by my successors. Inspired by Toshie's example, my exposure to Buddhist teachings through the art and my own special connection with Toshie, I eventually accepted the impermanence of what I had hoped would be a permanent space for Japanese art. This was an important lesson for me, not just as a curator, but as a person.

The Buddhist lessons I learned from Toshie and from developing and then losing the Japanese Gallery were comforting to me when Toshie herself passed away quietly in her sleep a few months before I began writing this memoir. Although I felt the pain of losing another family member—an adopted mother—I feel that our special relationship, or *en*, is not over. Whenever I curate an exhibition of Japanese art, I imagine showing it to her for her approval, just as Buddhist devotees of old could stare up at the temple ceiling and imagine themselves receiving the blessings of deities from distant temples. Because *en* can extend beyond a single lifetime, according to Buddhist teachings, perhaps I can continue to work for both of us—to build bridges—and verandas, even—between our cultures, for current generations and future ones, too.

PART III

Curating Beyond the Museum

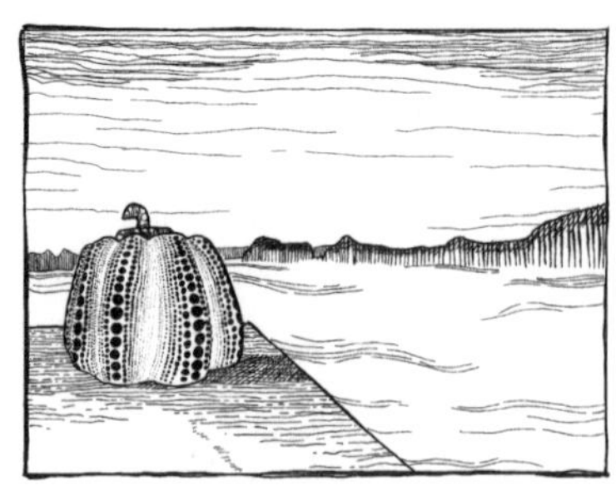

CHAPTER 12

The Polka-dotted Pumpkin Sculpture

One of my favorite expressions in Japanese is *"Ichi-go ichi-e"* (一期一会), meaning "one time, one meeting"—or "one meeting in a single lifetime." The phrase is linked with Zen Buddhist ideas of transience and of "living in the moment." It is also associated with the tea ceremony, or *chanoyu* ("hot water for tea"), in which a host prepares tea for special guests and serves it in a carefully prepared and ritualized setting.

"Ichi-go ichi-e" was coined in the sixteenth century by the hugely influential tea master Sen no Rikyū (1522–91), who had also studied Zen Buddhism. He used it to remind practitioners that, even though all of the participants may meet outside the tearoom, their shared experience drinking a bowl of tea together on that day in that tearoom using those specially selected tea utensils would happen only once. Each person should therefore fully savor that moment in time. To me, this phrase, which encapsulates the key Zen Buddhist idea of treasuring single moments of life, is one of Japan's great contributions to world spiritual culture.

I stood looking out over the Inland Sea as the sun began to lower behind some of the islands, dyeing the white stripes of cloud a soft pink at first. Then gradually, more and more orange seeped into the clouds, turning them the rich color of the grilled salmon I had eaten for lunch earlier that day. A few minutes later, the whole sky was aflame, as the pinks deepened to red, turning the chains of hilly islands floating in the sea below into dark silhouettes. I wasn't sure I had ever seen such an incredible sunset. Perhaps it was the glass of champagne that I was sipping that made it seem extra spectacular. It might have been because it was my birthday and I was celebrating it on the island of Naoshima, one of my favorite places on earth. As I made my way to dinner, I felt deeply happy to be able to witness this miraculous scene and to actually be able to enjoy it so much, even though I was so far from Theo.

This was the first time I had left my three-year-old son for a single night, let alone twelve whole days and twelve whole nights. When I left my position at Pacific Asia Museum two years before, I had imagined that working as a freelancer in Asian art would give me the best of both worlds. I really didn't want to miss a moment with my beautiful boy, but at the same time, I was not willing to give up the career I had worked so hard for. So far, life as an "Independent Asian Art Curator, Author and Educator"—the title I now put on my business cards— had been going fairly smoothly. While Theo was at daycare and then preschool, I continued to curate exhibitions on an adjunct basis for Pacific Asia Museum and a few other local museums and galleries and had begun writing about Asian art and culture for magazines and local and international websites. I also traveled to various local museums to lecture on aspects of Asian art and to train their docents when they had special exhibitions featuring Asian art. This all seemed manageable for the first year or so, as it still left me plenty of time to spend with Theo. Then, I received a phone call from the Santa Barbara Museum of Art asking me if I could lead a trip to Japan for their museum members.

I should have been excited. A few years before, I had been the study leader for one of their museum trips to Japan. Planning the itinerary, including some of my favorite places, had been so much fun, and then visiting these places with their museum members, staying in five-star hotels and eating delicious meals with them had been a truly wonderful experience! But, although I was delighted to be asked again, I was also terrified of the idea of leaving Theo. He was just a toddler. How could I abandon him when he was so small? What a terrible mother that would make me, heading across the world and leaving him behind! And what if something happened to me there? What if something happened to him? Plus, the trip was going to be in November, and it would mean being in Japan on the eleventh, my birthday—a day that I was expecting to celebrate with my family and enjoy being with my precious child. I really couldn't and shouldn't go.

But my husband, David, disagreed. It was a great job, well paid, and it should be a lot of fun. Plus, it would give me a little break from being a mom. He could take care of Theo, and we could all check in daily over the phone. The museum's travel team also encouraged me, offering to let me shorten my stay in Japan by a couple of days so that I could still perform my duties as a study leader but be away from Theo for less time. David promised that we could all celebrate my birthday together when I returned.

I half-heartedly accepted their offer, and started planning the trip, trying to make the itinerary so wonderful that I couldn't possibly miss Theo. The tour would start in Tokyo, where the group would have a couple of days to explore without me. Then, I would join them and give them an introduction to Japanese art. We would then travel by bullet train to Himeji Castle, after which we would continue down to Itsukushima (Miyajima), where I would give them a talk about Buddhist and Shinto art, followed by a visit to Hiroshima and the Peace Park. Next would be Naoshima, one of Japan's wonderful "art islands" in the Seto Inland Sea. These islands are famous for displays of contemporary sculptures and installations set in stunning natural landscapes and installed in three-hundred-year-old abandoned houses. The Bennesse House hotel on Naoshima Island, designed by Tadao Ando, allows visitors not only to stay in some of Japan's most innovative architecture but to live with the art, because each room is decorated with artwork by a renowned artist. There, I would give a lecture about Japanese aesthetics. I planned for us to be on Naoshima for my birthday! Surely, that would make being so far away from Theo bearable.

As the time of the trip drew closer, I became increasingly anxious. I couldn't imagine being away from him, not sleeping close to him, not checking in with him every morning. I worried that I was selfishly abandoning him for the sake of my work. Was I a bad mother? Would David be able to manage him on his own? Had I made a terrible mistake? I went a little insane the weeks before I left, going into super-organizer mode in an attempt to make sure we would all be okay. For David, I went grocery shopping, packed the fridge and freezer with food, wrote out a detailed menu for twelve days based on the ingredients I had bought and manically wrote out all sorts of instructions for him. He took them, nodded, and managed not to roll his eyes too much at the pages of instructions I'd left him with.

For Theo, I made a "book" of my trip to Japan, including a short text and photograph of where I was going to be each day so he could picture where Mummy was as I crossed Japan. I bought a little gift for each day and wrapped it up so that David could give him something "from Mummy" every day and then show him where I was in the book. I also promised to call every day, even though the time difference would be awkward, my nighttime would be their morning before drop-off at preschool. The night before I left, I was a neurotic wreck, terrified of the idea that something might happen to the plane or one of our trains or boats, and that Theo would be left without a mother. I paced around the house, muttering to myself as I packed and repacked. Sadly, I was unable to sit down and enjoy the exciting event that was playing out in the US that night. It was November 4, 2008. We had just held a general election and the people of the United States had just elected Barack Obama as our new president. David was beyond excited. Even Theo seemed excited. Rather than be able to enjoy this extraordinary, historic moment, I was consumed by anxiety.

The next morning, I got on the plane and flew off to Japan, feeling that I was leaving a huge part of myself behind. I made my way from the airport into Tokyo in a daze and checked into the hotel where the tour group was staying. Still feeling groggy from the flight, I left my luggage in my room and found the restaurant where I was supposed to meet the people for whom I had abandoned my young child. They all knew why I was joining them late and they cheered as I came in. They had already spent two days and nights in Tokyo and were very lively, regaling each other with the day's adventures and impressions. There were about fifteen travelers, as well as Theresa, the museum travel leader, the tour company representative, and the local guide and translator Kimiko. I knew one of the travelers already—a docent from Pacific Asia Museum who hadn't traveled much before but really wanted to see Japan. She had also been very nervous about the trip, but two days in, she seemed very excited to be on this adventure and much more relaxed. There was a young man traveling with his mother, several retired couples who were seasoned travelers and were keen to try every new experience we had planned, and a handsome gay couple who were designers and very excited to learn from me about Japanese art. Although my head was still foggy with jet lag, their enthusiasm about being in Japan was contagious, and I started to feel excited about my next ten days with them.

The next morning, I gave my first lecture introducing Japanese art to the group. They already had quite a few questions about the culture of the Imperial Court versus samurai culture, the influence of Chinese culture, the meaning of certain Japanese aesthetic terms and much more.

I was immediately impressed by the sophistication of their questions and comments and their general worldliness. Over the next week or so, as we visited museums, galleries and artist studios, I grew increasingly fond of my fellow travelers. I enjoyed watching their interest in Japanese art and culture grow. They were an extremely well-educated and well-traveled group, so our train and bus rides, lunches and walks overflowed with conversations, not only about Japanese art, but about politics (both Japanese and American), Japanese customs and habits (especially the high-tech Japanese toilets!) and, of course, Japanese food and sake. In response to some of the sake-related questions, I offered them a sake tasting. Drawing from the knowledge I had acquired planning the exhibition about sake at Pacific Asia Museum, I explained the importance of sake in religious and secular life, described sake production methods and offered them samples of the main types of sake. It was a small but lively gathering that bonded us all pretty quickly. By the eve of my birthday, when we landed on Naoshima, we were all very comfortable in each other's company.

My heart lightened as I stepped off the ferry and onto the island of Naoshima. The hilly island was covered with trees, and in the distance, I could see that many of them were beginning to take on their autumn colors. In the foreground, some slanted pines greeted us along the shoreline, and various large and colorful art sculptures dotted the gently sloping hillsides. There was something truly magical about this island, one of the nearly 7,000 islands of various sizes that make up the lush, green and mountainous landscape of Japan. Many of Japan's smaller islands are in the Inland Sea, a region full of natural beauty, but suffering diminishing populations as younger generations leave for the big cities. In the 1980s, the Bennesse Corporation, an educational publishing company based in Okayama, began developing several of the islands into "art islands," to help revitalize the region.

Naoshima was the first art island, created with several museums and sculptures by some of the world's most celebrated contemporary artists. Colorful sculptures by Niki de Saint Phalle, geometric kinetic works by George Rickey and many other notable works were positioned outside in the landscape and installed inside old, abandoned houses in the town. Later, nearby islands Inujima and Teshima followed suit. I had visited Naoshima once before and was blown away by its natural beauty and the high caliber of art to be found in the museums, on the hillsides and even in the Bennesse House hotel rooms! The most iconic of all the artworks on Naoshima is undoubtedly the giant yellow and black pumpkin by Yayoi Kusama that perches on a wharf close to the hotel. On my first encounter with the massive sculpture, I enjoyed the playfulness the polka-dotted pumpkin exuded, but the more I have learned over the years about the artist (particularly when writing an article for PBS SoCal about a 2017 exhibition of her work at LA's The Broad museum), the more I appreciate the depth and layers of meaning in her art.

Kusama is one of Japan's most extraordinary artists. She was born in 1929 in Matsumoto City in Japan's northern Nagano Prefecture to a family of affluent merchants who owned a plant nursery and seed farm. Although she grew up surrounded by natural beauty and escaped many of the horrors of World War II, her family life was deeply traumatic. Her mother was physically abusive and also sent Yayoi to spy on her father's extra-marital affairs, leaving the young girl with an obsessive and lingering fear of sex. At ten years old, she began to have hallucinations, including flashes of light, intense fields of dots, flowers, pumpkins speaking to her and patterns on fabric coming to life and engulfing her. She began to paint in response to her fears and hallucinations, often creating figures and then completely covering them in a sequence of nets and dots, a precursor to her famous polka dot patterning.

For Kusama, fields of polka dots, which she refers to as "infinity nets," are connected to her philosophy of "self-obliteration." The dots originated in her own hallucinations, in which everything around her appeared to be covered in patterns or dots, including her own body, which then appeared to disappear into nothingness. To overcome her own fear of these visions, she recreated them in her paintings. While living in New York in the late 1950s, she created a series of large *Infinity Net* paintings, in which she painted thousands of tiny white circles over a black canvas, almost completely obliterating the darkness and creating a sense of nothingness. She found the process liberating and empowering, as she was able to obliterate her own self, setting her creative spirit free and taking her stand in the world of art. She wrote in her 2013 autobiography *Infinity Net*, "I wanted to examine the single dot that was my own life. One polka dot: a single particle among billions." Dot patterns are now among the most recognizable features of Kusama's work.

And then there are the pumpkins. Known in Japan as *kabocha*, the fruit has been a recurring motif in her work for decades and is one of the most positive images that Kusama has retained from her childhood. During World War II, when much of the country's food supply was disrupted, the Kusama family storehouse was apparently always full, and often with pumpkins. As a young child, she spent hours drawing them, and her fascination has endured her whole life. She has described pumpkins as "such tender things to touch, so appealing in color and form." For the artist, they clearly represent comfort, humility and stability. Though much of her art originally evolved from her own personal pain and a desire for comfort and security, later in her life she has claimed that her overall goal as an artist has been to spread the joy and the love of being human. "My wish," she has written, "is for everyone to experience the love and joy that is around us."

On the morning of my birthday, I was scheduled to give the group a lecture on Japanese aesthetics. I shared with them some images that I believed illustrated Japanese terms like *wabi* and *sabi*, which are often hard to translate into English. For me, *wabi* can be translated as a "cultivated rusticity" as in the case of a rugged, hand-built tea bowl, which looks like it belongs on a humble peasant's table but was in fact crafted by a famous potter and sold for a small fortune. *Sabi* is a similar term that refers to a beauty that comes with age and loving use, like a bowl that has been broken but repaired with gold lacquer (*kintsugi*) so that the cracks and the repair are not only visible but enhance the bowl's beauty. Both *wabi* and *sabi* evolved within the context of the tea ceremony and in the connoisseurship of tea vessels, but their influence is felt throughout Japanese culture, from fashion to architecture.

Another term I shared was *asobi*, which means "playfulness." This term is not used to describe Japanese aesthetics, but it is one that I like to emphasize when talking about Japanese art, because I have long perceived a playful streak running through Japanese culture and art, for example, in the tradition of Otsu-e folk paintings.

After the lecture, I walked with some members of the group over to Kusama's pumpkin, where we took pictures and discussed whether the piece was an example of "*asobi*." Much of Kusama's work was born of her childhood trauma and resulting mental illness, so was this work playful and lighthearted, or was it rather a solid, comforting and reassuring sentinel standing guard over the island? Could she have created it as a metaphor for the union of nature (the pumpkin) and art (polka dots)—the very reason for the existence of Naoshima? I watched as they walked around the giant pumpkin taking in its form and surface patterning and then gazed beyond it at the scenery around them. I think we were all feeling the same sense of wonder at the moment we were in—standing in this beautiful natural environment taking in this unique and inspiring artwork.

Because it was my birthday, I spent the afternoon having a massage and soaking in the hotel's hot tub as a treat to myself, and then I called home to talk to David and Theo.

"Hi, Mommy!" came Theo's sweet little voice through the phone. "Happy Birthday!" I could feel the tears welling up. It was early in the morning the next day there, and his voice sounded sleepy.

"How are you doing, sweetie?" I asked. "Are you ready to go to preschool?" My heart ached to be able to touch his soft skin, stroke his silky hair, and cuddle him tightly.

"Yes. Yesterday I made a card for you. I drew a flower." He sounded very proud of himself. I immediately felt proud too.

"Thank you so much! I can't wait to see it. I'll be home in just a few more days."

Just then, David came on too, and together they sang "Happy Birthday!" to me. To distract myself from the tears that were forming in my eyes, I asked him how it was all going, and if he had enough food.

"You left enough food for a month! We are fine. Don't worry about us. Just enjoy yourself! You're on that art island place now, right?"

"Yes. It's so beautiful, I hope I can bring you both here one day. A bit expensive to stay, but we can visit it for a day trip sometime."

"Sounds great! I have to take Theo to school now and get myself to work. Have a great birthday evening! We love you!"

We all said goodbye, and I put my phone away. Knowing that Theo and David were doing well was the perfect birthday gift and, even more that the massage, it enabled me to relax.

I dressed for dinner and joined the group for champagne at sunset, followed by dinner in the hotel restaurant. That evening, the meal tasted particularly delicious, a multi-coursed feast made up of many tiny dishes of seasonal fish and vegetables, like the exquisite, multi-coursed *kaiseki* meals that are traditionally served before a tea ceremony. We lifted our chopsticks and began to select from the array of dishes in front of us. As always, the group was keen to understand what was in front of them, and we asked the waiter about the various ingredients—this mushroom, that pickle, the delicately seasoned chunk of pumpkin. I did my best to point out which serving dish I found particularly *wabi* or *sabi*, or perhaps even playful, so more *asobi*. The waiters brought in dish after dish bearing tiny portions, until we reached the final course with rice and miso soup. All the delicious food and sake and the animated conversation that danced around the table was making me feel quite light-headed and cheerful.

"I loved the gallery with the Monet water lilies best," said my docent friend, who by now had completely relaxed into the trip and was clearly enjoying her time in Japan.

"For me, it was the photographs of the sea and the horizon by Hiroshi Sugimoto arranged perfectly on the wall so you can actually see the horizon next to them," said one of the handsome young designers.

"I love the buildings. No one designs buildings like Tadao Ando," proclaimed an older architect. He had asked particularly astute questions during my lecture on aesthetics. "The beauty he is able to create using concrete is extraordinary! That's true *wabi*!"

"Yes! I agree with you all!" I jumped in, thrilled that they were all so excited about the artistic experience of being on this island. "But I have to say, my favorite piece has to be the pumpkin! It is so iconic of the island, and I can't help feeling she wanted us to feel happy when we look at it."

Just then, Theresa tapped on her water glass and stood up. "Before everyone leaves for the evening," she announced, "I think we'd all like to wish Meher a Happy Birthday!"

And suddenly, a waitress appeared carrying an elegant chocolate cake garnished with a single orchid flower and five candles. The group burst into song, and I started feeling tears welling up in my eyes. I inhaled deeply, blew out the candles and then thanked everyone for the wishes. Theresa walked over to me and gave me a big hug. She handed me a small, but heavy box. "We know it's been hard for you to be away from your little Theo, but we're so glad to have you with us here on this trip! We all thought you would like this."

I opened the box, and in it found the perfect present—a paperweight of the Yayoi Kusama pumpkin. I could no longer hold back my tears as I understood that leaving my precious little son and traveling so far away was not a mistake. Far from it. I held up the paperweight.

"This is perfect! Thank you all so much! I didn't think I'd be okay on this trip, but you're all so wonderful that it has actually been easy— and so special."

I looked around and saw the faces of this group of people who I hadn't known two weeks before. They were all smiling warmly at me.

"I know I already gave my lecture this morning," I added. "But there's another Japanese term that I want to share with you—*Ichi-go Ichi-e*. It means "one time, one meeting." It's a Zen Buddhist expression that basically means to live in the moment and enjoy the moment because this moment, with these people in this place, only happens once. I am really feeling that right now!"

This trip to Japan, which I took so reluctantly, had probably been the best thing I could do at this point in my career and as a mother.

With the blessing and support of my husband David and the warmth and encouragement of this kind group of people, I was taking some time out of motherhood to have experiences that added to my knowledge of Japanese art and culture and would make me a better art historian, curator and teacher. But, more importantly, this adventure had nurtured my soul and reminded me in many ways why I love Japan and Japanese art so much, making me a happier person, and therefore a better mother too. What's more, being far from the people I loved yet still being able to enjoy many moments very deeply had made me more mindful of the concept of *Ichi-go Ichi-e*. I couldn't wait to enjoy more such moments with my beloved son, but I was enjoying the present where I was right now. One day, I might even explain the expression to him and tell him about the very special moment I enjoyed when I celebrated my birthday with a group of people I barely knew on an art island with a giant polka-dotted pumpkin in the middle of the Japanese Inland Sea.

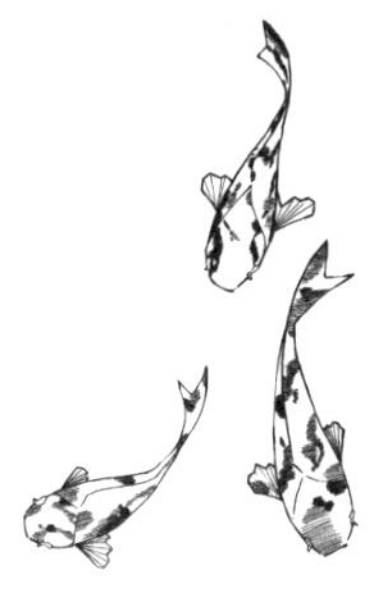

CHAPTER 13

The Origami Koi Pond

The Japanese expression *koi no takinobori* translates as "the carp's climb up the waterfall." It is based on a Chinese legend of carp (Japanese: *koi*) swimming up a waterfall at the headwaters of the Yellow River. Some of the carp were intimidated by the downward rush of water and swam back the way they came, but others fought against the current, gaining strength the more effort they made. Those who were able to ascend the falls and reach the top were transformed into dragons.

The Japanese adopted the legend and symbolism of these persistent and beautiful fish, adding them to their garden ponds and featuring them in paintings. The Japanese traditionally hang large carp streamers, or *koi nobori*, outside their homes on the fifth day of the fifth month to mark Boys' Day (now Children's Day), as a wish for the healthy growth and success of their children. Today, the expression, "*koi no takinobori*" is still popular as it reflects the national philosophy that, even if success looks impossible, it can be attained through hard work and perseverance.

———————— • ————————

One April morning in 2010, I sat at my desk sipping my morning latte and staring out of the window into the garden, searching for inspiration in the trees and sky. I had just dropped my son Theo off at his nearby preschool, and now it was time for me to start my workday, but I had no idea what to work on. A couple of birds perched on the feeder outside, and a butterfly fluttered past. Even they seemed busy and happily occupied doing what they were supposed to be doing. Often, these magical muses sparked an idea, but not today. I opened my desk drawer and pulled out a bar of chocolate. Perhaps that would help.

I was missing a sense of professional purpose. I envied my husband, David who had his lawyering work that kept him busy, made him feel useful and paid well. Even Theo's task for the day at preschool was clear—learn some new things and play nicely with others. When I was a full-time curator, I had known what my job was and had the museum's art collection to work with, a schedule to fill and a team to work with. It was much more straightforward. Almost four years into my work as a freelance art historian, I loved my work when I had it—writing articles, curating occasional exhibitions and preparing lectures. I could focus fully on it, without the constant interruptions of meetings or the dramas of office politics that often came with a full-time job. However, my projects were generally short-term and part-time, and, for the rest of my time, I found myself without work, income or company—until I picked Theo up from preschool and began my other job as a mother. Being a mother was challenging enough, and I often doubted myself. My professional self was also starting to wobble and feel a little adrift.

This situation was starting to cause some strain in my relationship with David. He was keen for me to work full-time again, even though I pointed out that there were very few full-time jobs in the Los Angeles area for my specific skill set. He had recently begun suggesting I explore alternative work options—even jobs that didn't require college-level skills, just so that I could earn a salary again—but I loved my work and did not want to give up my path. Furthermore, if I went back to full-time work, I knew that Theo wouldn't have much time with either parent. I remembered how much I'd enjoyed having my parents around when I was a child, and wanted him to experience that, too. My family hadn't had a lot of money, but we made do and had quality time together. Surely I could find a way to be present as a mother *and* keep working as a freelancer. I would have to somehow "reinvent" myself as an Asian art curator and generate more meaningful and lucrative work, but what on earth would "reinventing myself" look like?

Inspiration came later that day from an unlikely source—the TV. After dinner that evening, David, Theo and I sat down to watch a DVD a friend of ours had recommended. The film was called *Between the Folds*, and it bridged the art and science of paperfolding. The director, Vanessa Gould, had just won a Peabody Award for it. I was intrigued because I had loved origami as a child, folded origami cranes as an adult and I had recently been resurrecting my paper-folding skills to make flapping birds and water bombs for Theo and his friends. David was not as keen as I was to watch an art film, but he enjoyed documentaries, so he was game. Theo, only four years old, was not exactly a documentary film buff, so I crossed my fingers that it would hold his interest too.

For all fifty-six minutes of the film, the three of us sat riveted to the screen. Artists, mathematicians and scientists from around the world showed how their origami works had evolved from what most of us know as a traditional Japanese paper-folding craft into something quite extraordinary. Some of them used advanced math to make detailed calculations in order to create highly complex forms, like scorpions or dragons. Others wet the paper while folding to give a more sculpted look to forms like elves and seashells. Others still made their own special paper (including double-sided sheets for making a black and yellow toucan!) or colored their paper with pastels to create organic forms. One group in France even crumpled paper into mushrooms, and then blew into them to form sea creatures. Throughout the length of the film, I think the only word I repeatedly uttered was, "Wow!"

The artists talked about paper having memory, demonstrated examples of single-fold origami, and made kinetic sculptures that changed form as they were folded and unfolded. Amazingly, only one Japanese artist—Akira Yoshizawa, the "father of modern origami"—was highlighted. The rest were from North America, France, Israel, the UK, Europe and the Middle East. Although origami was born of Japanese paper folding, it had clearly gone global, and it had become a whole new kind of art. At the end of the film, I stood up and announced dramatically, "I have to curate an exhibition of this!"

As a Japanese art curator, I thought it was important to show how a Japanese art form was now impacting art and science around the world. To curate an exhibition that not only explored the history of origami, but also demonstrated its artistic evolution and its contemporary applications would be new and exciting—something no other Asian art curator had done before. I had to do it!

I rushed over to my desk, opened my laptop, and looked up one of the artists featured in the film—Dr. Robert J. Lang. A few years back, when I was at Pacific Asia Museum, a museum member had suggested to me that I curate a show of his work. Now, I understood why. His website showed many of his incredible super-complex and modular origami works, and more importantly, it also included a contact page. Still fired up from the documentary, I immediately poured all of my excitement into an email introducing myself, and explaining my idea of curating an origami art exhibition. To my surprise, he wrote back right away, explaining that there had been a couple of origami exhibitions in museums before, but that they had been curated by origami artists. He thought it would be great to have an exhibition curated from the perspective of a museum professional and art historian.

I had found my first major independent curatorial project.

After more emails and phone calls, and much help from Robert, I put together an exhibition proposal, which I showed to a colleague, Lisa, at the Japanese American National Museum (JANM) in the Little Tokyo District in Downtown Los Angeles. I had been talking to Lisa about a Buddhist-themed exhibition idea there, but that idea hadn't gained any traction. When I shared this proposal, she immediately answered, "Yes! We've been wanting to do an origami exhibition for years!"

"Is it okay that origami isn't directly linked to the Japanese American experience?" I asked, concerned about connecting the exhibition to the museum's mission.

"Hmm," she hesitated. Then, she ventured, "Well, a lot of this contemporary origami isn't traditional Japanese origami, right? It's something different, isn't it?"

"Yes!" I understood where she was going with this. "In a way, origami is sort of a metaphor for the Japanese American experience, isn't it?"

"Right. This community had its cultural roots in Japan, but most members consider themselves something more complex and global than solely 'Japanese.'"

Lisa believed my proposal would work for their members and shared it with her colleagues right away. Once JANM declared its interest in the exhibition, I approached traveling exhibition companies, and pitched an exhibition tour with JANM as the opening venue. Although a couple of companies showed interest, I decided to collaborate with International Arts & Artists (IA&A), a company based in Washington, DC. IA&A had presented several outstanding exhibitions of contemporary Asian art in recent years, and I had met some of their team when Pacific Asia Museum borrowed one of them a few years earlier. They were very excited very enthusiastic about the exhibition, so we got to work planning it.

During the planning, I enlisted Robert Lang as a key advisor. Viewed as the "rock star of the origami world" by origami enthusiasts around the world, Robert possesses a rare combination of artistic talent, a brilliant scientific mind (with a PhD from Caltech and years of experience working as a laser physicist for high-level organizations like NASA) and the ability to explain the mathematical complexities of origami to a lay audience. He can fold almost anything. He has folded scaly rattlesnakes and a praying mantis devouring her mate. He folds all sorts of animals and birds, such as moose, deer and cranes. He even created an origami cuckoo clock. And all out of a single square of paper—with no cuts or glue—a method that is considered almost sacred to many purist origami folders. Despite his busy schedule giving talks, appearing on TV shows, writing books and creating artworks, he was extremely generous with his time and knowledge.

"The first thing you have to do," he advised me early on, "is attend an OrigamiUSA convention."

"There's an Origami convention?" I asked, amazed at the concept.

"There are actually several every year in the US and other countries. This is the main one in this country. A few hundred folders will be there."

"So what exactly would I be doing there?" I asked, reluctant to have to fly across the country to spend time with people I didn't know. I was also concerned about the expense of a trip to New York at a time when I wasn't earning very much.

"Some of the top folders will be there, so hopefully you can meet them and invite them to be in the exhibition," he advised. "You'll also get a sense of how popular origami is right now. There's an OrigamiUSA convention coming up in June."

I managed to convince David that this trip would be worth the investment, and a few weeks later, I caught a red-eye flight across the country to New York. I had never been to a convention before, let alone an origami convention. At first, I just stood to the side and took in the scene. The place was teaming with people (mostly males, but many females too) of all ages wheeling carts containing their paper supplies and finished models made of all colors of paper. They went from workshop to workshop, learning from origami "masters" how to fold their signature models, or how to fold dollar bills and tea bag packets into unimaginable forms. There was a large room filled with hundreds of instructional origami books, and several authors were signing copies for their fans. I wandered around, amazed and inspired by the creative energy of the hundreds of teenagers, young adults and older people of all different ethnicities and backgrounds—all there to either teach or learn origami together for the weekend. Robert was right. The origami community was huge, diverse and extremely passionate about the art form!

Robert introduced me to an American college professor who teaches math using origami and makes extraordinary modular origami, in which multiple separate origami modules are assembled into complex polyhedra, and to a Japanese artist who runs a small museum in Tokyo called "Origami House" and mentors young, "superstar" folders. I also met a young American who had been an origami prodigy in his early teens, even teaching classes at an earlier convention, but had given it up to become a priest. However, years later, he had become disillusioned with his church and had recently given up that career. He told me that the first things he did after leaving the church, were to buy a cell phone and a ticket to the OrigamiUSA Convention. His excitement to be back in this community reflected the passion for this art form that I sensed all around me.

Although most of the participants were male, there were clearly a good number of talented female folders too. In the bathroom, I met a woman who was teaching a workshop on how to make an origami purse out of the top of an orange juice or milk carton. When I explained why I was there, she gave me one of her carton purses and the instructions as a gift. I also spoke to a mathematician known for building large modular structures using folded business cards. I was especially drawn to how she integrated recycling into origami art. When I told her about my exhibition plan, she pulled me aside and asked me to make sure that women were well represented in my exhibition. I could already see that the origami world was mostly dominated by men, but as I went on to develop the exhibition, I made sure to include as many outstanding female artists as I could. This is something I continued to do in future exhibitions too.

I left the convention overwhelmed by the size and complexity of the world of origami, but also very fired up. I could feel that this exhibition was going to be important—not just for me, but for the many enthusiasts out there. With Robert's guidance, I reached out to many of the top folders all over the world to invite them to participate. The final exhibition included the work of over 45 artists from countries as diverse as the US, Japan, Israel, Uruguay, Vietnam and South Africa. Most could communicate in English, but I had to write in French and Japanese to a few of them. It was challenging to resurrect my dormant language skills, but fun too.

I wanted the exhibition to illustrate the exciting world of origami at the start of the twenty-first century, and I hoped to demonstrate that origami was no longer just a Japanese handicraft, but it had become a sophisticated global artform, with many styles and sub-genres. As I communicated with the artists to secure their loans for the show, I also worked with IA&A to apply for grants for the exhibition, presenting it as the first museum exhibition to present origami as a global art phenomenon. Because I hoped that the exhibition would show how origami had evolved into an art form in recent decades, I was very frustrated when the National Endowment for the Arts (NEA) declined to support us because, as they stated in their letter, "origami is not really art."

Finally, we secured a substantial private foundation grant, and the traveling exhibition *Folding Paper: The Infinite Possibilities of Origami* opened at the Japanese American National Museum in Downtown Los Angeles in March, 2012. Thanks to the museum's talented staff, it looked even more spectacular than I had envisioned. The introduction outlined the history of paper folding in Japan and presented two figures who were key to its spread around the world—Yoshizawa Akira, the aforementioned "father of modern origami," and Sadako Sasaki, the little girl from Hiroshima who folded origami cranes. The next few sections introduced the main styles: the Super-complex Origami used to create realistic representations of various creatures, and Modular

Origami and Tessellations (surface patterns resembling tiling) used to create geometric structures and patterns. The final section presented applications of origami in medicine, architecture, space exploration and fashion. For the opening exhibition, the Swiss/South African artist Sipho Mabona installed 144 origami locusts folded from uncut sheets of US dollar bills. The spectacular large-scale work offered a sharp critique of capitalism, demonstrating that origami could also be used as a means for social and political commentary.

Many families visited the exhibition, and unlike many art exhibitions I'd curated and visited, it wasn't only the parents who were looking at the art. In fact, often younger family members rushed ahead from piece to piece, calling their parents to "come and look at this one!" On one occasion, I stood in one corner of the gallery and watched the visitors interact with the art and each other in the exhibition. I heard a lot of exclamations of "Wow! Look at this!" and "Can you believe this is just made of one sheet of paper?" and "Mom! Come and see this one!" I couldn't help smiling to myself. This was the loudest exhibition I had ever curated, the volume caused by pure excitement and joy at the works of the origami artists. As I had hoped, David and Theo also enjoyed the exhibition and remembered some of the artists from the documentary we had watched together. Friends who normally didn't get excited about my exhibitions also enjoyed it, and one of my colleagues, who I really respected, even commented, "This is a great exhibition. I wish I'd thought of it!" And the excitement continued as the exhibition traveled from museum to museum. The tour extended a year longer than the original three-year schedule and went to a total of ten museums, giving the exhibition the largest audience of any of my exhibitions—well over three hundred thousand people. This all felt very satisfying, but now what? It was just one exhibition.

The origami exhibition had given my professional confidence a big boost, but when it went touring around the country, I went back to my regular freelance work, so I still wasn't fully employed. This continued to be an issue at home—one of several issues that had been weighing on my relationship with David over the past couple of years. Even though we shared a deep love for Theo, we had been gradually drifting apart emotionally due to differences in our professional priorities, parenting styles and basic personality types. He believed in the importance of a stable profession and preparing for the future, while I was determined to stay in the field I'd trained for and felt passionate about, even if it meant less money and no retirement plan. As parents, we often disagreed about how engaged we should be in Theo's affairs. I thought he wasn't involved enough with his son, while he thought I should give Theo more space and let him make his own mistakes. I was basically an extrovert and desired regular conversation, engagement and intimacy, while he was far more introverted and preferred to re-charge by being alone. This often left me feeling rejected and isolated. So, I turned even more to my work to find joy, meaning and value, making me even more stubborn about not giving up my professional path for a job at a coffee shop or grocery store!

A few months after the *Folding Paper* exhibition left Los Angeles and started its tour, IA&A told me that, because of the exhibition's popularity, they would like me to develop another traveling origami exhibition—a sort of sequel. I jumped at the chance. Determined to drive home my argument that origami could be art, I developed a second contemporary origami exhibition proposal. This time, the exhibition, which I called *Above the Fold: New Expressions in Origami,* would feature fewer artists—only nine—and large-scale sculptures, installations, mixed media artworks and some conceptual pieces. The artworks would be presented primarily as works of contemporary art. The layout had no historical introduction, there was no linear order or narrative or sections—just bold, innovative art made of folded paper. We applied again to the NEA for a grant and held our breath. This time we were successful. Finally, the country's highest-level art "adjudica-tors" now viewed the works descended from this traditional Japanese craft as "art." I squealed when I received the news! This felt like a val-idation not only of origami as an art form, but also of my work in the art world. The past few years had felt like a professional struggle, like I was swimming against the art world current trying to succeed as a freelance Asian art historian. After the success of the first exhibition and now with the NEA's stamp of approval on the second one, I felt that I might be reaching a higher level as a curator.

The second exhibition opened in Springfield, Massachusetts in early 2015. I first saw it when it opened at the Japanese American National Museum in Los Angeles in the summer of 2016. It was completely different from the first exhibition. When visitors entered, they saw large paper artworks hanging from the ceiling. On one side, a delicate form made of pleated white paper swirled downward like an elegant dancer; on the other, a mysterious world took shape, inhabited by balloon-like creatures crafted from crumpled paper that had been inflated. The forms were illuminated to cast otherworldly shadows on the surrounding walls. The gallery's center was dominated by a massive twisted architectural structure, perfect for selfies (a new phenomenon at this time!), while all around, folded paper wall-hung works and sculptures invited contemplation of the natural world, literature and the complexities of religious conflict.

Robert Lang had lent his installation *Vertical Pond II*, which comprised sixty origami koi fish "swimming" along one wall. Robert is known for his lifelike folded paper models of all sorts of birds, beasts and bugs, and his models of koi in particular exude naturalism and elegance. For *Vertical Pond II*, Robert had gone beyond simply folding sixty origami fish. He had created a truly unique collaborative conceptual art installation. He worked with renowned origami artists and papermakers Michael LaFosse and Richard Alexander to craft sixty sheets of handmade paper, each colored by scattering blobs of black, orange and red pulp onto the molds as the sheets were being formed. Then, using a laser to carefully score the folding lines, he folded each of these sheets into individual koi. Each koi was placed at specific points on the wall and positioned to suggest fish swimming fluidly and spontaneously together in a pond.

Although each of the artworks in *Above the Fold* was spectacular in its own way, I noticed that many of the exhibition visitors seemed particularly drawn to Robert's installation, spending considerable time looking at each fish. Even though these were paper forms arranged vertically on a wall, visitors studied the koi as if they were standing in front of a real pond in a tranquil Japanese garden. One of the museum's security guards even shared with me that she loved the piece. In fact, she had a favorite fish—one with a single orange patch on its back—and she had named it "Spot!" I loved the uniqueness of each of the individual koi and the technical aspects of this extraordinary installation. However, the work also resonated with me because its allusion to the mythical struggle of koi swimming upstream echoed my own struggle to redefine myself as an independent curator as well as the challenges I was experiencing in my personal life.

The extraordinary artworks and magical worlds created by Robert and the other origami artists helped me find a new direction as a curator, and new ways to explore the impact of Japanese art in the world. I curated four more exhibitions of origami art, including one solo exhibition of Robert's work at the Alyce de Roulet Williamson Gallery at ArtCenter College of Design in Pasadena and published two books on the subject, including the *Folding Paper* exhibition catalog and a large book that showcases the work of twenty-five major origami artists, with the goal of elevating the perception of contemporary origami and the status of the artists. More importantly, however, the success of the two traveling origami exhibitions gave me the confidence to work with contemporary art and artists so that I could tell different stories about the global impact of Japanese art. I began proposing contemporary art exhibitions to local galleries and developed three more exhibitions of contemporary Japanese art that toured the country. Working with a team of art professionals on a fairly regular basis, I learned to conceive of Japanese art exhibitions on a larger, national scale, developing exhibition concepts and narratives and securing loans of artworks, while the skillful IA&A team promoted and coordinated the tour to museums. As a curator, I relished knowing that these exhibitions were out there in museums for years being seen by thousands of people in diverse parts of the country.

By gradually reinventing myself as a curator who could handle traditional and contemporary Japanese artworks, I was able to secure more work as a freelancer and improve my income somewhat. This wasn't enough to repair the cracks in my relationship with David, which had continued to fracture over the years. However, despite feeling like I was still swimming upstream, both in my working life and at home, I was starting to realize success in creating more innovative exhibitions and bringing Japanese art to wider audiences, which is what I had long been striving to do. Though the waters were still choppy, it seemed that I might just be making it a little farther up the proverbial waterfall.

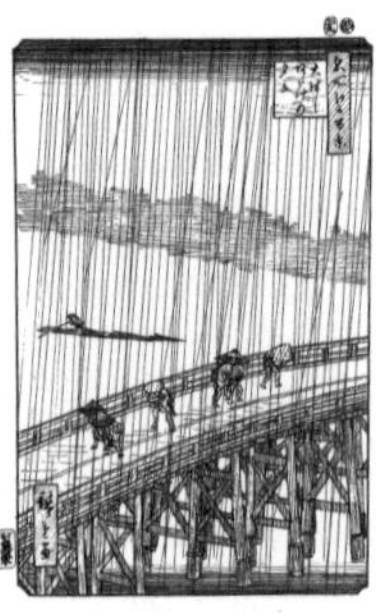

CHAPTER 14

The Woodblock Print

Japanese vocabulary relating to weather can be very poetic. For example, there are at least fifty words that describe different types of rain, including *kosame* (light rain), *samidare* (early summer rain), *harenochiame* (clear, then rain), *hisame* (cold rain), *nagame* (long rain), *yūdachi* (sudden evening rain) and even *keiu* (welcome rain). For the heaviest rain—often in the summer monsoon season—there is the simple term *o-ame* (big rain) and *doshaburi* (土砂降り), which is the equivalent of "raining cats and dogs" but literally means "raining earth and sand." This term suggests the devastation of heavy rain when it causes rivers to burst their banks and mountainsides to liquefy and slide downhill. To defend against this type of rain, the Japanese have encased many riverbanks and mountainsides in concrete, particularly in recent decades, as the threat increases. Although the delicate beauty of spring and dramatic colors of autumn have been the inspiration for more poems and paintings, the *o-ame* or "big rains" of the summer monsoons have also inspired artists and poets, often as a way to illustrate human resilience against the power of nature.

———◆———

The view across the Scripps College campus stopped me in my tracks. In front of me lay a perfectly manicured, lush, green lawn split in two by a central path lined with orange trees. Beyond the quad were the russet rooftops of the Spanish-style residence halls and a row of swaying palm trees, and in the distance, the spectacular San Gabriel Mountains reaching up into the bright blue sky. I scanned the entire vista, from right to left, breathing in its beauty, grateful to have found a position in such an uplifting setting at this moment in my life. Life could be much worse, I thought, allowing myself a few more minutes to take it all in before I headed to my meeting.

Though my career had recently seemed to be picking up, with more curatorial work and a new part-time position here at Scripps, my marriage to David had been on a downward track. After more than a decade together and several rounds of therapy, we had concluded that the tension in our relationship, though rarely expressed loudly, was not good for our thirteen-year-old son. Theo was struggling at school and seemed to be suffering from anxiety and low self-esteem. So, in the autumn of 2018, we decided to separate. We managed to be kind and caring toward each other in the process, but there were still floods of tears as we transitioned to a new reality, mine involving renting a new home. Theo was with me for only half of the time, and the rest of the time I was alone at home with two cats. I had found it hard to sleep in my new little house for the first few nights alone—strange thumps and creaks in the middle of the night and worries about the effects of splitting up Theo's life kept my mind awake. But as the weeks passed, I was getting used to my new normal.

My job at Scripps College was helping a lot. A few months before David and I had decided to separate, I was hired as their academic curator, a part-time position created to expose more students and faculty to the college's impressive art collection. The position gave me a steady part-time income in a curatorial position at a prestigious women's college, while I continued some freelance projects. It seemed perfect for me.

First, there was the setting. Scripps College was founded in 1926 as one of California's Claremont Colleges, a group of five private undergraduate colleges and two graduate colleges that operated in an intercollegiate system modeled on Oxford and Cambridge. Though worlds away from my own university days in Cambridge, I took comfort in the way that parts of the colleges do indeed have an old-world,

"Cambridgey" feel. Whenever I visited the wood-paneled Denison Library at Scripps, I was transported back to the centuries-old rooms of my beloved Emmanuel College. There were a few key differences, though. My time at Cambridge University cost me nothing (as a public university before the introduction of student loans in 1990 and tuition fees in 1998), and it didn't have the Spanish-style buildings, palm trees or the almost-year-round sunshine! I have no memories of wearing shorts and flip-flops when I was a student! But, like Emmanuel, this campus was idyllic.

Then, there were my colleagues, people who I already knew well and liked. I had been hired by Professor Mary MacNaughton, Director of the college's Ruth Chandler Williamson Gallery, which managed the college's art collection. I had known Mary since I had borrowed prints from Scripps for my Japanese folk painting exhibition over fifteen years before. Besides being gallery director, she was an inspiring art history professor who lovingly mentored her students and ran a robust summer internship program that enabled students to work with the collection and learn about art, art management and conservation. Mary had created the academic curator position with the help of Gabrielle Jungels-Winkler, an alumna who had become a major benefactor for arts education at Scripps. Gabrielle had graduated from Scripps in 1971 with an art history degree, and had recently endowed three art history positions at the college, including that of part-time Academic Curator. Sadly, Gabrielle had passed away shortly after I accepted the position, so I was unable to meet her and thank her in person, but her ardent support of art history at Scripps inspired me to want to succeed at this job.

At first, I had been excited at the opportunity to combine my curating skills with my teaching skills in this new position. I knew the Asian material in the collection quite well because I had taught two courses at Scripps when Professor Bruce Coats, the Asian art history professor, was out on sabbatical. During his thirty-five years at Scripps, Bruce had grown the college's collection of a few hundred fine Edo-period woodblock prints into a collection of close to three thousand single prints and printed books and published two outstanding catalogs on the subject. The timing felt right for me to be taking on this new position. Although I could continue my freelance work at home, it meant I wouldn't be spending as much time alone in my house. I would have an office of my own at Scripps and would be able to have lunch with my colleagues the two days a week that I was on campus.

After my initial enthusiasm, however, I soon realized that the academic curator position at a college is quite different from being a museum curator. Unlike a museum's art collection, a college collection functions primarily to educate the students, rather than to be organized into exhibitions. And, I wasn't a professor teaching classes where I could discuss the artworks. Instead, I had to reach out to the college faculty and persuade them to use the works from the collection in their classes. So, I researched the various classes being offered in the upcoming semester and emailed professors teaching studio art, art history, history, language, religious studies, economics, sociology, psychology, mathematics and science, pitching proposals for the types of artworks that I thought would fit in with their curricula. I was able to entice the professors of studio art, art history, religious studies and Asian history to incorporate some artworks from the collection into their classes, and the Spanish, French and Italian professors were delighted to bring their students into the gallery or storerooms to describe in their respective languages *"la cerámica," "les photographes," "le stampi Giapponesi."* However, my attempts to convince the economics professors, for example, to include Chinese silks and porcelains in a class about the history of trade with China never went anywhere; in fact, many of my emails remained unanswered. After six months or so of trying to convince them of the pedagogical potential of the works of art, I was feeling a bit deflated. Perhaps my sense of vulnerability and uncertainty in my own personal life was making me doubt my ability to make the academic curator position work.

After making my way across the beautiful campus, I arrived at Mary's office. The door was open, as it always was, and Mary stood at her computer typing away intently, her classically pretty face framed by perfectly styled light brown hair. Even when she was in deep concentration, her delicate features never looked harsh. I knocked and said a gentle "hello" so as not to startle her. She looked up, smiled, and welcomed me in. I pulled up a seat in front of her desk and waited for her to finish writing her email.

"I've asked Margalit to join us. I hope that's okay with you," she said, sitting down in her chair. Right on cue, Margalit appeared at the door, with her long mane of hair flowing at her sides, smiling widely, and carrying a small plate of cookies for us to share. I smiled back at her, always happy to see her and bask in her positive energy.

I had recommended Margalit to Mary when she needed a new assistant. She had worked for IA&A, the traveling exhibitions company I collaborated with, and we had bonded over our love of Japanese art and origami. She had since left the company and had been looking to move to California. I suggested she come and work for Mary, imagining that it might lead to more opportunities for her at Scripps. She had just joined the team, and now, she and Mary too seemed to have bonded over a common passion for art and love for the students. To my thinking, "the three Ms" made a lovely team!

"So, how has it been going with the faculty, Meher," Mary inquired. "Are you still feeling frustrated with your progress."

"Yes, I'm afraid so," I replied. "But I spoke to my counterpart at Pomona College, as you suggested. She said it took her about three years to get her colleagues to trust her ideas, which was a bit depressing to hear, but it made me feel better about my lack of progress. She suggested I attend faculty meetings, introduce myself, and pitch some ideas there. I think I'll try that, but meanwhile, I had an idea I wanted to run by you."

Mary took a cookie from the plate that Margalit had placed on the coffee table. "Sure. What are you thinking?"

"How about I give a series of short lunchtime presentations called 'Art Bites,' focusing on individual artworks in the collection? I could teach one 'Bite' a week in different locations, say at 12:30, after people have had lunch. One week, I could talk about a Chinese Tang ceramic horse. Another week, I could discuss a French photograph, and then a Japanese print and then a Mexican painting. They'd each be just fifteen minutes long, and people could get up close and personal with the art objects and ask questions. We can keep them pretty informal."

"I love it!" said Mary right away. "Let's get those started as soon as possible!"

That was one of the great things about Mary. She encouraged ideas and wasn't afraid to show her enthusiasm and support. Beside her, Margalit, echoed, "Me too! What a fun program for students and faculty! I'm sure they'd love learning from you about all these artworks. I can help you get the word out."

We brainstormed the idea a little more, and as we were finishing up, Mary added warmly, "Don't be too hard on yourself. You haven't even been here a year yet. It takes time to establish yourself. And you might not win over *all* the faculty. Not everyone sees art as a priority. I've struggled with that problem here at the Gallery for years. But there are many ways to get through to people with art. Stick with it. You'll get there."

I thanked her for her encouragement and started to head toward the door. I felt my spirits lifting, carried by their enthusiasm and support.

"Oh, I almost forgot!" she exclaimed, suddenly jumping up from her chair. "We received a donation of a couple of Japanese prints. Would you mind taking a look at them and telling me if you think we should accept them for the collection?" She walked over to a bookshelf where two frames were leaning facing the wall.

I knew that most of the artworks in the Scripps collection were donations from college alumnae or local collectors who preferred donating artworks to a college—where they could be viewed regularly by students—than to a museum, where most gifts are placed into storage and rarely shown. One of my roles as academic curator was to help build the collection and review offered donations to make sure they could be used for teaching. This part of the job felt more familiar to me because it more closely resembled a museum curator's work. It was certainly much easier than convincing a math professor to use ceramics or paintings in his class.

Mary turned the prints around and handed them to me. I gasped. They were both prints designed by Utagawa Hiroshige (1797–1858), and one was probably his most famous design. Called *Sudden Shower over Shin-Ohashi Bridge and Atake*, the print depicts pedestrians caught in a late summer evening downpour, or *yūdachi*, as they cross a bridge in Edo (now Tokyo). The way Hiroshige designed the rain as diagonal slashes across the scene almost makes us feel the rain lashing down on us. The print was from the artist's series *One Hundred Famous Views of Edo*, which was designed just before he died in 1857. His innovative technique, composition, and style inspired Vincent van Gogh to create a copy of the image using oil paints thirty years later, and also influenced American artist James McNeill Whistler's images of bridges over the Thames in London.

The print appeared to be in excellent condition, but it can be difficult, even for Japanese art historians, to tell if a woodblock print is valuable or not. Typically, with artists like Hiroshige, whose work was very popular during their lifetime, thousands of impressions were made of a single image. These prints were not actually made by Hiroshige himself. He would have provided the original design to a professional block carver, who then carved it into multiple wooden blocks, one for each color. The blocks were then used by a professional printer to print the final image. "First edition" prints are generally the most valuable versions today, if they have survived in good condition, without fading, being stained or eaten by insects. For popular images, another series of impressions might be made from the same blocks at a later date, and in some cases, entirely new sets of blocks were carved decades later. These prints can look very similar to the first-edition prints. However, Japanese print dealers and other experts can identify these distinctions and determine their value using clues in the paper quality, the tones of the pigment, the quality of the printing and even in details added to—or left out of—subsequent versions. I'd seen later editions and modern reproductions of Hiroshige prints, but my gut was telling me we had something special in our hands.

With Mary's permission, I removed the print from its frame and saw that it still had its original border. Over the century or so since Westerners started collecting these prints, some dealers and collectors would trim them, removing the borders and with them, important data about the print's age and authenticity. This border contained several seals, including a government censor's seal with a date. These looked correct to me. Now my heart was racing. Because this is one of the most popular of all Japanese prints, and it seemed to be an early version in very good condition, it could be quite valuable. I told Mary that I thought this print was excellent and worth accepting into the collection. Remembering that we already had another similar print in the collection, I persuaded her to let me show both versions of the print to a print dealer to determine their value and importance. The Los Angeles Fine Print Fair was coming up in a few weeks, and I suspected that Veronica Miller, a print dealer who I knew well and trusted, would be in town for the fair. She'd be the best person to ask.

The print fair was on a Saturday morning, and Theo was with David that day. Weekends without Theo usually made me feel sad, but this morning, I was excited to be heading to the fair to investigate this print. During the morning, though, a rainstorm had hit Pasadena. Even in January, it rarely rains in Pasadena, but it was already coming down heavily as I pulled into my parking spot at the convention center, so much that I was becoming nervous about our mission with the prints. Margalit had driven all the way from Scripps with the prints in her car. Even though the artwork was in an archival box, which was wrapped in multiple layers of plastic sheeting, even a little water could severely damage and devalue the prints. How could we get the art into the convention center safely? The rain pounded down while Margalit and I stayed in our respective cars and strategized over our phones. I had brought a large umbrella, and I held it over both of us while she clutched the box tightly, and we both ran practically glued together across the street to the entrance of the center, struck by the synchronicity of such rainy weather on the day we were to evaluate this iconic Hiroshige print.

Once safely inside, we wiped off the plastic sheet and were relieved to find that the boxes were completely untouched by the rain, so the prints would be fine. We called Veronica and found a table to lay out the prints for her inspection. When Veronica came out to meet us, she was immediately drawn to the print that was already in our collection. "This one is excellent," she declared. "Look at the yellow on the figures' hats and in the colophon. It's in great condition. All the colors are very sharp and the *bokashi* looks really good." *Bokashi* is the technique in which printers wipe some of the ink off the block to create a color gradient, particularly in the sky and on the water. Hiroshige's prints are famous for it. "And look at the rain strokes—the lines aren't broken, so the block was still in good shape. The two boats are missing, though, so it's not the earliest impression, but it's probably very close afterward. If I were to sell this print in Tokyo, I could fetch a lot for it." She named a price that I equated with that of a nice car.

"Wow!" Margalit and I both exclaimed in unison. Her evaluation confirmed this was indeed an important print—even more valuable than we had known. I made a mental note that we should make sure that it was well insured.

"What about this one?" I asked, pointing at the recent candidate for donation.

"This one is very good too. But look at how the yellow is paler and the colors aren't as rich and don't contrast as well as in the other print, and the *bokashi* looks heavier in the sky, making the whole print darker."

She leaned over to look at it more closely. "It's still quite an early version," she added. "But the colors aren't quite as sharp, and the contrast between the dark sky and the figures on the bridge isn't as well balanced. This is probably only worth a quarter of the value of the other print." I was very surprised at the difference in value determined by the color quality, the thickness of line and a few other seemingly minor details. It was fascinating to be able to compare the two prints, a real learning opportunity.

Then Veronica asked, "Can I show these to the Japanese art collectors' group coming to my booth in five minutes? I think they'd find this interesting."

"Of course!" we agreed and followed her inside, carrying our print box. At her booth, a group of several local Japanese art collectors waited. I knew some, but others I didn't recognize. Margalit and I both noticed the Japanese art curator from a major local museum, who was also a friend. We greeted one another warmly, and then Veronica brought out prints. One was another famous Hiroshige print of a flowering plum tree, *Plum Park in Kameido*, also from his *One Hundred Famous Views of Edo* series and also collected and copied in oils by Van Gogh. It was the first time I'd seen such a fine version of this print. We all oohed and aahed as the curator and Veronica took turns explaining the various details of this wonderful print. Then Veronica invited us to share the two Scripps prints as a bonus treat for the group. We opened the box, and I watched the collectors' faces as Veronica explained the differences between the two prints—as she had just done for us (but this time without revealing their values). Each member was genuinely fascinated by what they were learning from her—how a difference in color tone and density and balance could make one version of a print far superior to another—and much more valuable. One of the collectors, a slender, silver-haired woman called Pearl, gave us a particularly hearty thank you for sharing the two prints. She said she was looking for a home for her print collection and loved the idea of them being used for teaching. Perhaps she could come to Scripps for a visit some time.

Thrilled by Veronica's valuable information and Pearl's enthusiasm, Margalit and I packed up the prints and whispered to each other excitedly about all the ways we could use the prints to teach students. Not only would students in the Japanese print class enjoy comparing these two prints and learning about how their value is determined, but surely even students in a chemistry class would find it interesting to learn how pigments can change over time, affecting the overall appearance of important works of art. And perhaps even an economics professor might be persuaded to have a class on the market value of works of art, using these prints, some real and fake ceramics and different editions of a photograph! The prints had so much teaching potential! We couldn't wait to share our discoveries and ideas with Mary, who we were sure would be just as pleased as we were. I felt emboldened and positive about my role at the college, and keen to plan new classes to propose to the faculty. I was going to make this job work. I was going to make it *all* work.

Margalit bundled up our precious box, I picked up the umbrella, and we prepared to face the torrential rain again. When we got to the exit and looked outside, the skies had cleared up considerably. Instead of the deluge we'd faced before, we were met by some slender rays of sunshine peeking through gaps in the clouds and only the lightest of winter rain.

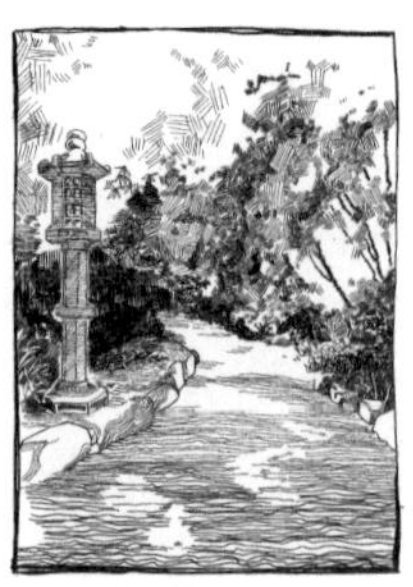

CHAPTER 15

The Garden

The word *ma* is one of the shortest yet most profound words in the Japanese language. This single-syllable word, written 間, can simply mean "a space," as in the space between objects or buildings or the opening of a doorway, as the Chinese character suggests. For centuries, the creation and expression of *ma* has been supremely important in painting, music, interior design, architecture, the tea ceremony, food and garden design.

Ma can also refer to an interval of time in music or dance, a pause between events, thoughts and even emotions, or even the white, unpainted space in a traditional ink painting. The term is often translated into English as "negative space," but it is in fact what animates the black strokes of an ink painting or energizes a musical phrase, triggering the memory of experiences and giving rise to emotions. Far from being empty, valueless or negative, the interval of space or time serves to define the things it separates, and it is just as important.

———◆———

Framed by parted *shoji* screens, the kimono-clad dancer glided slowly across the floor of the teahouse like an exquisite phantom floating in the evening light. He stamped on the floor and then gestured with the golden fan in his right hand as if to summon some spirit from another realm to join us in this sacred space. The classical dancer, or *buyoka*, Umekawa Ichinosuke was finishing up his third and final dance as part of a fundraiser event I had organized at the Storrier Stearns Japanese Garden in Pasadena. The audience was enthralled, holding their collective breath until he finally bowed at the end. They knew they were witnessing something special. For me, though, the performance was truly otherworldly. Umekawa Ichinosuke was the professional name of Futoshi, the son of my old friend Takeshi from Hita, the boy whose elementary school I had visited and to whom I had later taught English over twenty-five years ago! Seeing him perform in the serene space of this teahouse in this Japanese garden in Pasadena, I felt as if I had magically crossed both space and time.

The performance was in April, 2019. I had been working at Scripps College part-time for almost a year and was also organizing programs as a freelance creative director at the Storrier Stearns Japanese Garden in Pasadena. I had fallen under the garden's spell on my first visit in 2014, when I had arrived early for a meeting with the owner and had decided to explore the garden on my own. I was drawn to a pair of tall redwood trees and a stone lantern in front of the check-in area. I peered inside the open upper section of the lantern, where the light had presumably once been lit, and saw that someone had placed a couple of small pebbles there—an offering perhaps. I continued along the path, and a whole pond suddenly appeared to my left. I hadn't seen it because it had been hidden by the two redwoods and some adjacent bushes.

Red dragonflies flitted over the surface of the pond's lily pads and danced between the reeds, occasionally stopping to perch on a reed and take in the view themselves. A large yellow koi fish appeared from behind the reeds and swam toward me, opening its mouth as it looked up at me, hoping for some food. I apologized for my empty hands, then walked past thick spongy-looking grass and a gnarled old tree, until I arrived at a zigzagging concrete bridge.

I knew from my days working at Pacific Asia Museum that zigzagging bridges and winding entranceways were used in Chinese architecture and garden design to keep evil spirits away, because malevolent forces were believed to only be able to travel in a straight line. In Japanese gardens like this one, such bridges were also employed to force visitors to slow down and pay attention to their footing as they crossed the water. Moving slowly and carefully, I arrived safely on the other side. I turned to my right and saw a teahouse overlooking a second, smaller pond. I paused for a moment and took in the elegant scene before setting off again, winding my way past delicate plants, flowers and an enormous magnolia tree and into the open space in front of the teahouse. The wooden building with its veranda, sliding doors and interior tatami-mat floors reminded me of the many tea ceremonies I had attended in Japan. I could almost taste the bitter, thick green tea. I took a few deep breaths, inhaling the serenity of the spot, and then headed back to the main house for my appointment.

Connie Haddad, a petite octogenarian with wavy light-brown hair and wearing a long floral dress, met me on the veranda of the 1950s-style bungalow with French windows that looked out over the garden. She greeted me with a warm smile and welcomed me inside. I had been told about Connie and her husband Jim and their Japanese garden by Ken Brown, the Japanese art historian with whom I'd worked at Pacific Asia Museum on the Japanese folk painting exhibition. As the leading expert on Japanese gardens in the United States, he had explained that Connie and Jim had recently restored the Storrier Stearns Japanese Garden. Ken had helped them to apply for national historic landmark status and to form a non-profit organization to run the garden. He was now on the board of directors. He had told Connie about me because Connie was interested in adding art to the garden and he thought I might be able to help. It was currently only open to the public one day a week, and they were hoping to expand the garden's hours and present more programs. It wasn't the type of work I normally did as a curator, but I was intrigued to learn more about the garden and how I might use my skills to help.

Connie invited me inside for tea. I sat on the ornate French-style couch and watched her lay out tea and shortbread on the oval glass table. She poured tea and I helped myself to a biscuit. As we sipped tea, she shared the history of the garden with great energy and passion. It was completed in 1940 and had originally been commissioned by Charles and Ellamae Storrier Stearns. The fashionable couple had met later in life after several previous marriages between them. They lived a glamorous life traveling between the United States and France. The couple deeply admired all things "Oriental," and Ellamae had yearned for a Japanese garden and teahouse. She and Charles hired a Japanese landscape designer, Kinzuchi Fujii, to convert the tennis courts on their estate into a tranquil Japanese garden.

I asked Connie how she and Jim had come to own the property, and she explained that Charles and Ellamae died about ten years after the garden was completed. Because they had no children, their estate was put up for auction, and Jim's mother bought it, on a whim!

Jim's mother, Gamelia Haddad Poulsen was a Pasadena art dealer and had gone to the auction with the intention to buy some French chairs but, when nobody else bid on the property itself, she decided to purchase the whole estate. She sold off most of the property, but built herself a home in the garden where she lived for many years. Then, in 1975, the California Department of Transportation (CalTrans) decided to extend a local freeway and invoked eminent domain to buy almost half of the garden. Believing the garden to be a lost cause, Gamelia let it fall into ruin. She left the garden to Jim and Connie when she died in 1985, and for almost twenty years, the neglected garden ran wild. As the freeway plans stalled year after year, the parcel didn't seem like it was going to become a freeway either. It sat in sad, overgrown limbo.

But around the year 2000, the freeway extension plans appeared to be faltering, so Jim and Connie, who had recently retired, decided to restore the garden. They asked Japanese landscape designer Takeo Uesugi to help with the project. As a labor of love, he brought it back to its former glory.

"And now we are ready to share it with others!" Connie proclaimed, her face glowing with passion for this beautiful garden and all its potential.

When I asked her what she was thinking of, she sat up in her chair and spoke very quickly, her voice overflowing with excitement. "Well, we have a director, Deanie, who does a wonderful job of managing the garden and bringing in rentals to cover the operating costs, but she doesn't have time to run public programs too. We'd love to offer classes and lectures and other programs about Japanese art and culture," she explained. "And we've had a few musical concerts already. We want to have more of them and maybe even festivals that the whole family can enjoy." Her eyes sparkled as she described the origami workshops, goldfish fishing and other traditional Japanese activities she dreamed of offering children at a Japanese festival in the garden. She had put a lot of thought into these ideas and was keen to share them with someone who might be able to help realize them.

"What an amazing gift for the community!" I exclaimed, totally captivated by the garden's fascinating history, and already caught up in Connie's infectious enthusiasm and desire to share this cultural treasure with the local community. I related my experience with Japanese cultural programming at Pacific Asia Museum and at other local organizations. Keen to be of help with this wonderful project, I offered to assist for a few hours a week to develop programs that might draw more visitors to this beautiful space.

First, I set out to learn as much as I could about the garden, its history and its original creator, Kinzuchi Fujii. Jim and Ken's research on the garden's history had revealed that Fujii and his team had labored hard for five years to dig out the two ponds at the heart of the garden. They used the dirt from the ponds to build up hills on the eastern side and gradually created a traditional strolling garden, which typically includes features such as ponds with bridges and stepping-stone pathways. Around the pond they added a waterfall, stone lanterns and a small, covered bench for sitting, slowing down and enjoying the view. Using mules, they also carted in boulders and stones from nearby mountains to form the "bones" of the garden. For the "flesh" of the garden, they planted camellias, azaleas and other traditional Japanese plants, but they also incorporated local trees, like redwoods and sycamores, as well as trees from other parts of the US, like the now massive magnolia that overlooks the garden. The heart of the garden was the twelve-mat teahouse, originally designed by Fujii and then constructed in Japan. It was then disassembled, shipped to the US and rebuilt on a foundation of three giant boulders. In 1940, the garden was completed to the delight of his patrons.

But, tragically, Fujii was sent to an internment camp with 120,000 other Japanese Americans and never saw his garden masterpiece again. This shocking part of its story made me even more committed to sharing Fujii's garden with others. Even though there was nothing I could do to right the tragic wrong that had befallen Fujii and his fellow Japanese Americans, I could at least try to ensure that his name and legacy were seen and appreciated by as many people as possible.

I made new text panels with photographs about the garden's history that we could display for visitors to read.

Once I'd understood the garden's history, I read up on Japanese garden design—a new area of Japanese art for me. I learned that "strolling gardens," or *kaiyu-shiki-teien*, first appeared in the Edo period (1600–1868) on the estates of Japan's nobles and military lords to complement the *sukiya*-style villas of the upper classes. Visitors were encouraged to follow a path clockwise around a central lake, moving from one carefully composed setting to another. The designers of these gardens employed two techniques to compose these settings. One is *shakei*, or "borrowed scenery," which incorporated mountains or forests beyond the garden into the overall view, making the garden look larger. Here, the San Gabriel Mountains to the north helped make the garden more expansive. Another technique, *miegakure*, or "hide-and-reveal," uses winding paths, fences, trees, bamboo and buildings to hide certain natural details from view. A visitor will walk beside a fence or a bush, and then turn a corner, and something completely new will be revealed—like the pond on my first visit. During this research, I realized that, just like painters create images in ink on paper or silk in a way that guides the viewer's eyes across the surface, garden designers carefully consider composition, color and balance, adopting a three-dimensional approach to the use of space, or *ma*, that helps visitors move through it mindfully. They were also artists, and their gardens were true works of art.

After a few months, Connie and Jim were keen to add programs, so they increased my hours and gave me the title of creative director. While also going in part-time to Scripps College, writing articles and curating exhibitions from home, I planned Japanese art lectures, book signings, Japanese film screenings, music performances, cultural festivals and art fairs. Connie and Jim also allowed me to turn the living room into an art gallery called "En Gallery," because *en* means both "connection" and "garden" in Japanese. Here, I curated small solo exhibitions by artists whose work related to Japan, gardens and spirituality. In addition, I organized several fundraiser events with food and drink, a silent auction and performances in the teahouse, most notably by some exquisite geisha from Kyoto as well as by Umekawa-san, the classical Japanese dancer from Hita. They also decided to open the garden on certain weekdays as well as Sundays to allow more people to visit. They brought in another staff member, Virginia, to manage the garden on those days. The level of activity at the garden and the number of visitors rose considerably, as Connie and Jim had hoped.

However, the open-day overhead, staff wages and program costs were more than the revenue from private rentals for weddings, retreats and film shoots could cover. Jim, Connie, the staff and the board of directors had many discussions, meetings and strategic planning sessions to figure out how to raise more funds or cut costs, but we were unable to find a solution that we all agreed on. Then, in March of 2020, everything suddenly came to a grinding halt. Not just in the garden, but all over the world.

The lockdowns and restrictions in activities caused by the COVID-19 pandemic not only kept people isolated in their homes for months, but the pause around the world also dramatically impacted most businesses and non-profit organizations. Like most cultural organizations, the Storrier Stearns Japanese Garden closed its gates for several months, and the weddings and other private events that had been planned for the next year were all canceled. Connie and Jim had to let most of the small staff go. Deanie decided to take partial retirement, Virginia looked for a position elsewhere, and I left to work on a couple of Japanese art exhibitions and start this book, though I remained involved as a board member. We all wondered if the garden would be able to survive without a staff to run it and the income from wedding rentals and regular admission fees. For several months, as with many non-profit organizations, the Storrier Stearns Japanese Garden held its breath.

Later in 2020, noticing that other gardens were becoming popular destinations for people looking for safe outdoor places to visit, Jim and Connie began opening the garden on Sundays only, for visitors with reservations, with one masked staff member checking people in at a distance. The garden would simply be a garden—a beautiful respite from the stress and anxiety of the time and a place of healing. Immediately, people started coming back—in greater numbers than ever before. The garden, with its winding paths and appearing-and-disappearing views of the pond and teahouse, all conceived to encourage guests to slow down and take in the smaller details of nature, began enchanting dozens of new visitors every Sunday. Small groups, couples and families—who had been cooped up indoors for months and unable to travel anywhere—were eager to be outdoors and thrilled at the opportunity to immerse themselves in another culture for an hour or two. Some even brought lunch with them so they could enjoy a picnic in a safe outdoor space that was also an exotic location—a real treat for people who were missing foreign travel. After a few more months, Jim and Connie decided to open for the whole weekend, and then Friday evenings too, and this brought even more visitors, many of whom shared their appreciation for being able to spend time in a serene place. Whenever the garden was open, it generally had more guests than before. The word was spreading about this beautiful, healing natural space.

During this time, I also made several visits to the garden on weekends, often masked and careful to keep my distance from others. I was no longer working there organizing events, but, like other visitors who had been facing fear and loss, I also sought its serenity. For me, the pandemic had begun with the fear of COVID-19 itself and a deep sense of personal loss. My father had been suffering from dementia over the previous decade or so. During those years, my sister Roshan, brother Alan, and I had been maintaining contact via regular phone calls and occasional visits to Cambridge. During those moments of contact, we had experienced the prolonged heartbreak of witnessing our brilliant father going from being "a bit forgetful" to increasingly confused and finally uncertain of who we were. On one call before he was admitted into an assisted living facility, Dad's speech had been incoherent, but he had still sounded cheerful and hummed a jolly Scottish-sounding tune to me. It had reminded me of the Scots evenings he and Mum had organized when we were children. I had listened with tears rolling down my cheeks but smiling that the part of him that still knew who I was wanted to share this gift of music with me. Just two weeks into lockdown, Jacqui called to tell us Dad had died in his sleep.

There was no way to go to Cambridge for the funeral. Jacqui, who had cared lovingly for him for many years now and visited him daily in his care home, had to arrange his cremation at the most difficult of times, when everyone was keeping their distance from each other and people from different households weren't permitted to embrace. Jacqui sent us a video of the cremation over WhatsApp, and Roshan and I in Los Angeles, and Alan, who was in Mexico at the time, watched this enormous life event on the tiny screens of our cell phones. At this painfully isolated moment, we grieved as best we could using our devices, sharing memories about Dad over cell phones and posting loving memorials for him on social media. When it became possible again, I found solace and space for my thoughts in nature and in the Japanese garden.

In early 2021, after the garden had been reopened for a few months, the remaining staff and trustees of the Japanese garden met over Zoom for a board meeting. We went over the garden's financials together and were surprised to discover that not only was the garden helping to emotionally heal the people who visited it, but it was itself healing financially. Its budget was now in the black. Only being open on weekends and Friday evenings and scaling back on programs was costing the garden much less to operate—*and* it was still attracting a healthy number of visitors. Jim and Connie were relieved that so many people, including families with small children, were relishing their time in the garden, even without special events and activities. In the past, our guests had enjoyed our music concerts, lectures, festivals and fundraiser events, but it seemed that maybe we didn't need to hold so many programs and events. Although the occasional event was a special treat, I was realizing that for most of the time, it wasn't necessary to supplement the garden with anything. The garden itself was enough.

A Japanese garden, like any other work of art, can and should be enjoyed for what it offers that is unique and meaningful. Just like a painting built up with brushstrokes and added color, a Japanese garden has "bones" made up of stones and pathways that form its basic structure, and water and plants that are added to create texture, color and tone. In a strolling garden, all these elements are best enjoyed by simply walking along the paths, stepping carefully on the flat stones and over the bridges, and stopping to enjoy the many delightful views and exquisite plants, the scent of the occasional flower and the sounds of passing birds. A visitor may simply sit and enjoy a view. And, because the garden is a living thing, it is constantly growing and changing with the seasons and passing years, so no two visits to the space will be the same. Savoring the beauty of a Japanese garden is soothing to the soul. It doesn't overload the senses with colors and sounds and busy-ness. It is a place that offers space for breathing and for reflecting on one's life and loved ones, both present and lost. It is a place to pause and just be.

When life started normalizing again after the pandemic, I continued my involvement with the garden as a board member. I promised Connie that I would still schedule the occasional concert, help with our annual tea festival and organize a few other programs every year. No more than that. I had moved on in my professional life, and because of the forced pause of the pandemic, I had also changed my thinking about how best to appreciate the garden and share it with others.

Like many Japanese gardens, the Storrier Stearns Japanese Garden is a perfect manifestation of the principle of *ma*. This unique garden is an in-between space—in between Japan and the United States, nature and art, and everyday life and an escape. It is a special—almost magical—space that allows people to pause in their daily lives and enjoy simply being. And that is plenty.

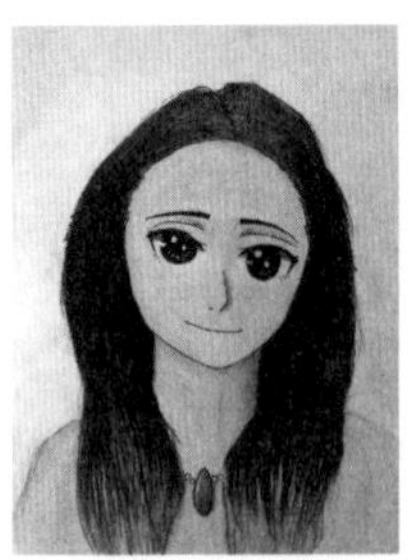

CHAPTER 16

The Anime Drawing

Like most languages, Japanese has absorbed many words and phrases from other languages over the centuries. Most notably, some fifteen hundred years ago, the Japanese adopted the Chinese writing system and integrated many Chinese words into their language. More recently, over the last one hundred fifty years, words from many European languages have also been Japanized. These foreign loan words, or *gairaigo* (外来語), literally "outside coming word," are typically written in an angular script called *katakana*, a syllabary (*a, ka, sa, ta* rather than a, b, c, d) that is reserved for foreign words and names, and also used for emphasis, like all caps in modern English.

Gairaigo words can be entire foreign words like "camera"—*kamera* (カメラ), or "computer"—*konpyūta* (コンピュータ), or they can be abbreviated foreign words like "television"—*terebi* (テレビ). There are also hybrid *gairaigo*, like the word *karaoke*, made up from the Japanese word *kara*, meaning "empty," combined with *oke*, an abbreviation of "orchestra," and *anime*, an abbreviation of the English word "animation" that refers specifically to Japanese animated TV shows and films. All these new words are examples of a language and culture blending and growing as it encounters other languages and cultures and is enriched by the collective creativity that is the very best of globalism.

—◆—

178

"I hate art!" Theo proclaimed defiantly.

My eight-year-old son stood by the front door, hands on his hips and pouting, clearly not intending to put his shoes on anytime soon. I had suggested that we go see a new exhibition at the Los Angeles County Museum with my sister, Roshan and her daughter, Kaia. I thought it might be something the kids would enjoy. Roshan had seemed keen too, and Kaia would no doubt go along with the plan, as she was an easygoing nine-year-old. But clearly Theo wasn't convinced. "Why are you always dragging me to museums? Museums are so boring! I'd much rather stay at home and play Pokémon!"

Ever since Theo was a baby, it has been hard for me to keep my two careers/jobs—art historian and mother—separate from each other, and often I didn't want to. Once, when Theo was just two months old, I led a docent tour at Pacific Asia Museum with him strapped onto me sleeping. Later, when he was a toddler and young child, I would regularly take him to museums and galleries to see art, often with Roshan and Kaia. For a few years now, it had been fun sharing my love of art with the kids and encouraging them to look at things they might otherwise ignore. Because Theo had been increasingly resistant to these visits, I would try to make them more enticing by bringing his friends along too. I also arranged after-school art clubs for him and his classmates, taught origami to his elementary school class every year, and even invited his whole elementary school to see my *Folding Paper* origami exhibition one evening. This all may have been a bit much for him. Clearly, my efforts to convince him of the value of art and museums were not having the desired effect. I wondered if all my efforts were actually putting him off art.

Like many kids of his generation, Theo would much rather be staring into a screen. As a young child, he enjoyed Disney movies and various cartoons on TV, but, as the years passed, he grew increasingly interested in Japanese animation, which was growing in popularity in the US. When he was about four years old, he discovered Pokémon. Pokémon (derived from "pocket" and "monsters") is a massive media franchise that began in 1996 as a video game series and then expanded rapidly to include trading cards, animated TV shows and movies, and all sorts of toys, clothing and other merchandise. In 2016, most of the planet learned the word "Pokémon" when the game Pokémon Go briefly took over the world, with one billion downloads of the mobile game globally. That's one eighth of the planet's entire population! For Theo, the colorful characters and their powers and evolutions were a source of endless fascination, and the idea of "collecting them all" hooked him on various versions of the game, TV shows and movies. This was also the start of his love of anime—his "gateway anime," if you will.

Anime, or Japanese animation, began in the early twentieth century, but really took off after World War II, when American popular culture began flooding into Japan. American comics and cartoons inspired Japanese artists and publishers to create Japanese versions that drew from the country's own rich graphic art traditions, folklore and artistic styles, and responded to current social trends and anxieties. These Japanese comic books, or *manga*, began to flourish in the 1950s and 60s, with content created both for children and adults. The illustration style featured certain visual conventions that were also adopted into Japanese animation, which was also growing an avid audience during these decades. Characters were given large eyes, small mouths and emotional detailing, such as sweat drops for anxiety, popping veins for anger and bold parallel lines denoting horror, shock or disgust. Strong lines and expressive dialogue bubbles were combined with unique frames and abstract background mood effects. Most of these conventions continue today in Japanese comic books and anime, and are globally recognizable as Japanese in style. I had some experience of manga and anime while living in Japan. I had been shocked to see businessmen on buses and trains reading sexy or violent manga, and I had been puzzled by some of the wacky-looking cartoons I'd seen on TV. Admittedly, my Japanese language skills were not advanced enough to understand what the comic books or animated TV shows were about, but I had little interested in these childish or violent aspects of Japanese popular culture. I was far more taken by traditional ceramics, Buddhist art and textiles.

But now, as a mother of a young boy, anime, and occasionally manga, had entered my home. First it was Pokémon, which seemed cute and harmless. In a few years' time, Theo was starting to watch more complex, sophisticated creations like the TV series *Naruto* and *Sword Art Online*, which he watched and talked about excitedly with friends. Theo explained the basics of *Naruto* to me: a boy who is possessed by the spirit of a nine-tailed fox demon aspires to become the head of a clan of ninja. Now, as someone who had studied foxes in Japanese folklore as part of my undergraduate degree, I found this premise intriguing, so I was pleased that it would teach him about Japanese culture and lore. When I asked him about *Sword Art Online*, he explained that it was about group of kids playing a video game becoming immersed in a fantasy world from which they can't escape. I wasn't as thrilled with this premise, because I was starting to worry that this might actually happen to Theo!

Then, in the summer of 2019, when Theo was thirteen and in between the seventh and eighth grades, he insisted I watch some *anime* series with him. David and I had separated, and I was recovering from surgery after badly tearing tissue in my shoulder (caused by years of wear and tear and some over-zealous stretching in a yoga class), so I was off work and confined to the house. Theo saw his chance.

"Come on, Mom. I want you to watch some anime with me. You'll see how amazing it is."

Because I didn't really have much to do other than recover, and it would allow me to learn about my son's world and interests, I agreed. Theo sat down next to me and aimed the remote control at the TV, calling up one of the increasing number of channels that were now streaming content. One, Crunchyroll, seemed to have hundreds of anime shows available. Theo clicked on one called *Haikyū!!*, and we sat back and watched it begin.

The show was about a high school boys' volleyball team, and the main character was short in stature, but determined to be the best player in the country. Because Theo was also short, I was immediately interested in the protagonist's journey. In fact, I found most of the characters likable. The storytelling was quite compelling, and the animation very skillfully rendered. Soon I was rooting for their team as they headed for the national championships. Then, we watched *Yuri!!! on Ice*, a surprising series about competitive ice skaters that hinted strongly at a gay romance between a Russian skating champion and a younger Japanese skater. I found myself pulled into the story by the unique characters and romance, and the breathtaking animation.

"The animation is so good because the animators worked with skating choreographers," Theo explained.

"Really?" I answered, eager to learn more. "How did they do that?"

"It's based on real skaters spinning," he added, excited to be able to tell me how the show was made. "Look at how they made the characters spin!"

"Wow! That's fascinating!" I replied, impressed—both at the creativity of the productions, and at Theo's knowledge and enthusiasm for the creative process behind the series. It was dawning on me as an art historian that there was much more to anime than I had imagined. And as a mother, I was realizing that Theo wasn't just watching these shows passively; he was paying attention to the storytelling, the character development and to the artistry that went into making them.

The same summer, Theo became a huge fan of *One Piece*, a spirited and very long-running animated series about "Monkey D. Luffy," a young lad who turns into rubber after eating a "devil fruit." Luffy aspires to become the King of the Pirates and travels the world with pirate crew of oddballs and misfits. Theo adored the main character, an energetic, optimistic fellow with a hilarious, stretchy superpower and a deep loyalty to his friends. He binge-watched the series and regaled me with tales of the characters' adventures in different fantastic worlds. The premise was ridiculous, but he was utterly captivated. Again, I worried that he might become obsessed by this TV show. But then, he began to draw.

As he absorbed these animated TV shows, Theo was also carefully observing how the characters were drawn, and this inspired him to break out his sketchbooks and pencils and attempt to draw the characters himself. He turned to YouTube videos made by artists to learn how to draw a face. He followed their instructions, sketching face after face on individual sheets. Gradually his lines became quicker, cleaner and more confident, and he not only copied characters from anime, but started to draw his own characters and create story ideas around them. He stuck the faces on his wall above his desk, and over the summer began writing a fantasy story starring the various characters he had designed. Soon, he became interested in using better pencils and markers for drawing. Then, in the lead-up to his birthday, he surprised me by asking for a large set of beautiful, high-quality pencils as a gift. And my now fourteen-year-old son, who just a few years ago had declared that he hated art, started adding color to his drawings.

Over the next year or so, his love of anime, his passion for storytelling and his character-drawing skills increased exponentially. When the COVID-19 pandemic hit, he managed to persuade friends to watch anime too, and some of them joined him in his enthusiasm. At this time, anime was enjoying a global boom, helped also by the series *Demon Slayer*, a beautifully animated series with sympathetic characters and a nuanced exploration of the nature of good and evil. During lockdown, streaming platforms like Netflix and Crunchyroll increased their offerings, and millions of house-bound kids around the world became captivated by anime. For many teens in the US, Japan had become more than a source for sushi, ramen and other delicious food. It was also the home of the world's coolest entertainment— anime, manga, video games and all of its related music. For Theo, anime was beginning to represent not just a pastime but a world he wanted to be part of. He was no longer simply a "weeb"—a name anime fans often use to refer to themselves; he was being pulled by anime into the world of Japanese culture and art. He was even studying Japanese—at a younger age than I was when I began the language. And I hadn't forced him to do any of this!

One day during the pandemic, Theo asked me to text him a photograph of myself. A day or two later, he came up to me at my desk and presented me with a portrait he had drawn of me—in the style of a manga or anime character. My features were simplified, my eyes were huge and my pupils were dark with little white specks in them, making them sparkle. My nose and mouth were rendered with thin lines, and my head tilts slightly to one side, giving me a look of kind concern. He had "mangafied" or "anime-ted" me! (I thought I'd made up these terms, but they are already out there on the internet!) I loved the portrait, in part because I am his mother and will probably love most of the art he creates, but also because it was born from a love of Japanese art that we share, albeit very different aspects of it. I proposed that he take commissions from people for similar manga portraits and posted his picture of me on my Facebook page. Immediately, several friends asked for portraits, and in a few months, he had drawn and sold ten of these portraits. He started talking about becoming an artist and wondering how he could make a living this way. Other parents may not have been excited at this prospect.... I. Was. Thrilled.

And thanks to Theo's enthusiasm for anime, my art historian self could no longer ignore this aspect of Japan's artistic culture. It was now clear to me that manga and anime are even more developed as art forms in Japan than comic books and animation are in the United States. In the US, comic books peaked in the 1940s, but in Japan, manga have been increasing in popularity and sales steadily since the 1950s, and are a huge part of the nation's publishing industry. Here, when we think of animation, we think of TV cartoons for children or films by Disney, Pixar or DreamWorks, and a handful of animated TV series for adults, like *The Simpsons*, *South Park* or *Family Guy*. But in Japan, not only is there a rich variety of cartoons for young children, but a wide assortment of anime series for teenagers and young adults too, and numerous animated films created by such acclaimed animator/directors as Hayao Miyazaki and Studio Ghibli as well as animation studios like Kyoto Animation and CoMix Wave Films.

Just as I had dragged Theo around museums when he was young, hoping that he would realize the importance of art, Theo convinced me to watch his favorite anime to understand the significance of Japanese animation. At this point, I have watched a rather embarrassing quantity of anime—some duds, for sure, but many series that are beautifully designed and explore intriguing aspects of traditional culture, folklore and the supernatural. Thanks to his persistence, I now see anime as a continuation of earlier Japanese artistic traditions—such as the woodblock prints of the Edo period. Those traditional artworks, designed by some of Japan's most celebrated artists like Hokusai and Hiroshige, are today appreciated, collected and exhibited in the world's museums as works of art. But at the time they were created, they were made for the enjoyment of the general population as entertainment. They played a central role in Japan's popular culture—just like manga and anime do today.

So, in the fall of 2023, when I was asked by a colleague if I would be interested in working as a curatorial consultant on a retrospective exhibition of a Japanese animator at the Academy Museum of Motion Pictures, I jumped at the chance. The exhibition was the brainchild of TOHO Animation, the studio that produces films by Shinkai Makoto, a renowned animator who brings to life his magical storytelling using exquisitely animated scenes of Tokyo and rural Japan, skillfully rendering light, shadow and rain. The streaming service Crunchyroll had been hired to create an amazing one-day event in Los Angeles to promote Shinkai and his latest film *Suzume*, and Shinkai would be there to meet film critics and fans. Like his previous film, *Your Name*, the new film had gained significant global attention, particularly among younger filmgoers, and the 2024 Academy Awards were just a few months away. This was a chance for me to not only grow as an art historian and curator, but also to look cool to my son!

But I had to sign a non-disclosure agreement, or NDA, about the project, a very Los Angeles "entertainment industry" thing that I had never been required to do before. I had told Theo that I might be working on an anime-related exhibition, but I couldn't tell him any more than that. I did ask him for help with one aspect of the work, though. I wrote a panel for the exhibition describing the general animation process in Japan, something he had researched deeply. He reviewed my text and made some helpful suggestions. When the exhibition finally opened—for one day only—I was able to reveal to Theo the identity of the animator. He loved Shinkai's work (we had watched *Your Name* together), so he was thrilled to come and see the exhibition.

We walked through the aisles of the show together, and I watched Theo's reaction to the artworks. From the start, I could tell he was more interested than he'd been at any of my other exhibitions. At one point, he stood thoughtfully studying some character design sketches of a teenage girl wearing a winter jacket and scarf shown in different poses—her figure from the front and the back, and a close-up of her face shown from the front and then from the side. He took out his phone and snapped a picture, saving the image to review later. He moved onto the next image, this time a head-and-shoulders drawing of a young man, eyes wide open in surprise, with director's comments scribbled next to it by Shinkai. He took another picture and nodded to himself as if he'd understood something important.

At the end of the exhibition, Shinkai Makoto himself made an appearance to meet and greet fans for a photo-op. He was talking graciously to every fan, signing their posters and then smiling with them for pictures taken by a professional photographer. Everyone had a few minutes with him. I was over the moon to meet him. Working on this exhibition, I had come to appreciate his storytelling skills and his creative process as an animator. To me, he was quite clearly a contemporary artist on par with woodblock print artist Hiroshige, particularly in his depictions of Tokyo in all its changing atmospheric conditions and moods. Theo, too, was excited to meet him because Shinkai was one of Japan's greatest living animators, and now Theo was beginning to think that he might also want to become an animator. When it was our turn to meet him, Theo introduced himself in Japanese and bowed deeply to Shinkai. I thought my heart would burst!

I had watched my son for eighteen years struggling to figure out who he was and to find his place in the world. Just as I had encountered rejection because I looked different than my childhood peers and felt like I didn't fit in, Theo had often felt that he wasn't as smart or talented as his peers. Now, just as I had discovered the Japanese language and Japanese art and found my place in the world as a Japanese art historian, he was discovering his talents as an artist while developing a deep passion for Japanese animation. As I write this, Theo has started art school and is embarking on his path as an artist, storyteller and animator. Maybe he, too, will travel to Japan to study Japanese animation. Or maybe he will decide, at some point, that anime and things Japanese were just a phase—and he will find his creative muse elsewhere. And that will be fine. All I can hope is that his journey is as full of gifts as mine has been—of fascinating places and words, and of exquisite works of art that tell intriguing stories, and of people who believe in him, support him and help him find his way.

And I will continue to walk my own path in the world of Japanese art, one that has introduced me to not only some of the world's most extraordinary paintings, sculptures, ceramics and other works of art, but many exceptional people, too. I may never be able to repay all the kindness and generosity these people have extended to me along the way, but by exhibiting, writing and lecturing about Japanese art, I am endeavoring to share with others Japan's remarkable artistic traditions and new creations. And somehow, on this perhaps unlikely cultural journey, I have managed to find my place as a global citizen the way my parents promised I would—as an Indian-born, California-based, Scottish-Persian historian of Japanese art!

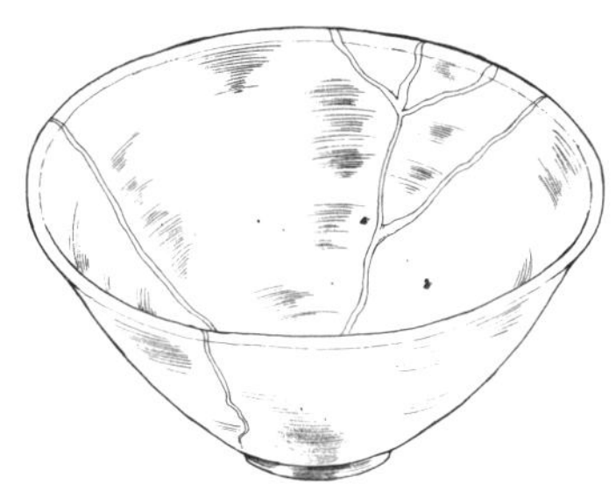

Afterword:
The Kintsugi Tea Bowl

One of my favorite art terms and concepts in Japanese is *kintsugi* (金継ぎ), meaning literally "to join with gold." The term refers to a technique that has traditionally been used in Japan to repair broken ceramics with gold lacquer, extending the utility of the vessels and often enhancing their beauty.

Since the late sixteenth century, the tea ceremony, in which a host formally serves tea to guests in a tea house, has brought together ceramics, flower arrangement, architecture, garden design and other art forms in a social and spiritual ritual that has profoundly impacted Japanese culture. As a result, the tea bowls, dishes and other ceramic vessels used in the practice have been so highly treasured by Japan's tea masters, collectors and connoisseurs that—even when broken—they are not discarded. Instead, because of the prominence of the aesthetics of *wabi* (humble, austere beauty) and *sabi* (beauty that comes with age and loving use) in the tea world, these beloved vessels have been repaired whenever possible. Often, the elegant, vein-like lines of the gold lacquer repair are so exquisite—and the story of the breakage is so intriguing—that the ceramic's value increases with the *kintsugi* repair.

One evening, a couple of years ago, Theo was helping me get dinner ready. I asked him to get me a bowl out of my cabinet, but I had forgotten how tightly packed the shelves were. I heard something hit the floor with a dull crack, followed by Theo exclaiming, "F**k!" I looked over and saw him crouching and picking up several pieces. "I'm so sorry!" he said, looking at me with pleading eyes. "I broke one of your special bowls." He knew how much I treasured my Japanese ceramics. I refocused my eyes from his worried face to the four large, pinkish-brown shards he now held in his hands. I felt my heart tighten a little. The tea bowl was one that I had made in Hita when I was twenty-five years old, so over thirty years ago—in another lifetime almost. My teacher, Mr. Anai, had said it was one of my best pieces, and had insisted on coating it himself with a special glaze, a bit like the rich, creamy glazes of Shino wares from the Mino region. My tea bowl had attracted a lot of attention at the farewell exhibition that my three teachers arranged to showcase my artistic efforts in Hita, and a friend who practiced the tea ceremony had asked me to give it to her. I was flattered but told her that because it was my best work with Mr. Anai, I wanted to keep it.

"It's okay. It's not your fault." I reassured Theo. "I should have taken more care with it and stored it properly." I shared some of the bowl's story with him, but didn't want him to feel bad, so I added, "But it's just 'stuff.' It's not worth getting upset about 'stuff.'" On one level, I do genuinely believe that, and I can often let go of objects quite easily—adding a Marie Kondo-like "thank you" when I part with them. However, this particular "stuff" tugged at my heart a little, so I gathered up the large shards and put them in a box. Perhaps I could have the tea bowl repaired on my next visit to Japan. I put the box deep in another cupboard so I wouldn't have to think about it again for the time being.

Earlier this year, at the opening event for a small exhibition that I had curated at a gallery in Pasadena, I met a Japanese artist, Shingo Murayama, who was serving tea to guests. Next to his table, he was displaying some ceramic dishes and bowls that had been cracked and repaired with *kintsugi*. When I asked him about them, he explained that he had learned a way to do *kintsugi* that was similar to the traditional method of mixing gold powder with sticky lacquer, but easier and quicker. My heart jumped, and I told him about my bowl and asked if he could "*kintsugi*" it for me. He said he'd be happy to, but it would take him a couple of weeks.

When it came time to pick up the bowl, I rushed back to the place we had met, eager to see the result. Shingo pulled it from a box. It was wrapped tightly in bubble wrap. "I hope you like the repair," he said humbly, handing it to me. I opened the package as slowly and carefully as my eagerness would allow and then held my bowl in both hands in front of me. It was whole again! But, no, it was more than whole. It was now truly beautiful—much more than it had been before! Veins of gold ran across its surface, not hiding, but highlighting its cracks, telling the bowl's story in brilliant, calligraphic lines. I had made this vessel as a young adult on an adventure in Japan, my kind and generous teacher had glazed it for me to make it extra special, and I had kept it for decades. It had been accidentally broken by my beloved son, and now it had been transformed into a true work of art by a Japanese artist. My eyes started welling up with tears. This was why I loved Japanese art so much. Because the Japanese have a way to take something damaged and not only repair and preserve it, but make it even more extraordinary and valuable by "joining it together with gold."

This is how I felt Japanese art had worked for me in my life. I was a person of many cultures, whose life and identity were unified and given meaning and purpose through Japanese art. Born in India to a Scottish father and a Persian mother, raised in Scotland, Canada and then England, I didn't feel like I truly belonged in any of these cultures. But my parents—particularly my father, whose wise words I had often chosen to live by—had promised that I wouldn't always feel culturally disconnected, that one day I would find my place and feel comfortable as a citizen of the world. I had discovered the Japanese language and then Japanese art, and it had resonated with me on such a profound level that I felt compelled to build a career around it. I have been doing this now for more than thirty years, and am always cognizant that I am representing a culture that I wasn't born into. I am particularly honored, therefore, when Japanese friends and visitors, including government officials, praise my work.

Just a few months earlier, a college gallery director (herself white) told me that she and her team thought it might be problematic for them to host an exhibition I'd curated about Japanese art—because

I was "white" and not Japanese or Japanese American. I was quite shocked. First, I have never considered myself white. I am brown. Second, I understand that some people do appropriate aspects of other cultures in insensitive ways, but I have always felt a heavy responsibility to represent other cultures well, especially Japan. I had adopted Japanese culture as my professional focus, in large part thanks to a Japanese government program devised to bring foreigners to Japan to teach the Japanese about the world, and then upon their return home, teach people there about Japan. For me, the JET Program had really worked—I was spending my life promoting Japan's art!

Finally, to me as an art historian, it is very clear that in the world of art, music and entertainment, people from different cultures have admired and drawn inspiration from each other for millennia. Our world has been so interconnected for so many centuries that it is often impossible to refer to a song or dance or painting as being purely of one single people or place. In the early nineteenth century, Japan's most famous artist—Katsushika Hokusai, who designed the woodblock print widely known as *The Great Wave*, and whose work is considered by many to be quintessentially Japanese—incorporated elements from Chinese paintings and even Dutch engravings into his paintings and print designs. And a few decades later, in Europe, the Dutch artist Vincent van Gogh—one of the world's most beloved artists—was so inspired by Japanese art that he wrote, "All my work is based to some extent on Japanese art." I strongly doubt any museum would call either of these artists' work "cultural appropriation" and refuse to show it.

The human creative spirit finds inspiration all around it, and has long fed on this inspiration to make something different and new. In the realm of cultural studies, many people like me have fallen in love with distant cultures, their arts, languages, music and food, and have devoted their lives to sharing their knowledge with others. As long as the source of the inspiration is appreciated, respected and credited, then cultural borrowing need not be harmful. Instead, it can benefit and enrich everyone. For me, the many golden connections of Japanese art have given my life such meaning and a sense of wholeness that I feel compelled to share them with others—so that they, too, can learn from and enjoy these rich artistic traditions.

Acknowledgments

This book is all about gratitude—or *kansha* (感謝)—toward the people who introduced me to Japanese art, to those in Japan who taught me how to make art and those in the UK who taught me how to study its history, and to the colleagues, collectors, museum supporters and artists in the UK, US and Japan who helped me become a curator. I am deeply grateful to everyone mentioned in this book—and to the many others I wasn't able to include—for guiding me on my journey through Japanese art.

I have written several books and many articles about Asian art and culture, but those have generally involved "telling" with words and "showing" with illustrations. This book has been an entirely different animal—a tiger rather than a house cat—one far more terrifying and requiring expert skills to wrangle. First, I would like to thank Sascha Brown Rice. I first shared with her the idea for this book on New Year's Day, 2020 and asked her to be my writing coach. We didn't start right away, because of COVID-19, but we eventually did in 2022, from which time she patiently guided me to use words to "show not tell," one slow chapter at a time, crafting the book into something hopefully worthy of sharing with others. Many thanks also to Eric Oey and Jon Steever of Tuttle Publishing for seeing the potential for this book among a wider audience, and to Jon for masterfully guiding it through the editing and production processes. Thank you also to my sister, Roshan, for generously reading through the manuscript to check for accuracy in the family story and to her and my dear friends, Lynn Paul and Amy Miller, for advice, feedback and support. Thank you also to Elisa Parhad for brainstorming publishing ideas with me. And many thanks to editor Avalon Radys for reviewing my manuscript and providing excellent structural and content feedback, and to Coco Harris and Katie Harp from Beta Reading Services for their invaluable suggestions and encouragement. And my deepest gratitude to Pico Iyer, for most generously agreeing to write the Foreword to this book. It is a true honor.

For the images in this book, I am indebted to several people. The wonderful line drawings of the artworks in the book are the work of Greyson Sloan and Kate Lin. For the photographs of the artworks, I am grateful to Executive Director Dr. Bethany Montegano and Collections Manager Annie Yihong-Kuang Lee, at the USC Pacific Asia Museum. At Scripps College, I am thankful to Dr. Erin Curtis, Director of the Ruth Chandler Williamson Gallery, and John Trendler, Collections Data Specialist and Curator of Visual Resources. At the Japanese American National Museum, thank you to Vice President of Exhibitions and Art Director Clement Hanami and Archivist Jamie Henricks for the image of Sadako Sasaki's folded crane. Thank you to Dr. Robert J. Lang for the image of his *Vertical Pond II* installation and to Futoshi Shigeishi for photographing his father's sword and the Onta-ware dish. The rest of the images were taken by me, and as with the text, I take all responsibility for them.

I also want to thank the JET Programme, which was established by the Japanese Government with the goal of "promoting grass-roots international exchange between Japan and other nations." If not for this program, I would not have flown off to Japan after graduating from university—one of 2,284 graduates from eight countries—and spent two years working for the government in rural Japan, surrounded by Japanese art and culture. I may not have fallen deeply in love with Japanese art and decided to devote my career to it. This farsighted international exchange program, which now welcomes nearly six thousand graduates from fifty-one countries, exemplifies how direct, person-to-person contact helps foster true intercultural understanding and enriches all involved.

Lastly, I thank my family—my Scottish and Persian parents, Tom and Feri (Fereshteh), who made me so culturally complicated, but then armed me with the tools to thrive as a global citizen, my sister, Roshan, and brother, Alan, who have supported me and my gallivanting, while also doing a lot of their own, and my American family, David and Theo, who have sustained me and enriched my life in the ways that really matter.

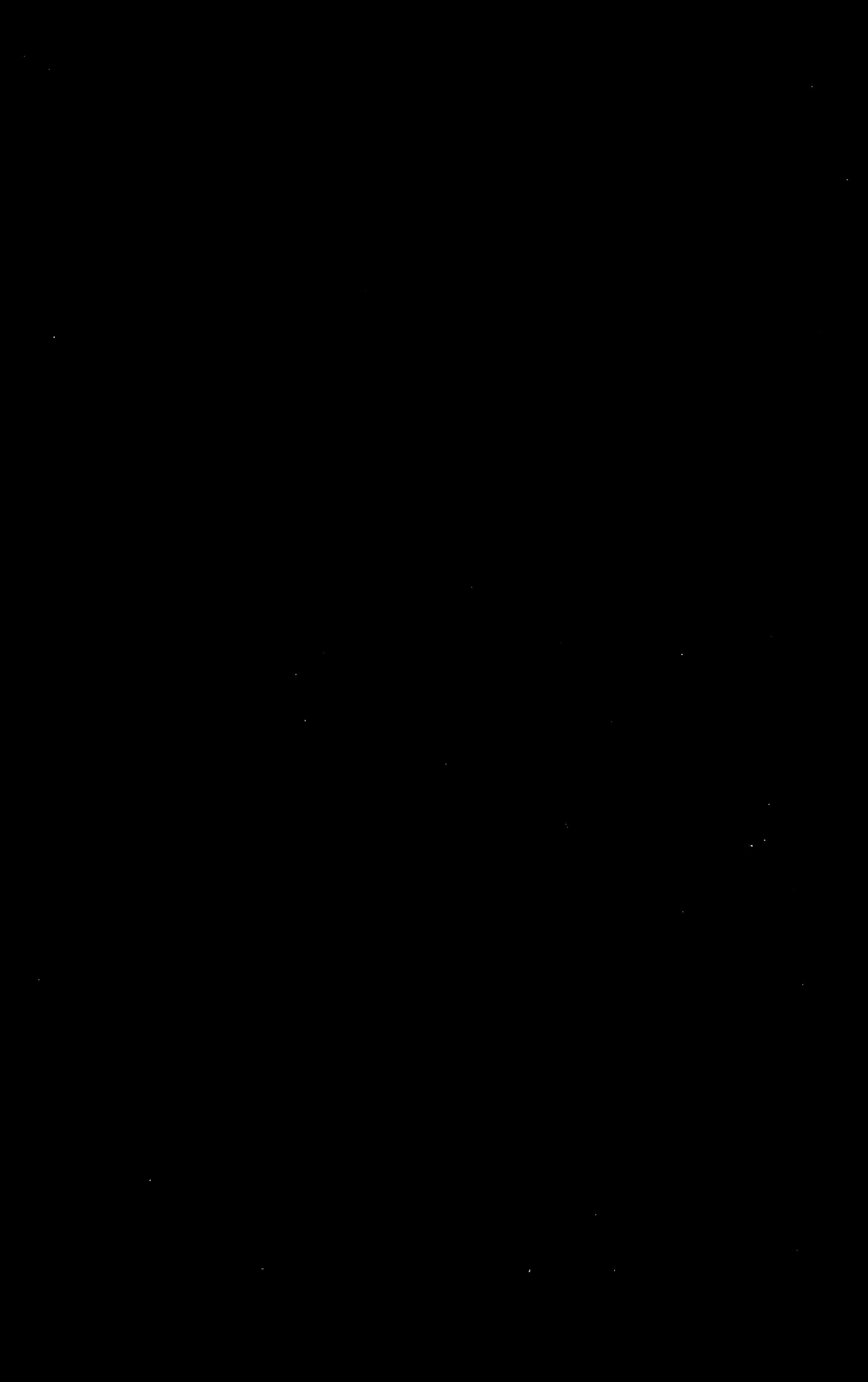

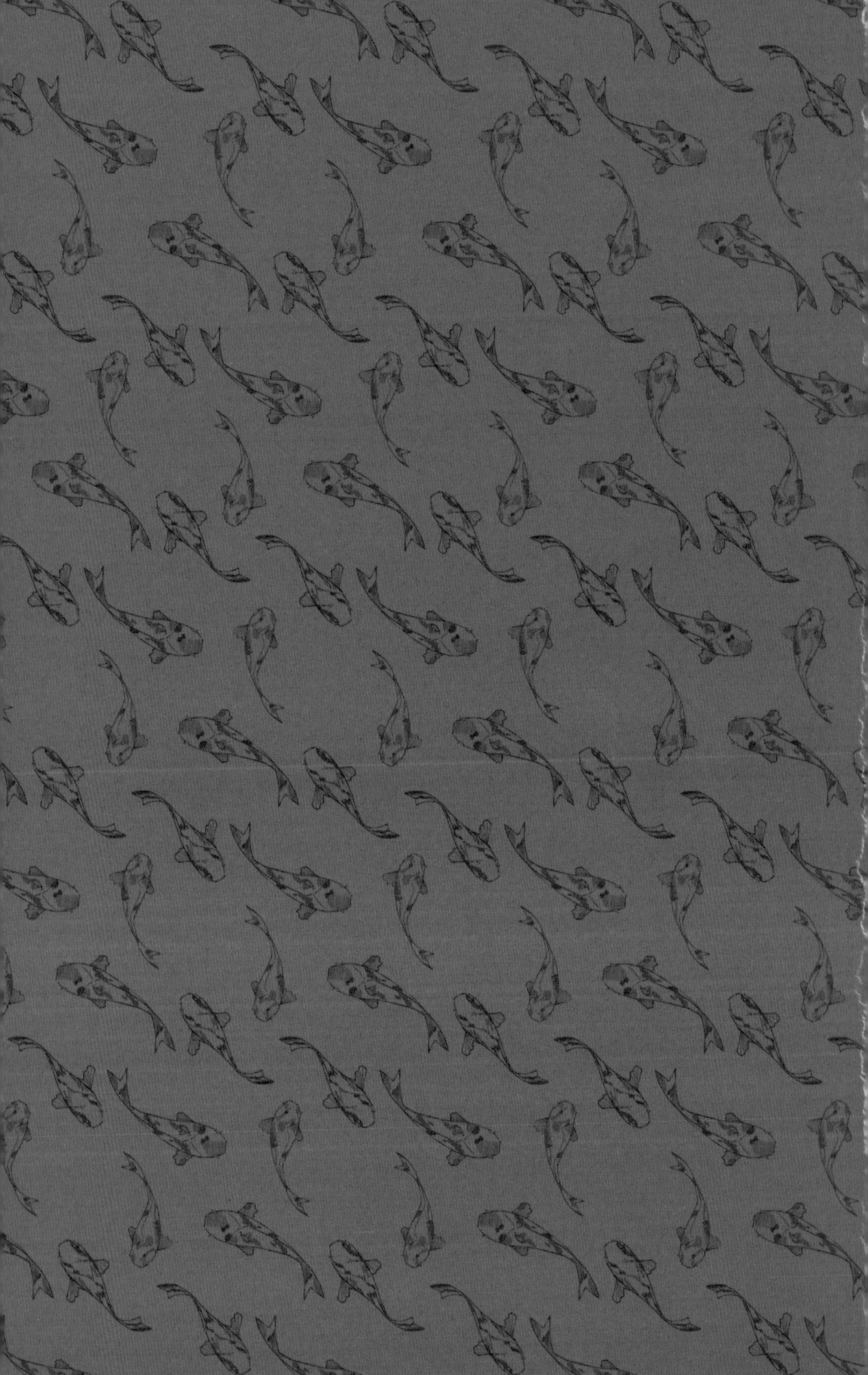